Emotions, Values, and the Law

John Deigh

Emotions, Values, and the Law

OXFORD
UNIVERSITY PRESS
2008

OXFORD

UNIVERSITY PRESS

Oxford University Press, Inc., publishes works that further
Oxford University's objective of excellence
in research, scholarship, and education.

Oxford   New York
Auckland   Cape Town   Dar es Salaam   Hong Kong   Karachi
Kuala Lumpur   Madrid   Melbourne   Mexico City   Nairobi
New Delhi   Shanghai   Taipei   Toronto

With offices in
Argentina   Austria   Brazil   Chile   Czech Republic   France   Greece
Guatemala   Hungary   Italy   Japan   Poland   Portugal   Singapore
South Korea   Switzerland   Thailand   Turkey   Ukraine   Vietnam

Copyright © 2008 by Oxford University Press, Inc.

Published by Oxford University Press, Inc.
198 Madison Avenue, New York, New York 10016

www.oup.com

Oxford is a registered trademark of Oxford University Press

Library of Congress Cataloging-in-Publication Data
Deigh, John.
Emotions, values, and the law / John Deigh.
p.   cm.
ISBN 978-0-19-516932-4
1. Emotions.   2. Intentionality (Philosophy).   3. Values.
4. Ethics.   I. Title.
BF531.D385   2008
128'.33–dc22   2007038784

1   3   5   7   9   8   6   4   2

Printed in the United States of America
on acid-free paper

For Lynn

Preface

Philosophy progresses very slowly. Its movement, like that of continents along the earth's crust, becomes evident only after long periods of seemingly stationary activity. For much of the last century and continuing to the present, such movement has gone on in Anglo-American moral philosophy. While the standard and seemingly stalemated clashes between the believers in moral law and the believers in utilitarian ethics or between what Mill calls the intuitive and inductive schools of the discipline have continued to occupy center stage, a change in how we conceive of the phenomena that these clashes are about has been taking place in the background. In the space of about eight decades, the understanding of these phenomena as products of reason or will, operating independently of feeling and sentiment, has yielded ground to an understanding of them as manifestations of the work of emotion. Beginning with the first exposition of an emotive theory of moral language in Ogden and Richards, arguments in Anglo-American moral philosophy concerning the nature of these phenomena have come increasingly to rest on theses about human emotions. And while such arguments were at first the exclusive property of the inductive school, the emergence of more complex conceptions of the emotions has enabled the intuitive school to make such arguments of its own. As a result, questions about the nature of emotions and their place in the thinking and practices that morality encompasses are now very much a focus of study and debate among moral philosophers who work in the analytic tradition.

The first five essays in this collection concern these questions. They belong to the movement whose course I have just sketched. The first essay, "Emotions: The Legacy of James and Freud," explains the revolution in our thinking about emotions that chiefly arises out of the work of William James and Sigmund Freud. Of course, neither James nor Freud wrote under the influence of analytic philosophy. James completed his writings on emotions more than a decade before its founders came along, and Freud's views are the product of the intellectual traditions of the European continent. Indeed, Freud's importance to the revolution in our thought about emotions should remind us that even before Anglo-American moral philosophy began shifting its focus onto them, thinkers on the European continent going back at least to Nietzsche had already initiated such a shift, and their work undoubtedly influenced thinking across both the Channel and the Atlantic. The impact of Freud's work alone on twentieth-century thought about human psychology and culture is so great that it leaves no discipline to which these subjects are central undisturbed.

The three essays following the first concern a single problem in the study of emotions. How are we to understand their intentionality? This is perhaps the hardest problem for the philosophical study of emotions. What makes the problem so hard is the resistance that the most natural under-standing of the intentionality of emotions meets when it is applied to emotions of other animals than human beings or to emotions of humans in their first year or two of life. For the most natural understanding of an emotion's intentionality is that it consists in some kind of propositional thought about the object at or toward which the emotion is felt, yet propositional thought presupposes linguistic capacities and seems therefore to be thought of a kind that beasts and babies are not or not yet capable of having. The problem becomes especially acute when one considers emotions like fear and anger that beasts, babies, and adult human beings are all capable of experiencing. The second essay, "Primitive Emotions," sets out this problem and exam-ines attempts at its resolution that proceed either from the thesis that the intentionality of emotions consists in propositional thought or from the the-sis that other animals besides human beings experience emotions. Attempts at resolution that proceed in the first way represent cognitivist theories of emotion. Attempts that proceed in the second way follow from theories of emotion that grow out of Darwin's work on the expression of emotions in humans and other animals. Neither of these theories' attempted resolutions is successful, and what we see in their failure, I argue, is the depth of the problem.

In the third essay, "Cognitivism in the Theory of Emotions," I survey different cognitivist theories in analytic philosophy and critically examine those that by the end of the twentieth century had come to dominate the philosophical study of emotions. The examination is more thorough than that of the second essay and includes extensive probing of the difficulties in these theories' accounts of the intentionality of emotions. I conclude, as in the second essay, that these accounts are unsuccessful. This essay is the oldest in the collection. Since its appearance some of the chief defenders of the theories I criticize have responded with further development of their views. Their responses consist mainly in bringing out the perceptual character of the cognitions that they identify either as emotions or as the essential cognitive component of emotions. These are significant developments in the defense of cognitivist theories. Nonetheless, I am unpersuaded that they succeed in answering my criticisms. Despite the greater emphasis on the perceptual character of these cognitions, the theories still assume a conception of them as evaluative thoughts, and for reasons that I advance in the fourth essay, linguistic capacities are necessary to having such thoughts. Hence, their accounts of the intentionality of the emotions of beasts and babies remain problematic.

The fourth essay, "Emotions and Values," offers a resolution to the problem of understanding the intentionality of emotions that is distinct from the attempted resolutions I examine in the second and third essays. The resolution it offers depends on the relation of emotions to evaluative thought. That I look to this relation for a resolution does not, of course, distinguish my view from the cognitivist theories I criticize. In particular, it does not distinguish it from those cognitivist theories that accept the ancient Stoics' identification of emotions with evaluative judgments. These theories too make use of the relation of emotions to evaluative thought in giving their accounts of the intentionality of emotions. But unlike their view, I do not take the relation to explain the intentionality of every emotion or hold that evaluative thought is implicit in every experience of emotion. Rather, I maintain that the connection between emotions and evaluative thought is forged through the education of emotions that children undergo at an early age. Accordingly, there is a radical difference between the intentionality of emotions prior to their education and their intentionality subsequent to it. Only the latter is identical with evaluative thought. It presupposes that the subjects of the emotions it characterizes have linguistic capacities. The former, by contrast, does not. Being the same as the intentionality of the emotions of beasts, it does not imply evaluative thought but is to be understood, instead, as given in the sensory experiences that these primitive, which is to say, uneducated emotions comprise. The explanation of how the connection between emotions and evaluative thought is forged thus becomes crucial to resolving the problem.

Any account of evaluative thought and its relation to emotions must contend with the view that the values, whether positive or negative, attributed to objects in such thought are mere figments of our feelings toward those objects. Such subjectivism in the theory of values has a long history. In modern philosophy, Hume is its most celebrated defender. The account of evaluative thought I give presupposes the same conception of such thought as that on which the cognitivist theories of emotion descending from the ancient Stoics proceed. It thus opposes Hume's view. The argument of the fourth essay begins with criticism of this view. The main targets of the criticism are subjectivist theories of value that take Hume's analogy between values and secondary qualities as their point of departure. The analogy not only informs Hume's projectivist account of evaluative thought but also extends to accounts of such thought on which it is true or false according as it corresponds or fails to correspond to properties in the objects that the thought ascribes to them. The latter are the so-called "response dependent" theories of value that have attracted significant support among contemporary moral philosophers. These accounts too are targets of my criticism. Hume's analogy, I argue, is refuted by considerations of the learning through which a child acquires values, acquires, that is, a capacity for evaluative thought. The overall thrust of my account of the intentionality of emotions, then, is to justify an understanding of values as objective properties that one can comprehend independently of the emotions through which we commonly experience these values and that is consistent with naturalism in the theory of values.

My account of evaluative thought in "Emotions and Values" is general. While my aim is to advance our understanding of how we are capable of perceiving moral and aesthetic values, I take as the major hurdle to achieving this aim explaining how we can understand the evaluative thoughts that figure in our emotional responses to objects as perceptions of properties that those objects have consistent with our understanding of those properties as natural properties. They are natural properties of the objects that have them, that is, in the same sense as the toxicity and digestibility of the objects that have them are natural properties. Consequently, I do no more than gesture toward how this explanation works specifically in the cases of moral and aesthetic perceptions. The fifth essay, "The Politics of Disgust and Shame," does more. It extends the explanation specifically to the perceptions of moral value in those experiences of disgust in which the emotion is a moral emotion. I do this in the context of discussing Martha Nussbaum's critique of the use of disgust and shame in politics and law. Nussbaum, in her critique of disgust, draws on the work of the social psychologist Paul Rozin, whose account of the emotion is congenial to her own cognitivist theory. In criticizing Rozin's account, I observe that it does not apply to the full range of experiences of disgust, including, in particular, disgust at the actions of "sleazy politicians," which Rozin aptly calls "moral disgust" (while acknowledging that it lies outside his account). Using my account of how the connection between emotions and evaluative thought is forged through the education of emotions, I show how, through such education, a liability to disgust at putrid things is extended to morally corrupt acts and morally corrupt people. And I then explain the importance of this extension for understanding the programs of such conservative political thinkers as Sir Patrick Devlin and the force of Nussbaum's critique of their views.

As we come increasingly to understand the phenomena of morality as manifestations of the work of human emotion, the importance of voluntary action in our conception of these phenomena should diminish. I do not believe this is an inevitable consequence of greater focus on the emotions in our study of these phenomena, but I do think it is predictable inasmuch as this greater focus should weaken the tendency to fall back on the traditional notion of the will as the site of basic moral assessment. It is also, I think, salubrious in that it marks greater maturity in our thinking about morality. The wisdom of abandoning the traditional notion of the will as necessary to grasping the moral character of human action is a theme that runs through the collection's last five essays. While these essays do not jointly make an extended argument for this theme, they cumulatively contribute to its advancement by finding its place in several different areas of morality. Taken together, then, they represent a working out of Bernard Williams's sage observation that "the idea of the voluntary...is essentially superficial."[1]

Each of the sixth, seventh, and eighth essays deals with a distinct bit of morality. The sixth concerns the authority of law. In this essay, "Emotions and the Authority of Law," I explain the law's authority as arising out of strong emotional bonds that the people whom the law governs have to their political institutions. My thesis follows the ideas of Jeremy Bentham and John Austin, who proposed to explain the same phenomenon, under the concept

1. Bernard Williams, *Shame and Necessity* (Berkeley: University of California Press, 1993), p. 67.

of sovereignty, as arising out of the habits of people in a political society to obey the coercive general commands of a certain individual or assembly. The concept of an emotional bond, I believe, improves on that of a habit of obedience, which, as critics of Bentham and Austin have shown, is insufficient for explaining the phenomenon of supreme authority in a polity. Like Bentham and Austin, though, my explanation is meant to supersede explanations on which the law's authority is due to the consent of those who are subject to it. Political authority, I maintain, when it is supreme or ultimate and not delegated or conferred by a higher authority, is a construct of collective emotion and not the result of separate acts of individual will spread across a population. The topic of the seventh essay, "All Kinds of Guilt," is guilt felt over thoughts, feelings, and conditions that are involuntary or the result of events for which one has no responsibility. Many commentators regard such feelings of guilt as irrational. Following Herbert Morris's lead, I argue to the contrary that one can make sense of them without attributing irrationality to their subjects, but in contrast to Morris's view, I make sense of them by appealing to norms of common sense morality that regulate nonvoluntary behavior and feelings. In the eighth essay, "Promises Under Fire," I highlight acts of surrender in war as examples of valid promises made under coercive circumstances, and I then use Hume's view of what makes promises obligatory to explain how such coerced promises create obligations despite their being made involuntarily. I take the success of this explanation as an argument for Hume's view and argue as well that an opposing view, powerfully expounded by T. M. Scanlon, is less successful at explaining how such coerced promises could be obligatory.

The last two essays in the collection mount a more direct challenge to the moral significance of the traditional notion of the will. The notion is particularly at home in the criminal law and in the political and economic institutions that have arisen out of classical liberalism. The essays argue against taking this notion as bedrock in our conception of the principles of justice that should regulate these institutions. In the ninth essay, "Moral Agency and Criminal Insanity," I consider the question of what justifies having a separate defense of insanity in the criminal law: why, that is, does the criminal law need a separate insanity defense for protecting mentally ill offenders from being unjustly convicted of and punished for their offenses? In answering this question, I argue for seeing the advent and continued support for such a defense as based on our realization that some voluntary actions are undeserving of punishment, despite being intentional, because they spring from mental disorders that negate the actor's capacity for moral agency. In effect, then, I argue for separating the capacity for moral agency and therefore the preconditions of moral responsibility from having a will. The criminal law is more just when it uses exercises of the former rather than exercises of the latter to determine when an offender is responsible for breaking the law.

The tenth essay, "Liberalism and Freedom," concerns the ideas of individual freedom in the tradition of liberalism. The kind of freedom that classical liberalism extols and seeks to protect from government intrusions is exemplified by freedom of contract. The nineteenth-century reforms in Britain that placed limits on this freedom in the interest of protecting workers from accepting employment conditions that damaged their health and placed them at risk of crippling injuries were advocated by liberals such as T. H. Green who extolled and sought to secure for workers and tenant farmers through government regulation of private contracts a different kind of freedom. This kind of freedom is often characterized as positive in contrast to the kind of freedom, often characterized as negative, with which classical liberalism is concerned. Classical liberals' love of this negative freedom, I argue, rests on their assumption of the simple faculty psychology that Locke inherited from Descartes in which the human soul has the twin powers of understanding and will, and their opposition to government regulation comes from their seeing it as interference with an individual's will through coercive threats and other means of thwarting it. The promotion of positive freedom through the nineteenth- and early twentieth-century reforms of welfare state liberalism, by contrast, rests on an assumption of a more complex psychology in which the idea of a well-integrated and intellectually developed personality replaces that of the will as the basis of human freedom. Thus, the moral progress that the enactment in liberal democracies of these reforms represents can be understood as an advancement as well in our understanding of human psychology such that having and freely exercising a will is no longer the essence of the capacity for self-government whose attribution to individual men and women is a fundamental doctrine of liberalism, whether classical or reformed.

These essays are collectively the result of more than a dozen years of philosophical work. I have, in the course of writing them, greatly benefited from the observations and criticisms of so many people that I fear I have not remembered everyone who has helped me. I am grateful to all who have and to the several philosophy departments, law schools, and academic societies to whom I presented these papers and from whom I received valuable responses in the subsequent discussions of them. I owe special thanks to Jonathan Adler, Robert Audi, Susan Bandes, Lawrence Becker, Jeffrey Blustein, Daniel Brudney, Marcia Cavell, David Copp, Russell Dancy, Meir Dan-Cohen, Derrick Darby, David Dolinko, Joshua Gert, Harvey

Green, Patricia Greenspan, Christopher Gowens, Ishtyaqui Haji, Bennett Helm, Eva Kittay, Richard Kraut, Jeffrie Murphy, Herbert Morris, Martha Nussbaum, Tim O'Keefe, Philip Pettit, Bernard Reginster, Michael Ridge, Robert Roberts, Connie Rosati, Michael Smith, Nic Southwood, Jim Sterba, Michael Stocker, Jon Tesan, and Meredith Williams. Michael Stocker read and commented on all of these essays, some in different drafts. His comments were of great help to me, and I am much in debt to him for his generosity and encouragement. Robert Solomon and Richard Wollheim also gave me many helpful comments on these essays, and sadly their recent deaths prevent me from thanking them again on this occasion.

I have had the good fortune to receive institutional support from the universities with whom I have been affiliated while working on these essays and am grateful to both Northwestern University and the University of Texas at Austin for this support. Twice in the last ten years I have been a visiting fellow for three months in the philosophy program of the Research School of Social Sciences at the Australian National University, and thanks to the wonderful academic environment and philosophical community the School provides, I was able to bring two of the essays in the collection to completion during my visits.

I wish to thank Peter Ohlin, my editor at Oxford University Press, for his interest and support as well as his valuable assistance in putting this collection together. Molly Wagener and Christi Stanforth also helped with the Press's editing and production of the collection, and I thank them too for their valuable assistance. I am grateful as well to Michael Sevel for his help in proofreading and constructing the index. Finally, I am indebted to Feris Greenberger for finding the photograph of the teenage girl in the throes of Beatlemania that appears in chapter 2.

Three of the essays, "The Politics of Disgust and Shame," "All Kinds of Guilt," and "Promises under Fire," were contributions to symposia on the work of Martha Nussbaum, Herbert Morris, and T. M. Scanlon respectively. These scholars have all replied to my discussions of their work, and their replies raise challenging questions about the cogency of the positions for which I argued. Interested readers can find these replies in the same issues of the journals in which my essays originally appeared. I have enjoyed years of friendship with Martha Nussbaum and Herbert Morris. While my views differ from and on some points oppose theirs, I have learned a great deal from them. They read and commented on many of these essays, and their influence on my thinking and its product in these pages will be evident to anyone who knows their work.

At a conference on emotions several years ago, I became engaged in discussion with a young scholar who was very enthusiastic about the studies of brain activity that use MRI technology to locate the sites of emotional arousal in the brain. These results, she thought, advanced significantly our understanding of emotions, and she was somewhat taken aback when I expressed skepticism about this. A study of love, she told me, has, by using this technology to create photographic images of a person's brain when the person sees his beloved enter the room, determined in which part of the brain this emotion is felt, and wouldn't my beloved be distressed to discover that an image of my brain did not show activity in this part when she appeared in my visual field? "When you've been married as long as I have," I quickly replied, "love won't be a matter of there being activity in a certain part of your brain on seeing your spouse enter the room you're in." Lynn Hill has for many years shared the pleasures and frustrations of my philosophical efforts as I have shared those of her mathematical ones. The value of such mutuality is beyond words. While I have no idea of what part of my brain my dedicating this book to her has occurred in, I do know that the dedication comes from deep within my heart.

Contents

Sources

Essay 1, "Emotions: The Legacy of James and Freud," appeared in the *International Journal of Psychoanalysis* 82 (2001): 1247–1256. It is reprinted by permission of the Institute for Psychoanalysis, London, U.K.

Essay 2, "Primitive Emotions," was written for and published in *Thinking about Feeling: Contemporary Philosophers on Emotion*, Robert C. Solomon, ed. (New York: Oxford University Press, 2004).

Essay 3, "Cognitivism in the Theory of Emotions," was a contribution to a symposium on emotions and cognition at the 1994 meeting of the Pacific Division of the American Philosophical Association in Los Angeles. It appeared in *Ethics* 104 (1994): 824–854. It is reprinted by permission of the University of Chicago Press.

Essay 4, "Emotions and Values," in an earlier draft, was presented at a conference entitled "Minds in Context: Morality and the Imagination" at Franklin and Marshall College in 1998. Later drafts were presented at the sixth annual Kino-eye Conference at the Museum of Contemporary Art in Antwerp in 2005 and a conference on mind, self, and identity at the University of Aarhus in 2007. It has not been previously published.

Essay 5, "The Politics of Disgust and Shame," appeared in a symposium issue on the work of Martha Nussbaum in the *Journal of Ethics* 10 (2006): 383–418 and is reprinted by permission of Springer.

Essay 6, "Emotions and the Authority of Law: Variations on Themes in Bentham and Austin," appeared in *The Passions of Law*, Susan Bandes, ed. (New York: New York University Press, 1999), pp. 285–308. An earlier and shorter version was given at a conference on law and emotion at the University of Chicago Law School in 1998. It is reprinted by permission of New York University Press.

Essay 7, "All Kinds of Guilt," was first presented at a conference on guilt, shame, and punishment organized by George Fletcher in honor of Herbert Morris. It took place at the Columbia University Law School in 1998. I presented the paper again the following year at a symposium on the work of Herbert Morris at the Pacific Division Meeting of the American Philosophical Association in Berkeley. It was published in *Law and Philosophy* 18 (1999): 313–325 and is reprinted by permission of Springer.

Essay 8, "Promises under Fire," appeared in *Ethics* 112 (2002): 483–506. It was a contribution to a symposium on T. M. Scanlon's *What We Owe to Each Other*. It is reprinted by permission of the University of Chicago Press.

Essay 9, "Moral Agency and Criminal Insanity," was the keynote address of the nineteenth annual meeting of the Association for the Advancement of Philosophy and Psychiatry 2000. An earlier version was my contribution to the twenty-third annual Midwest Philosophy Colloquium at the University of Minnesota, Morris, in 1999. It has not been previously published.

Essay 10, "Liberalism and Freedom," is a slightly longer version of a paper of the same title that was published in *Social and Political Philosophy: Contemporary Perspectives*, James Sterba, ed. (London: Routledge, 2001), pp. 151–165. It is based on my comments on Eva Kittay's "What (Welfare) Justice Owes Care," which were given at a conference on alternative conceptions of justice at Notre Dame University in 2000. It appears here by permission of Taylor and Francis Books.

Emotions, Values, and the Law

1

Emotions

The Legacy of James and Freud

The theoretical study of emotions in both philosophy and psychology has undergone revolutionary changes over the last one hundred years. In the eighteenth and nineteenth centuries, emotions were commonly conceived of as discrete, episodic, and purely affective states of consciousness, states whose connection to cognition, physiological activity, and conduct was that of either cause to effect or the converse. By now they are generally understood as complex states of mind whose existence is not separable from that of other mental states, restricted to episodes, purely affective, or connected to cognition, physiological activity, and conduct strictly as a cause or an effect. To explain these changes, one needs to go back to the work of two giants of late nineteenth- and early twentieth-century thought, William James and Sigmund Freud. Both James and Freud introduced into psychology conceptual innovations of the highest order, and through these innovations they radically and permanently altered our understanding of the human mind. The new ways of thinking about the mind that developed under the influence of their work freed philosophers and psychologists from the constraints of the old, classical empiricist conception that was born of the Cartesian revolution in philosophy and that had framed and guided psychological studies for over two hundred years. In the study of emotions, in particular, the removal of

3

these constraints opened up possibilities both for recovering conceptions of emotions that preceded the Cartesian revolution and for developing wholly new ones. In each case, the result was to deepen significantly our understanding of the place of emotions in human thought and action.

James's and Freud's innovations in psychology directly opposed the fundamental tenets of the classical empiricist conception of the mind. The mind, on this conception, is a single field of thought and feeling, entirely conscious, and transparent to itself. Further, its states are either simple or complex, and if complex, then fully analyzable as combinations of simple states. They are, as Hume wrote, like players in a theater, who "successively make their appearance; pass, repass, glide away, and mingle in an infinite variety of postures and situations" (1978, p. 253). While these theses reflect Descartes' influence on classical empiricist psychology, the program of representing all mental states as either simple or complex and, if the latter, then fully analyzable as combinations of the former became a staple of classical empiricism as a result of Locke's relentless prosecution of it in his *Essay Concerning Human Understanding* (1975), the first great work of empiricist psychology in the modern period. Thus, when James, in the famous ninth chapter of *The Principles of Psychology*, "The Stream of Thought," insisted that thinking was a continuous flow and not a series of discrete states, he had Locke's program squarely in his sights (1950, v. 1, pp. 229–271). And although James did not challenge the Cartesian conception of mind as unitary, entirely conscious, and transparent to itself, his representation of conscious thought and feeling as surface phenomena encouraged such a challenge. It left psychology with the choice of either understanding the mind as the site of epiphenomena or reconceptualizing it in ways inhospitable to the Cartesian conception. Freud, in developing his ideas of repression and the dynamic unconscious and his corresponding division of the mind into conscious, preconscious, and unconscious parts, produced just such a reconceptualization.

The central points of Freud's challenge to the Cartesian conception of the mind are too familiar to need reviewing here. One detail worth noting, however, is Freud's including emotions as well as thoughts among the unconscious states that figured in his explanations of certain forms of human thought and behavior. Their inclusion, which was corollary to the postulation of a dynamic unconscious, made clear the brute incompatibility of this postulation with the Cartesian conception. That there were unconscious thoughts and unconscious thinking was, by the late nineteenth century, a common, though not uncontroversial, hypothesis in psychology (1950, v. 1, pp. 164–176). It was offered to account for such experiences as that of having a thought slip from one's mind and become frustratingly beyond recall until all of a sudden one remembered it or that of discovering, upon waking from a deep sleep, the solution to a problem one had struggled with unsuccess- fully before falling asleep. And it was not particularly hard to make sense of such unconscious thoughts and thinking without doing great violence to the Cartesian conception. One simply abstracted them from their being con- scious and then supposed their residing in some uncognized region of the mind. Since such thoughts and thinking could readily become conscious without otherwise being changed, one could then treat them entirely on analogy with conscious thoughts and thinking and therefore as requiring only some loosening of the Cartesian equation of mind with consciousness. One could not, however, similarly make sense of unconscious emotions. The reason is that emotions, understood as conscious states, are feelings, and one cannot abstract a feeling from its being conscious. Nothing would remain. Hence, to propose, as Freud did, that certain forms of human thought and behavior were explained by unconscious emotions was to reject taking con- scious states of mind as the model for all unconscious states and so to break completely with the Cartesian conception.

Here too James's criticisms of Locke's program helped ease the way to the kind of theoretical innovation that Freud's idea of an unconscious emotion represented. For Locke's program imposed on psychology a conceptual appa- ratus that had no tolerance for such an idea. Its grip on psychology, therefore, had to be relaxed for the idea to be admissible, and James's criticisms effec- tively weakened this grip. They targeted, in particular, Locke's assumption of simple mental states, mental atoms, as James liked to call them, which Locke identified with certain sensations and their copies in imagination and intellect. Thus, for Locke, simple sensations were the primary states of mind, and they fell into either of two types, sensations of external objects and unlo- calized feelings of pleasure and pain, which Locke called 'internal sensa- tions' (1975, pp. 229–230). Sensations of sight, sound, smell, taste, and touch belonged to the former. Basic emotions belonged to the latter. Locke, then, following his assumption that all human thought was built up from these simple sensations, treated them as individual units of thought that recurred in different combinations and arrangements, as Hume's simile of players in a theater aptly illustrated. This scheme, James argued, by supposing that "sen- sations came to us pure and single" (1950, v. 1, p. 233), seriously misrepre- sented actual sensory experience. Sensory experience is no more made up of individual units of sensation than rivers are made up of individual drops of water. Both are Heraclitan. One never, James insisted, had the same sensa- tion twice. Indeed, sensations, according to James, were unrepeatable expe- riences. And what was true of sensations of external objects was true of the internal sensations as well. "The trouble with the emotions in psychology," he wrote, "is that they are regarded too much as absolutely individual things" (1950, v. 2, p. 449).

We are led to think otherwise, James observed, by our habit of identifying sensations of sight, sound, taste, and so forth by their objects. We speak of the same sounds when we hear the same thing on different occasions, a musical note, say, or a bird's chirp. Inattentive to variations in our sensory experience, we say that the sensations are the same when, in fact, there is no individual sensation on any of these occasions and therefore no relation of identity holding between sensations on different occasions. What is the same is the object of sensation. When we listen to the performance of a sonata, for example, we hear the same notes repeated at different intervals and in different arrangements, yet it would be wrong to think that each time we heard some note during the performance, we had a distinct auditory sensation that was separate from and a successor of an equally distinct auditory sensation we had in hearing the previous note and that was identical to an auditory sensation we had when we last heard this note. The experience of hearing the sonata does not consist of separate, individual sensations of sound experienced sequentially and repeated at different intervals. It is only the tendency to confuse these sensations with their objects that leads us carelessly to think of the experience in this way and to speak of having the same sensation when we hear the same note. With regard to emotions, moreover, Locke's treatment of them as separate, individual sensations that recur at different times cannot even be excused as a careless confusion of sensations with their objects. Instead, it appears to be an artifact of his having conceived of them as a type of sensation and thus on analogy with sensations of external objects. Hence, his treatment directly inherits the misconceptions James exposed in his treatment of sensations of external objects.

Once this Lockean conceptual apparatus lost its hold on psychology, it became possible to conceive of mental states as something other than units of thought and feeling. In particular, it became possible to conceive of emotions—hope, love, joy, fear, hatred, sorrow, anger, and the like—as something other than individual sensations or feelings each identifiable by a distinctive sensory tone or quale. One might, then, following James, conceive of emotions instead as feelings of the bodily processes that were set going by certain perceptions (e.g., feelings of one's body's trembling and one's face's reddening upon hearing an insult or stiffening and paling upon seeing a viper) (1950, v. 2, pp. 449–450). By so conceiving of emotions, one could, as James did, continue to identify them with sensations and feelings without supposing that they occurred as units in a sequence of individual states of mind. Alternatively, though, one might conceive of emotions as states of mind that, though characteristically manifested by certain sensations and feelings, were nonetheless distinct from them and so identifiable by other marks. This alternative is the conception implicit in Freud's recourse to unconscious emotions in his explanations of certain forms of human thought and behavior. For Freud such emotions were unconscious states disposing the mind to undergo certain processes that, if allowed to run their course, would terminate in feelings but that were prevented from running their course by repression. Hence, for him they were distinct from feelings. And while he recognized the oddity of this conception, he did not, contrary to what many have assumed, regard the term 'unconscious emotion' as merely a convenient expression that, taken literally, meant nothing.

This last point is essential. One could not understand how his use of the term signified a complete break with the Cartesian conception of the mind if it did not hold. Yet it is bound to provoke an objection. For Freud is commonly seen, largely in light of his remarks in the third part of his 1915 essay "The Unconscious," as having concluded that strictly speaking, there are no unconscious emotions. Indeed, a number of influential psychoanalytic writers have attributed just this conclusion to him (Schur, 1969; Pulver, 1971; Spezzano, 1993; Lear, 1990; see also Sachs, 1974, and Gardner, 1991). Freud, they maintain, drew it because he saw that on his own understanding of emotions as discharges of instinctual energy, no emotion could occur without its subject's being to some extent conscious of it.[1] This interpretation, then, directly threatens the point essential to understanding Freud as having in his use of the term 'unconscious emotions' broken completely with the Cartesian conception of the mind. Consequently, to sustain the point, it is necessary to revisit these well-known remarks of his 1915 essay.

The specific passage that is usually cited to support the interpretation occurs midway through the essay's third part, where Freud writes:

> Strictly speaking, then, and although no fault can be found with linguistic usage, there are no unconscious affects as there are unconscious ideas. But there may very well be in the system Ucs. affective structures which like others become conscious. The whole difference arises from the fact that ideas are

---

1. An especially crisp example of this interpretation is Lear's. He writes, "[R]oughly speaking, Freud treated emotions as feelings. Either they are feelings or, more strictly, they are processes of discharge which feelings accompany. Either way, we must in some way be aware of an emotion when it is occurring. So Freud thought. And thus Freud, who argued so vigorously that mental life should not be equated with conscious mental life, was, by his own conceptualization, forced to equate emotional life with conscious emotional life" (1990, p. 88).

> cathexes…whilst affects and emotions correspond to processes of discharge, the final manifestations of which are perceived as feelings. (1915, p. 178)[2]

The passage does suggest the interpretation, but not unambiguously. Freud is clearly here denying that the states of mind to which the term 'unconscious emotion' applies are analogous to the states to which the term 'emotion' in its standard use applies. In this respect, unconscious emotions are unlike unconscious ideas. But Freud is not saying that the term 'unconscious emotion' applies to no states of mind. Else he would have to admit that fault could be found with his using it.

To see what Freud is saying in this passage, one has to read it in light of several things: the text that precedes it, the argument of the whole paragraph in which it occurs, and the two previous paragraphs, which serve to define this argument's point. Its point is to show that the term 'unconscious emotion', unlike the term 'unconscious instinctual impulse', is not just loose phraseology or a harmless misnomer. Its point, that is, is to show that the term has a genuine application. It denotes certain states of mind. And the mental states it denotes are described in the text that precedes the passage in question. Freud writes:

> Thus it cannot be denied that the use of the terms in question is consistent; but in comparison with unconscious ideas there is the important difference that unconscious ideas continue to exist after repression as actual structures in the system Ucs., whereas all that corresponds in the system to unconscious affects is a potential beginning which is prevented from developing. (1915, p. 178)

An unconscious emotion, in other words, is a state of potentiality, a state defined by its power to produce certain things, the realization of whose productive power is prevented by repression. Freud's identification of the term's meaning thus falls directly out of his applying his postulation of a dynamic unconscious to affective states of mind.[3]

---

2. Pulver (1971) does not rely on this passage but relies instead on Freud's assertion in the paragraph preceding the passage, "It is surely of the essence of an emotion that we should be aware of it" (1915, p. 177). Yet Freud, in this paragraph, is only setting up the problem psychoanalysis faces in view of its "being accustomed to speak of unconscious love, hate, anger, etc." and so does not intend the assertion Pulver cites to be taken as his final word on the question. He makes the assertion and follows it with the observation about psychoanalysis being accustomed to speak of unconscious emotions to make clear how sharp the problem is.

Other passages that might also be cited to support this interpretation occur in *The Ego and the Id*. For consideration of these, see fn. 4 below.

3. When Freud later replaced his topographical model of the mind, on which the mind was divided into its conscious and unconscious parts, with his structural model, on which it was divided into three agencies, ego, id, and superego, he became able, using this new model, to delineate more exactly what he had in mind in characterizing unconscious emotions, on the

To be sure, Freud's understanding of such states as discharges of instinctual energy encourages the supposition that he conceived of the state of potentiality to which he meant the term 'unconscious emotion' to apply as neurological rather than mental. Accordingly, one might suppose that the difference between unconscious emotions and unconscious ideas with which Freud was concerned is that only the latter, and not the former, are to be conceived of as mental states. Yet there is a powerful reason for rejecting this supposition. It is that Freud's express purpose in showing that the term 'unconscious emotion' had a genuine application was to uphold the practice in psychoanalysis of explaining certain forms of human thought and behavior as symptoms and products of unconscious love, hatred, anger, fear, and so forth.[4] The force of these explanations, in many cases, lay in their revealing a meaning or purpose in thoughts and behavior that otherwise seemed meaningless and pointless. Such thoughts and behavior could appear, for instance, to be the products of inner compulsions and fixations that were themselves inexplicable, and by finding their source or motive in emotions whose operations were blocked from consciousness, these explanations rendered the thoughts and behavior intelligible as products of human endeavors. The explanations, however, could not have done so if what they cited as the source or motive behind these thoughts and behavior was conceived of as a neurological state. For the neurological properties of a state cannot explain

---

old model, as "affective structures [that can] become conscious" and "a potential beginning which is prevented from developing." This advance is evident specifically in the way he construed the term 'unconscious sense of guilt' on the new model. Thus, with the new model in place, he says specifically about sensations and feelings, "We...come to speak in a condensed and not entirely correct manner of 'unconscious feelings' keeping up an analogy with unconscious ideas which is not altogether justifiable" (1923, p. 22), and also about the discovery of the unconscious workings of conscience and their momentous effects, "But this new discovery...compels us, in spite of our better critical judgment, to speak of an 'unconscious sense of guilt'" (p. 27). He later explains, "The normal conscious sense of guilt...is based on a tension between the ego and the superego and is the expression of condemnation of the ego by its critical agency" (pp. 50–51), and this tension between the two agencies then serves, in his theory, to give meaning to the term 'unconscious sense of guilt'. It exemplifies an affective structure that can become conscious and, when it does, is expressed in feelings of guilt and a conscious sense of guilt. Freud then solidified this distinction between a conscious and an unconscious sense of guilt by expressly identifying the latter with the need for punishment (see 1924, p. 166). In this way, he rendered the term 'unconscious sense of guilt' as having genuine meaning.

4. "But in psychoanalytic practice, we are accustomed to speak of unconscious love, hate, anger, etc., and find it impossible to avoid even the strange conjunction 'unconscious consciousness of guilt,' or a paradoxical 'unconscious anxiety.' Is there more meaning in the use of these terms than there is in speaking of 'unconscious instincts?'" (1915, p. 177). (The argument to show that such terms have a genuine application then ensues.)

its transmission of meaning or purpose to its products. Hence, the states that were cited, unconscious love, anger, fear, etc., had to be conceived of as mental. Only as such could they be understood as having the power to transmit meaning or purpose to their products.

The conception of emotions implicit in these explanations was, therefore, a genuine alternative to James's. On its account, emotions are mental states defined both by their power to generate processes of discharge that terminate in feelings and by their role as the source of the meaning those processes transmit to the feelings in which they terminate. The conception, then, differs from James's in three ways. First, it takes the relation of feelings to emotions to be that of expression rather than identity (see Wollheim, 1999, pp. 1–11). Hence, it allows one to attribute an emotion to someone without implying that the person feels the emotion, an attribution that is impossible on James's conception.[5] Second, it gives emotions a role in the explanations of thought and behavior, whereas on James's conception, emotions are effects only and never explain anything. Indeed, James made a point of noting how his conception contradicted common sense in its view of the relation between an emotion and its behavioral expression. Fleeing, he said, precedes and causes fear, weeping precedes and causes sorrow, and not the other way round (1950, v. 2, pp. 449–450). On the conception implicit in Freud's explanations, the common sense view of this relation is preserved. Third, the conception explains the feelings of emotion as meaningful phenomena rather than as phenomena that merely register the occurrences of bodily processes. Accordingly, one identifies the feelings by the emotion they manifest—that is, as feelings of shame, guilt, anger, etc.—and then identifies the emotion by the meaning it transmits to those feelings. Shame, for example, is identified by a sense of being or having appeared unworthy of others' esteem and by the need to hide or cover up what one sees as shameful. On James's conception, by contrast, the feelings that an emotion consists in have no such meaning. Hence, their identity as feelings of shame, say, or fear is superficial, a point that ultimately proved fatal to this conception.[6]

Clearly, the thrust of James's conception, in keeping with his general views in psychology, was to render emotions epiphenomenal. As a result,

5. Thus, Freud, in a well-known passage in *The Ego and the Id*, could write of a patient whose illness was due to a sense of guilt, "But as far as the patient is concerned this sense of guilt is dumb; it does not tell him he is guilty; he does not feel guilty, he feels ill" (1923, pp. 49–50).

6. Experimental work by Stanley Schacter and Jerome Singer (1962) is generally thought to have established that the bodily processes a person who is feeling some emotion undergoes are not by themselves sufficient to determine the type of emotion the person is feeling.

under this conception, the importance of emotions as an object of study diminishes considerably. For this reason, the conception is likely to be current in periods in which or among thinkers for whom skepticism about the mind as an object of scientific study prevails. Epiphenomenalism, after all, is only a short step away from eliminating psychology in favor of neurophysiology or replacing the study of the mind with the study of behavior. Such skepticism was, for a good part of the twentieth century, a major trend in Anglo-American philosophy and psychology, perhaps even the dominant one. But no more. Confidence in taking the mind and its states and processes as objects of scientific study is now strong. Their study now flourishes in both disciplines. And the conception of emotions that has come to enjoy wide acceptance in the theories that these studies have produced, while not the same as the one implicit in Freud's explanations, is similar to it in several major respects.[7] Specifically, it shares with the one implicit in Freud's explanations the three characteristics that distinguish the latter from James's conception and that represent its complete break with the Cartesian conception of the mind: (1) that the relation of feelings to emotions is not that of identity but of expression, (2) that emotions are explanatory of thoughts and behavior, and (3) that the feelings expressing them are meaningful.

What accounts for their meaningfulness, their import, to use Charles Taylor's useful term, is the main question with which the theories that now dominate the study of emotions in philosophy and psychology are concerned (Taylor, 1985). The answers they give, while differing in specifics, largely converge on the thesis that some form of evaluative thought is an essential element of an emotion. On these theories, for instance, thoughts about good fortune are essential to joy, and thoughts about loss are essential to grief. Accordingly, the import of the feelings expressing joy or grief derives from these thoughts. Feelings of joy thus concern something good happening to one, and feelings of grief concern the loss of something dear to one. The feelings that express emotions are therefore importantly different from feelings and sensations that merely register some physiological disturbance. The latter, being symptoms of some bodily state, do not concern anything. They have no import. When after sudden exertion, say, one is short of breath and feels weak or wobbly, the feeling is symptomatic of respiratory difficulty and nothing more. If, by contrast, upon a sudden attack of panic one is short of breath and feeling wobbly, the feeling is not just a symptom of respiratory

---

7. Among those in philosophy, see de Sousa (1987); Greenspan (1988); Nussbaum (2001); Roberts (1988); and Solomon (1976). In psychology, see Arnold (1960); Lazarus (1991); Ortony et al. (1988); and Oatley (1992).

difficulty. It concerns, rather, something of which one is intensely afraid, and what determines the object of one's fear is the thought that one is in danger. The object of one's fear, in other words, is what one thinks is endangering one. And the same pattern of analysis, so these theories hold, applies to emotions generally. Every emotion, that is, is necessarily about something, however vague or indeterminate, and what it is about is determined by the evaluative thought it contains. Consequently, such a thought is an essential element of the emotion.

To take such a thought as an essential element of an emotion, and not merely a common concomitant, is therefore to understand an emotion as a cognitive state. This understanding represents a recovery of ideas about emotions that were prominent in the thought of the ancients. Indeed, Aristotle is often cited in the expositions of the theories that now dominate philosophy and psychology as a source of their central thesis. And the boldest of them go so far as to endorse the ancient Stoic theory on which emotions are taken to be identical to evaluative judgments of a certain kind (Nussbaum, 2001; see also Nussbaum, 1994, chs. 9–13; Deigh, 2000). Most of the now dominant theories, however, are not so bold and give accounts of emotions that include, as essential elements, other things besides evaluative thought and articulate some complex relation among these elements. Agitation of the mind, autonomic behavior, and impulses to action are the usual additions. But even in these theories, evaluative thought is the primary element in the mix, for it is the element by which each emotion is principally identified. It is the element the theories principally use to define different types of emotion (Deigh, 1994, pp. 835–842).

A theme that runs through all of these theories is that emotions, like other cognitive states, belong to rational thought and action. They are in this respect on a par with beliefs and judgments, decisions and resolutions. They are, that is, states that one can regard as rationally warranted or unwarranted, justified or unjustified by the circumstances in which they occur or the beliefs on which they are based. Thus, fear would be warranted if its object evidently posed some threat to one and unwarranted if it evidently posed no threat. Likewise, anger would be justified if it were a response to a genuinely demeaning insult and unjustified if based on one's mistaking an innocent remark for such an insult. In addition, to say that emotions belong to rational thought and action is to say that their cognitive content is combinable with the cognitive content of other states and that through such combinations the mind moves rationally to new cognitive states or to action. Thus, the evaluative thought essential to a juror's pity for some plaintiff is that the plaintiff's suffering is undeserved, and this thought can combine with the belief that the defendant in the case is responsible for the suffering to yield a judgment in favor of a larger assessment of damages to be awarded the plaintiff. In general, the theories make sense of these rational movements or transitions of thought, as well as the rational warrants for and justifications of cognitive states, by assuming that the states' cognitive content is conceptual and the thinking by which the transitions from one state to another occur aspires to be logical. In general, that is, the theories assume that the mind, when in good working order, functions rationally and that rational functioning consists in transitions of conceptual thought that, when coherent and cogent, are logical. Hence, in understanding emotions to be cognitive states on a par with beliefs, judgments, and the rest, these theories incorporate emotions directly into such rational functioning.

The upshot of this understanding is that the mind, as soon as it becomes susceptible to emotions, if not before, is not only capable of conceptual thought but actually possesses the concepts out of which the evaluative thoughts essential to these early emotions are formed. It follows, then, on this understanding of emotions, that a child at an early stage of infancy possesses the concepts out of which evaluative thoughts are formed, since children even at such an early stage of life experience emotions. Indeed, if our susceptibility to these emotions is an inherited trait, it follows that the concepts a child possesses at this early stage are innate. These are particularly striking consequences, for one does not ordinarily think of infants as capable of conceptual thought. What these consequences bring out, then, is the intellectualism at the heart of the cognitivist theories that support this understanding of emotions. Because these theories explain the workings of the mind as rational functioning and understand rational functioning to consist in transitions either between cognitive states whose content is conceptual or from such states to action, they must assume that the mind has the conceptual resources to function in this way from the time it begins to convert sensory stimuli into thought and action. This intellectualist assumption then surfaces immediately when one puts the theories' understanding of emotions as primarily cognitive states and their treatment of the content of cognitive states as conceptual together with the observation that human beings begin to experience emotions early in their infancy.

And once one grasps the intellectualism at the heart of these theories, it becomes clear that their conception of emotions is significantly different from the one implicit in Freud's recourse to unconscious emotions to explain certain forms of thought and behavior. While both conceptions represent emotions as states that explain thoughts and behavior and that are expressed by feelings and while both take emotions to be the source of the import of these feelings, that import, on the conception implicit in Freud's explanations, derives ultimately from instincts or drives and not evaluative thoughts. It derives ultimately from the former since, on Freud's theory, the motivating force of an unconscious emotion is always traceable to a basic instinct in whose aim the meaning of the thought or behavior the emotion explains originates. And it does not, therefore, derive ultimately from the latter, since instinct and thought cannot both be the ultimate source of the same thing. The reason is that instincts, being springs of animal behavior that operate independently of learning, memory, and understanding of the ends at which the behavior is directed, operate independently of thought. What is instinctual is the opposite of what is intelligent. The one is reflexive. The other requires thinking. Instincts, then, do not transmit meaning to the emotions they prompt through transitions of thought. Rather, they transmit it directly and, hence, independently of thought. The difference between the conception of emotions implicit in Freud's explanations and the one supported by the cognitivist theories that prevail in contemporary philosophy and psychology reflects this opposition between ultimate sources of meaning. It thus reflects a fundamental division in psychology.

These cognitivist theories, therefore, only partially fulfill Freud's legacy in psychology. They proceed on a conception of the mind that is incompatible with the Cartesian conception, and in this respect they are Freud's offspring. But because of their central thesis, that evaluative thought is an essential element of emotions, they fall on the other side of the divide in psychology from the one on which Freud's theory falls. They fall on the intellectualist side, and Freud's theory, as we have seen, opposes intellectualism.[8] Indeed, their lineage is an odd mix of Freud and Descartes, for Descartes was a major architect of intellectualism in modern psychology. His famous statement—I am a thing that thinks (*sum res cogitans*) (Descartes, 1975, p. 153; see also p. 101)—captured both his belief that the mind is unitary, entirely conscious, and transparent to itself and his belief that the mind is essentially an organ of rational thought. Hence, to be free of these strains of Cartesian

8. For an attempt to revise Freud's theory in a way that removes this opposition, see Lear (1990), pp. 88 ff. Lear is guided in this attempt by the thought that one can divorce Freud's theoretical understanding of emotions from his practice of explaining certain thoughts and behavior as products of unconscious emotions and then use a cognitivist conception of emotions in place of the former to reconstruct Freud's theory as the theory supporting the latter. The difficulty with this attempt, though, given Freud's opposition to intellectualism and so the impossibility of grafting the cognitivist conception onto his theory, is that the reconstruction teeters between losing contact with his theory and being incoherent at points at which it makes contact with it.

psychology, a theory of the emotions must not only proceed on a conception of the mind that contradicts the first of these beliefs but also reject any thesis, like the central thesis of cognitivist theories, that presupposes the second. A theory, for instance, that grouped the emotions into those in which rational thought is an element and those in which it is not and that took the latter as inborn and the former as arising from the latter through experience and learning would, given a general conception of emotions as being expressed by feelings and not identical with them, meet these conditions. Such a theory, though not wholly matched by any currently influential theory, largely matches the one Antonio Damasio (1995; see especially chs. 6–7) expounds in his aptly titled work *Descartes' Error*. By capturing Freud's signal idea that emotions precede and shape rational thinking and not conversely, it escapes the intellectualism in psychology that Freud strongly opposed and thereby promises a more complete fulfillment of his legacy.

REFERENCES

Arnold, M. (1960). *Emotions and Personality*. New York: Columbia University Press.

Damasio, A. (1995). *Descartes' Error*. New York: Avon Books.

de Sousa, R. (1987). *The Rationality of the Emotions*. Cambridge, MA: MIT Press.

Deigh, J. (1994). Cognitivism in the theory of emotions. *Ethics* 104: 824–854. (Ch. 3, this volume)

———. (2000). Nussbaum's defense of the stoic theory of emotions. *Quinnipiac Law Review* 19: 293–307.

Descartes, R. (1975). *The Philosophical Works of Descartes*, trans. E. S. Haldane and G. R. T. Ross. Cambridge: Cambridge University Press.

Freud, S. (1915). The unconscious. In *The Standard Edition of the Complete Psychological Works of Sigmund Freud* (hereafter cited as *SE*), gen. ed. James Strachey, vol. 14. London: Hogarth Press, 1953–1971.

———. (1923). The Ego and the Id. In *SE*, vol. 19.

———. (1924). The economic problem of masochism. In *SE*, vol. 19.

Gardner, S. (1991). The unconscious. In *The Cambridge Companion to Freud*, ed. J. Neu. Cambridge: Cambridge University Press, pp. 136–160.

Greenspan, P. (1988). *Reason and Emotions*. New York: Routledge Press.

Hume, D. (1978). *A Treatise of Human Nature*, ed. L. A. Selby-Bigge. Oxford: Clarendon.

James, W. (1950). *The Principles of Psychology*, vols. 1 and 2. New York: Dover.

Lazarus, R. (1991). *Emotion and Adaptation*. New York: Oxford University Press.

Lear, J. (1990). *Love and Its Place in Nature: A Philosophical Interpretation of Freudian Psychoanalysis*. New York: Farrar, Straus and Giroux.

Locke, J. (1975). *An Essay Concerning Human Understanding*, ed. P. H. Nidditch. Oxford: Clarendon.

Nussbaum, M. (1994). *The Therapy of Desire: Theory and Practice in Hellenistic Ethics*. Princeton, NJ: Princeton University Press.

———. (2001). *Upheavals of Thought: The Intelligence of Emotions*. Cambridge: Cambridge University Press.

Oatley, K. (1992). *Best Laid Schemes: The Psychology of Emotions*. Cambridge: Cambridge University Press.

Ortony, A. et al. (1988). *The Cognitive Structure of Emotions*. Cambridge: Cambridge University Press.

Pulver, S. E. (1971). Can affects be unconscious? *International Journal of Psychoanalysis* 52: 347–354.

Roberts, R. (1988). What is an emotion: A sketch. *Philosophical Review* 97: 183–210.

Sachs, D. (1974). On Freud's doctrine on the emotions. In *Freud: A Collection of Critical Essays*, ed. R. Wollheim. Garden City, NY: Anchor Press, pp. 132–146.

Schacter, S., and J. Singer. (1962). Cognition, social, and physiological determinants of emotional state. *Psychological Review* 69: 379–399.

Schur, M. (1969). Affects and cognition. *International Journal of Psychoanalysis* 50: 647–653.

Solomon, R. (1976). *The Passions*. New York: Doubleday.

Spezzano, C. (1993). *Affect in Psychoanalysis: A Clinical Synthesis*. Hillsdale, NJ: Academic Press, pp. 64–66.

Taylor, C. (1985). Self-Interpreting Animals. In *Human Agency and Language: Philosophical Papers 1*. Cambridge: Cambridge University Press, pp. 45–76.

Wollheim, R. (1999). *On the Emotions*. New Haven, CT: Yale University Press.

2

Primitive Emotions

Two facts about emotions stand out among the many that a theory of the subject ought to cover. The first is that emotions are intentional states in the sense that they are directed at something. Hope, for example, is a state of mind directed at a future condition or event. One hopes for sunny weather on the day of the picnic or calm seas on the day of the regatta. In this respect, hope is unlike giddiness or drowsiness, states of mind that can occur undirected at anything. The difference is nicely illustrated in the opening scene of Shakespeare's *Romeo and Juliet*, when two servants of the house of Capulet and two servants of the house of Montague cross paths. "Do you bite your thumb at us, sir?" Abram, one of the Capulet servants, asks Sampson, the offending Montague retainer. "No, sir," replies Sampson. "I do not bite my thumb at you, sir. But I bite my thumb, sir."[1] Sampson's reply, as we know from an aside to his confederate, is insincere. His thumb biting is aimed at the Capulet servants, and we understand its being aimed at them by recognizing the state of mind it expresses. It expresses contempt, an intentional state, and its target, so to speak, that at which it is directed, is the Capulet pair.

1. William Shakespeare, "Romeo and Juliet," I, i, 42–48, J. E. Hankens, ed., in *William Shakespeare: The Complete Works*, A. Harbage, gen. ed. (New York: Viking Press, 1969), p. 860.

If Sampson's reply had been sincere, then his thumb biting would not have expressed this intentional state, though it might still have signified a state of mind, like chronic and undirected jitters. But in this case, the state it would have signified would not have been an emotion.[2]

The second fact about emotions that a theory of the subject ought to cover is that emotions are common to both humans and beasts. This is not to say that humans and beasts are liable to the same set of emotions. On the contrary, the set to which humans are liable is much greater than the set to which beasts are liable. Shame over a moral failing, for instance, is an emotion to which humans are liable and beasts are not. It is to say, though, that some emotions are common to both sets. These are, in many cases, what I will call primitive emotions. They are the emotions liability to which is instinctive. That is, a human's or beast's liability to them is an inherited trait whose development, to the extent that it depends on the existence of environmental conditions, depends only on those necessary for meeting basic biological needs. Fear, anger, and delight all have primitive forms. The terror of horses fleeing a burning stable, the rage of a bull after provocation by a tormentor, and the delight of a hound in finding and retrieving his quarry are all examples.

A successful theory of emotions must account for both of these facts. It cannot skirt them. Yet accounting for both has proven to be surprisingly difficult. Some theories, particularly the cognitivist theories that have been so influential in philosophy and psychology over the last thirty years, use the first fact as their point of departure and leading idea, but they then have trouble accommodating the second.[3] Other theories, particularly those that have developed under the influence of Darwin's seminal work, *The Expression of the Emotions in Man and Animals,* take the second fact as their springboard, but they then have trouble accommodating the first.[4] The reason, in either case, is the gap between the way intentional states of mind are typically understood and the way primitive emotions are typically understood. The problem of closing this gap seems to outstrip the resources of these theories. The point is not generally recognized, however. It tends to lie beyond the theories' horizons. The object of this essay is to bring it forward and to vindicate it.

2. I am ignoring the possibility of objectless emotions here. Whether there are such emotions and how, if there are, their existence can be squared with this first fact are issues on which theorists of emotion disagree. Their disagreement, however, does not affect the argument of this essay. For discussion of these issues, see my "Cognitivism in the Theory of Emotions," *Ethics* 104 (1994): 824–854 (ch. 3, this volume).

3. See ibid. for a survey and critical discussion of these theories.

4. Charles Darwin, *The Expression of the Emotions in Man and Animals,* 3rd ed., with introduction, afterword, and commentary by Paul Ekman (New York: Oxford University Press, 1998).

The gap appears most clearly when one considers the trouble that cognitivist theories have in accounting for primitive emotions. On standard cognitivist theories, an intentional state of mind is either a thought or a compound state that includes a thought as a component, and in either case the content of the thought is represented as a proposition. Consider again the hope of a picnic planner for sunny weather. The emotion contains a thought about the advantages of sunny weather for picnicking, and the content of that thought is naturally represented by a proposition in which being sunny is predicated of the day of the picnic. Indeed, sometimes we make the propositional character of such thoughts explicit, as when we describe a person who is planning a picnic as hoping that the day of the picnic will be sunny. But propositional thought presupposes linguistic capacities, which are unique to human beings and, in fact, human beings who have grown past infancy. Consequently, if one represents the thought content of every intentional state as a proposition, one cannot account for primitive emotions. One's theory of emotions in that case will be like the theory of the ancient Greek and Roman Stoics. They held that emotions were judgments, which is to say, affirmations and denials of propositions, and therefore that beasts and babies were incapable of emotions. Such a view is no longer tenable, however. Like Descartes' cognate view that human beings alone among the animals of the world have minds, it has passed into history. So cognitivist theories of emotion must give up taking the thoughts emotions contain as in every case a proposition. They must find a way to explain some of those thoughts as nonpropositional so as to avoid making the possession of linguistic capacities a condition of being liable to emotions.[5]

This demand may not seem all that difficult to meet. After all, you might think that a defender of a cognitivist theory could just assume that the thoughts primitive emotions contained were like the thoughts contained in the distinctively human emotions that her theory takes as the paradigms of its subject, except that they lacked propositional form. Indeed, you might think that the thoughts contained in the former were just unencoded versions of the thoughts contained in the latter. To think this, however, would be a mistake. The concept of an encoded thought is that of a thought expressed in the words of some language or its equivalent.[6] When the thought is a complete

5. The best and most sustained effort at providing such an explanation is Martha Nussbaum's in her *Upheavals of Thought: The Intelligence of Emotions* (Cambridge: Cambridge University Press, 2001), pp. 89–138. I have discussed Nussbaum's explanation and raised some objections to it in my "Nussbaum's Defense of the Stoic Theory of Emotions," *Quinnipiac Law Review* 19 (2000): 293–307. For Nussbaum's replies, see "Reply" in ibid., 349–370, esp. pp. 358–362.

6. By an equivalent, I mean a code like Morse code whose meaningful strings of symbols one must translate into a language to recover their meaning.

one, then it is expressed by a complete, declarative sentence of that language. Consequently, if there is a version of this thought that is unencoded, it must be a complete thought in abstraction from every complete, declarative sentence that expresses it, and this is just what logicians mean by a proposition. A proposition, on their understanding of it, just is the meaning of a complete, declarative sentence of some language. It is what one grasps when one understands the sentence and what one preserves when one accurately translates it into a sentence of another language. If the translation is accurate, then the two sentences have the same meaning. They express the same proposition. Hence, defenders of cognitivist theories cannot use the idea of an unencoded version of an encoded thought to explain the thoughts that primitive emotions contain. For this idea just is the logicians' idea of a proposition.

Nonetheless, you might still think that the difficulty is not that great. For you might think that, even if the thoughts primitive emotions contain are not unencoded versions of the thoughts contained in the distinctively human emotions that cognitivist theorists take as the paradigm of their subject, we can still understand them as like the thoughts contained in the latter except that they lack propositional form. But to think that we could so understand them is to suppose that there is some way in which they and the thoughts that these distinctively human emotions contain are alike, and it is unclear what the form of this likeness could be. Of course, both are alike in being identical with or a component of an intentional state of mind, but to say that they are alike in this way is merely to reaffirm what is true of both types of emotion in virtue of their being intentional states. It is merely to reaffirm that intentional states are or include thoughts. A more specific account of what makes them alike is necessary if their being alike is to explain the character of the thought that primitive emotions must contain in virtue of their being intentional states, and no such account seems available.

The difficulty is an old one. It goes back to the problems on which Locke's doctrine of abstract ideas came to grief. Locke, you may recall, advanced this doctrine in opposition to the Cartesian belief that some thoughts, the intellective ideas, did not originate in sensory experience while others, in particular those that are the product of our imagination, did. On Descartes' theory of human cognition, the intellective ideas were radically unlike the ideas of imagination. They were clear and distinct. The latter were confused and obscure. And what explained the difference was the dependence of the latter on the operations of the body's sensory apparatus. These operations produced sensory images and internal feelings, and the ideas of imagination were composed of memories and replicas of these images and feelings. The intellective ideas, by contrast, did not depend on the operations of the body's sensory apparatus and were comprehensible apart from the sensory images and internal feelings they produced. This distinction corresponds to a distinction between thoughts common to both humans and beasts and thoughts that are distinctively human, though of course no Cartesian would have embraced this latter distinction since it presupposes what they denied, namely, that beasts had minds. Locke, however, did not deny that beasts had minds. On the contrary, he took sensory experience to be common to both humans and beasts and, in consequence, held that both were capable of retaining the resultant ideas in memory and of discriminating among them.[7] Distinctively human thought, Locke maintained, consisted in applying the power of abstraction to these ideas, for humans alone possessed this power.[8] Humans alone, that is, had the power of attending exclusively to some feature of an idea while neglecting all the others. An abstract idea, then, was an idea that one held in memory or formed in imagination and that one understood to represent generally a property of things that corresponded to the feature of the idea one had abstracted. Accordingly, Locke identified the ideas that came immediately from sensory experience as thoughts common to both humans and beasts and abstract ideas as thoughts that were distinctively human. At the same time, abstract ideas, on Locke's view, were not radically unlike other ideas. To the contrary, they were ideas of memory and imagination to which the power of abstraction was applied. Thus, Locke defined a kind of idea that was distinctively human in ways analogous to Descartes' intellective ideas and that was nonetheless like the ideas that were common to humans and beasts.

Yet for this definition to cover the same cognitions that Descartes explained as intellective ideas, it had to capture the thoughts that words and sentences express when they are used with their customary meaning. This requirement is evident from Descartes' point, at the start of Meditation VI, that our knowledge of the difference between a chiliagon and a myriagon cannot come from comparing the ideas we form of these figures in our imagination, since any idea we form in imagination of either figure will be indistinguishable from the idea we form of the other.[9] Our knowledge must come instead, Descartes observed, from our comparing the intellective ideas we have of these

---

7. John Locke, *An Essay Concerning Human Understanding*, P. Nidditch, ed. (Oxford: Clarendon Press, 1975), pp. 157–158 (bk. II, ch. xi, secs. 5–7).

8. Ibid., pp. 159–160 (bk. II, ch. xi, secs. 10 and 11).

9. René Descartes, *Meditations on First Philosophy*, in *The Philosophical Works of Descartes*, E. Haldane and G. R. T. Ross, trans. (Cambridge: Cambridge University Press, 1911; reprinted with corrections, 1975), I, pp. 185–186.

figures or, as we would now say, our concepts of them. The knowledge, then, to which Descartes appealed in this passage consists in our conceptual understanding of these figures, and this is the same as our understanding of what it means to say that a figure is a myriagon and not a chiliagon. It is the same, that is, as our understanding of what thought the sentence 'A myriagon is not a chiliagon' expresses when the sentence is used with its customary meaning. Nor was Descartes' point peculiar to mathematical objects. One could make the same point about our knowledge that a coyote is not a dog. So the success of Locke's opposition to Descartes' theory depended on his capturing with his definition of abstract ideas the thoughts that words and sentences express when they are used with their customary meaning.

Locke of course, though he may not have recognized the force of Descartes' point, meant his definition of abstract ideas to capture such thoughts.[10] In this regard, he initiated a long tradition in modern empiricist philosophy of programs for reducing what words and sentences mean to a set of sensory images and internal feelings common to all speakers. He supposed that the thoughts we express in language precede and are independent of our knowledge of language, and he further supposed that we came to have such thoughts by first making comparisons among the great many sensory images and internal feelings that fill our minds and then exercising the power of abstraction to isolate in thought those features and facts that interest us and that we use words and sentences to denote. In short, he conceived of the thoughts we express in language as wholly independent of our linguistic capacities, for he conceived of the powers of comparison and abstraction as operating independently of such capacities. Hence, Locke's doctrine of abstract ideas, if it were sound, would close the gap between the way we typically understand emotions as intentional states and the way we typically understand primitive emotions. On his doctrine, the thoughts we attribute to emotions in virtue of their being intentional states do not presuppose linguistic capacities and are therefore attributable to primitive emotions as well as to the distinctively human ones that cognitivist theories take as the paradigms of their subject.

The difficulty with the doctrine, however, is that it fails to account for the thoughts we express in language. Specifically, the power of abstraction, when understood as a power that operates independently of linguistic capacities, cannot yield such thoughts. It cannot, for instance, yield the thought we express when we say that a coyote is not a dog. For no amount of abstraction from the sensory images of dogs will isolate in one's thought features that

---

10. Locke, *Essay Concerning Human Understanding*, p. 159 (bk. II, ch. xi, sec. 9).

show, in view of one's abstract idea of a coyote, that a coyote is not a dog. The reason, moreover, is not or not merely that whatever features one abstracts will be at too great a level of phenotypic generality to be features that coyotes lack, though this is no doubt true. The reason, rather, is that we distinguish coyotes from dogs because of their genotype and regardless of any phenotypic difference between them. A coyote is not a dog because none of the ancestors it has in common with dogs was a dog, and no dog has a coyote as an ancestor. Descartes, then, was right to treat intellective ideas as radically unlike the ideas that come from sensory experience and are held in memory or produced in imagination. What we now call concepts and the propositions they help to constitute are not explicable on Locke's doctrine of abstract ideas.

The failure of Locke's program and of programs like it to reduce the thoughts we express in language to sensory images and internal feelings means that Descartes' theory of human cognition survives the attack that its traditional empiricist opponents made on it. What is more, the failure of their attack leaves unopposed the view that the thoughts we express in language are radically unlike the thoughts common to both humans and beasts. And in the absence of a viable alternative to this view, cognitivist theories of emotions must therefore abandon giving a uniform account of the thoughts in virtue of which emotions are intentional states. They must, in other words, take the thoughts in virtue of which primitive emotions are intentional states to be radically unlike the thoughts in virtue of which the emotions they take as paradigms of their subject are intentional states. Yet how they can do this consistently with their signature thesis that the thoughts in virtue of which emotions are intentional states are the principal determinants of the nature of emotions is a significant challenge. It is hard, after all, to maintain that one has satisfactorily explained the nature of something if one also allows that its nature could be determined by either of two radically dissimilar things.

Let us leave it to the defenders of these theories to stew over this problem and turn next to theories of emotions that take the second fact, that emotions are common to humans and beasts, as their guide. As I said at the outset, these theories draw their inspiration from Darwin's work on the expression of emotions in humans and other animals, and accordingly I will refer to their defenders as Darwinians.[11] Darwin himself was unconcerned with the

---

11. Among the Darwinians, I include Silvan S. Tomkins, Robert Plutchik, Carroll E. Izard, and Paul Ekman. For representative writings, see S. S. Tomkins, *Affect, Imagery and Consciousness* (New York: Springer, 1962, 1963), vols. 1 and 2; R. Plutchik, *Emotions: A Psychoevolutionary Synthesis* (New York: Harper and Row, Publishers, 1980); C. Izard, *Human Emotions* (New York: Plenum Press, 1977); P. Ekman, "Biological and Cultural Contributions to Body

question of the nature of emotions. He reflexively accepted the empiricist conception of them that was the orthodoxy of his time.[12] This conception identifies emotions with feelings as distinct from thoughts. They are, in Locke's words, "internal sensations," a phrase that nicely reveals the assimilation of emotions to sensations characteristic of traditional British empiricist psychology.[13] Consequently, on this traditional psychology, emotions, being pure feelings, are mental states that are not essentially directed at anything. Hence, the standard British empiricist conception immediately runs into trouble when applied to the first fact, that emotions are intentional states. For this reason, among others, it now has few defenders. In particular, the Darwinians do not defend it. Though they are inspired by Darwin's work, they assume a different conception from his. Nevertheless, it too has trouble accommodating the first fact. To understand why will require some explication of their program, and to do this it is best first to explain how it emerges from Darwin's.

Darwin was chiefly concerned with involuntary expressions of emotion. He was particularly interested in the involuntary facial expressions common among human beings. The study of these has a long history, going back at least to Descartes' explanations of how emotions are manifested in laughter, tears, blushing, paling, the wrinkling of the brow, the quivering of the lips, and so forth.[14] Darwin did not follow Descartes' lead, however. Indeed, as far as I can tell, he was unaware of Descartes' work, though he does mention the work of the seventeenth-century painter LeBrun, who had based his teachings of how to paint the face on Descartes' theory.[15] In any case, Darwin's interest in his predecessors in this field was more local. The main writer whose views interested him was Charles Bell, a prominent physiologist whose book *Anatomy and Philosophy of Expression* Darwin praised for having "laid the foundation of the subject as a branch of science."[16] What especially

---

and Facial Movement in the Expression of Emotion," in *Explaining Emotions*, A. Rorty, ed. (Berkeley: University of California Press, 1980), pp. 73–102; and P. Ekman, "Expression and the Nature of Emotion," in *Approaches to Emotion*, K. Scherer and P. Ekman, eds. (Hillsdale, NJ: Lawrence Erlbaum Associates, 1984), pp. 319–343.

12. Darwin, *Expression of the Emotions*, p. 33 n.

13. Locke, *Essay Concerning Human Understanding*, pp. 229–230 (bk. II, ch. xx, sec. 3).

14. René Descartes, *The Passions of the Soul*, in *The Philosophical Works of Descartes*, E. Haldane and G. R. T. Ross, trans. (Cambridge: Cambridge University Press, 1911; reprinted with corrections, 1975), pp. 380–390.

15. See Stephanie Ross, "Painting the Passions: Charles LeBrun's *Conférence sur l'expression*," *Journal of the History of Ideas* 45 (1984): 25–47.

16. Darwin, *Expression of the Emotions*, p. 7.

interested Darwin in Bell's work was Bell's view that the musculature of the human face was unique to human beings. Nothing like it, Bell maintained, occurred in other species. Moreover, Bell regarded this fact, or rather what he mistakenly thought was a fact, as evidence of God's design in creating human beings. God, Bell held, gave human beings these special facial muscles for the purpose of expressing the emotions distinctive of humankind. Needless to say, Bell's thesis offered Darwin a ripe opportunity for showing, in a new area of natural history, the superiority of evolutionary theory to explanations that appealed to God's design.[17] *The Expression of the Emotions in Man and Animals* was the result of Darwin's having seen this opportunity and seized it.

Darwin focused his study on facial expressions that seemed purposeless. Of course, if Bell were right, their purpose would be to express emotions just as nodding and shaking one's head express affirmation and negation. The point, in either case, is to communicate an attitude or thought. But on this view, the connection between a movement of the face and the emotion it expresses would be entirely arbitrary: as long as God's design of our facial muscles had as its sole purpose to facilitate our expressing emotions, raised eyebrows might just as well have expressed dejection as surprise, a curled lip might just as well have expressed admiration as scorn. Darwin thought, to the contrary, that one could see a purpose in many of these movements that would be well suited to the prehistoric environments in which the distant ancestors of modern human beings lived, even though it was ill suited to the environments of modern human life. Accordingly, he proposed that human beings inherited the disposition to make these movements from their ancestors, who had themselves acquired it because of the usefulness of the movements in their prehistoric environments. On this explanation, then, the connection between surprise and raised eyebrows, for example, was not arbitrary because the movement was advantageous in the circumstances that typically provoked surprise in prehistoric environments. Thus, raising one's eyebrows, Darwin observed, is necessary to opening one's eyes widely, and wide-open eyes enable one to scan one's surroundings quickly, something it would be very useful to do in circumstances in which unexpected sights and sounds were often omens of danger.[18] And though these circumstances may not be so common in modern life as to explain why raised eyebrows accompany surprise, they were common enough in the life of our prehistoric ancestors to explain why they acquired the disposition to raise their eyebrows when surprised.

17. Darwin, *Expression of the Emotions*, pp. 17–19.
18. Ibid., pp. 280–281.

Darwin, in offering these explanations, usually characterized the ancestors who first acquired the disposition as themselves hominids. Sometimes, though, to reinforce his explanations, he cited similar facial and bodily movements of other primates, thus implying that the ancestors who first acquired the disposition to make these movements were not hominids. And sometimes he appealed to the bodily movements of animals even lower down on the phylum that expressed the same emotion. Thus, to explain why our hair stands on end when we are frightened, Darwin noted that the same thing occurs in many other animals and that, though it serves no purpose in our life, it does serve the purpose in theirs of discouraging predators and cowing rivals. This is because their hair typically constitutes a coat and consequently, when erect, makes them appear larger and fiercer.[19] In these cases, then, the ancestors from whom humans inherited the disposition are the progenitors of many other animal species as well.

Clearly, Darwin could not argue for the superiority of these explanations to theological ones like Bell's if the dispositions to make the movements that were their explananda were not inherited. He could not argue for their superiority, for instance, if human beings acquired these dispositions by mimicking their parents' behavior or following their parents' instructions. Evolutionary theory, in that event, would be inapplicable. Hence, Darwin had to establish that the movements on which he focused were the products of inherited dispositions. Obviously, in a case like bristling hair that, as an expression of emotion, is common to many species, the evidence that the underlying physiological mechanism is inherited is irrefutable.[20] But in many other cases, such as raising one's eyebrows as an expression of surprise or curling one's lip as an expression of scorn, the burden of establishing that the disposition to make these movements is inherited is more difficult to meet. Darwin was aware of this burden and devoted a good deal of his research to meeting it. Specifically, he recognized that he needed to isolate the involuntary expressions that were the proper object of his study from expressions that were merely conventional. The latter, he observed, were most likely to be learned in childhood and to vary across cultures. For example, as we saw in *Romeo and Juliet*, biting one's thumb was an expression of contempt in Shakespeare's Verona. It does not, by contrast, express contempt, at least not conventionally, in contemporary

19. Ibid., pp. 99–100.
20. "With mankind some expressions, such as the bristling of the hair under the influence of extreme terror or the uncovering of the teeth under that of furious rage, can hardly be understood except on the belief that man once existed in a much lower and animal-like condition." Ibid., p. 19.

America. Rather, the conventional, vulgar expression of contempt in America is displaying a fist with a raised middle finger. True expressions of emotion, therefore, Darwin declared, differ from conventional ones in being instinctive or innate. As such, they are likely to be invariant across human cultures. Or at any rate, showing that the same movements were recognized in many different and disconnected cultures as expressing the same emotion would be powerful evidence that the disposition to make those movements, when experiencing that emotion, was inherited.[21] A substantial part of Darwin's work, then, entailed gathering and presenting such evidence for a broad range of movements, particularly facial movements, that express emotions.

It is this part of Darwin's work that inspires the Darwinians. Their program for studying the emotions follows his account of the true expressions of human emotion and uses the same principle he used to organize the chapters that presented his account. Thus, the Darwinians focus on human emotions and divide them into a small number of basic, general categories, each of which is defined by facial movements that, according to their research, qualify as the true facial expressions of all emotions that belong exclusively to that category. There are some disagreements among the Darwinians about how many basic categories there are and what emotions belong to them, but these disagreements are minor. A typical Darwinian division includes, as its basic categories, joy, anger, disgust, surprise, fear, distress, and sadness.[22] Each of these is then understood to cover a range of cognate emotions. The category of joy covers happiness, delight, gladness, satisfaction, and so forth; that of anger covers annoyance, indignation, rage, resentment, and so forth. And what makes the emotions in a given category cognate, that is, what explains why they belong to the same basic category, is that their true facial expressions consist of the same facial movements. To be sure, some emotions also have conventional facial expressions, but these are irrelevant to the determination of the basic category to which they belong. Holding one's nose, for instance, is a conventional expression of distaste, which is a mild form of disgust. But it is not by virtue of this expression that distaste, on the Darwinians' program, belongs in the category of disgust. Rather, its membership in this category is

21. "Whenever the same movements of the features or body express the same emotions in several distinct races of man, we may infer, with much probability, that such expressions are true ones—that is, are innate or instinctive. Conventional expressions or gestures, acquired by the individual during early life, would probably have differed in different races, in the same manner as do their languages." Ibid., p. 22.

22. There appears to be some uncertainty among the Darwinians about whether and how to distinguish the last two categories.

due to its being expressed by wrinkling one's nose, raising one's nostrils, and lowering the inner corners of one's eyebrows.[23]

What separates the Darwinians from Darwin is their belief that the study of an emotion's true expressions illuminates the very nature of the emotion. Darwin, as I noted, conceived of emotions as analogous to sensations in accordance with traditional British empiricism, and on that conception an emotion's true expressions no more illuminate its nature than swollen gums illuminate the nature of a toothache. The Darwinians, however, conceive of emotions differently. An emotion, on their conception of it, is a neurophysiological event whose manifestations typically include the facial and overt bodily movements that are the emotion's true expressions.[24] The event that is the emotion occurs when certain neurophysiological mechanisms are activated, and activating the mechanisms produces these movements along with covert physiological changes such as changes in heartbeat and electrogenic activity.[25] In human beings, the most perspicuous true expressions of emotion are facial movements, and the Darwinians take these to be the determinants of the neurophysiological mechanisms whose activation, on their conception, produces the emotion. These movements, that is, in virtue of being the emotion's true facial expressions, fix as the referent of the basic category

23. See Ekman's comment about these facial movements in Darwin, *Expression of the Emotions*, pp. 256–257.

24. This conception is implicit in the Darwinians' belief that they are studying the very nature of emotions by studying the true expressions of emotion. In their statements of what an emotion essentially consists of, however, some of the Darwinians add other components besides neurophysiological processes. Izard, for instance, includes subjective feelings or some inner experience. See Izard, *Human Emotions*, p. 4. But he seems to include this component as a concession to common sense. It is not well integrated into his study of the facial expressions of emotion, which is the major part of his research. Furthermore, he does not entertain the possibility of the subjective experience of an emotion occurring in the absence of the activation of the neurophysiological mechanisms that produce the expressions of the emotion. His ignoring it strongly suggests that the subjective feeling is merely a parasitic element in his conception, for it is hard to see how someone could acknowledge the possibility that the subjective feeling or inner experience of anger, say, could occur in the absence of the activation of the neurophysiological mechanisms that produce the expressions of anger without having to conclude that the subjective feeling, the inner experience, is the emotion and the operations of the neurophysiological mechanisms that produce its expressions are just its normal material base. Ekman evades defining what an emotion is. Emotion, he says, is complex, and there are many things that are relevant to its study such as subjective experiences and coping behavior. See Ekman, "Biological and Cultural Contributions to Body and Facial Movement in the Expression of Emotion," pp. 79–82. But his research, which concentrates on facial expressions and correlative processes in the autonomic nervous system, leaves no doubt that he is working with a conception of an emotion as a neurophysiological event.

25. See Ekman, "Expression and the Nature of Emotion," pp. 324–328.

to which the emotion belongs those neurophysiological mechanisms whose activation produces the emotion. In this way, the true facial expressions of an emotion are evidence of its very nature. Indeed, one philosophical enthusiast for the Darwinians' program has declared that the success of their program establishes the basic categories into which they divide the emotions as natural kinds by virtue of this reference fixing character of the facial movements that define the basic categories and the applicability of evolutionary theory to the neurophysiological mechanisms reference to which they fix.[26]

It should be clear, then, that the Darwinians view their division of the emotions into these basic categories as corresponding to major real differences among the emotions. Because they hold that the different facial movements that define the categories determine, for each category, the neurophysiological mechanisms whose operations the emotions in that category consist of, they understand the real distinction between joy, say, and all of its cognate emotions, on the one hand, and sadness and all of its cognate emotions, on the other, to be a distinction between the neurophysiological mechanisms that produce the facial movements defining those categories. And the same is true of other major differences they find among the emotions. The Darwinians recognize minor differences among the emotions too. Thus, they explain differences among the emotions that belong to the same category—distaste and revulsion, for instance, which are forms of disgust—as reflecting differences in the intensity, duration, and course of the neurophysiological events that constitute these emotions. And they explain differences among emotions that belong to two or more categories—horror, for instance, which is a mixture of fear and disgust—as reflecting differences in the combination of neurophysiological mechanisms whose operations those emotions consist of. These explanations follow more or less directly from how the Darwinians explain the major differences among emotions and, consequently, do not introduce any substantially new premises into their program. Thus, in considering how well their program accounts for the two facts I have highlighted, we can concentrate exclusively on their explanations of these major differences.

That the Darwinians can readily account for the second fact, that emotions are common to humans and beasts, is evident. The mechanisms to which they attribute the major differences among the emotions have the same place in their theory that the inherited dispositions to make facial movements have in Darwin's explanations of the true facial expressions of emotions. Indeed, on the Darwinians' most ambitious hypothesis, they suppose that each of

---

26. Paul Griffiths, *What Emotions Really Are* (Chicago: University of Chicago Press, 1997), pp. 11–14.

the basic categories into which they divide the emotions corresponds to a complex program that is genetically hard-wired in the brain, as it were, and that coordinates activation of the different neurophysiological mechanisms whose operations an emotion consists of. These affect programs, to use the term those who advance the hypothesis favor, are inherited dispositions, and the ancestors from whom human beings inherited them are the progenitors of many different species of animal.[27] Hence, the Darwinians, given their conception of an emotion as a neurophysiological event that occurs when an affect program is activated, can account for there being emotions common to humans and beasts by identifying many of the emotions that belong in one or another of their basic categories as emotions to which some beasts are liable in virtue of their having affect programs that are homologous to the human affect programs to which those categories correspond. The question, then, is how, given this conception of emotion, the Darwinians can account for the first fact, that emotions are intentional states.

To do so, they must explain intentional states differently from the way standard cognitivist theories of emotion explain them. That is, they must explain differently how emotions are directed at objects. Standard cognitivist theories, as I observed earlier, explain this feature by attributing propositional thought to emotions, for they take the emotions distinctive of human beings as the paradigm of their subject, and the thought content of these emotions is propositional. The Darwinians, by contrast, start with a conception of emotions as common to humans and beasts and indeed as having first occurred in beasts millions of years before the first language-using animals appeared on the earth. They will therefore have no interest in this or any explanation that is based on the emotions distinctive of human beings. Instead, they must give an explanation of how emotions can be directed at things that is immediately consistent with the emotions of beasts. The explanation they give, that is, must immediately fit what goes on, say, when a dog, angered by a stranger's invasion of his territory, growls or barks at the stranger. The dog's anger, in this case, is directed at the stranger, and what the Darwinians must explain is how to understand this feature of the dog's emotion, given that it cannot be explained by a belief the dog has or a judgment he makes *that the stranger has invaded his territory*.

What is going on in a dog's mind when he growls at someone? Suppose, for example, you need to enter your neighbors' yard, but just as you approach the gate, their dog growls at you. What excites the dog's growling is his perception

---

27. See Ekman, "Biological and Cultural Contributions to Body and Facial Movement in the Expression of Emotion," pp. 80–84. Ekman cites Tomkins as the source of the idea of an affect program and the inventor of the term.

of you as you are about to encroach on his territory. He senses something invasive about your behavior that he would not sense in someone he knows and has affection for. Your appearance in his perceptual field triggers this sensitivity, and as long the condition lasts, so does the growling. In fact, you could be someone whom the dog knows and likes but initially does not recognize. In that case, upon recognizing you, the dog will immediately change his attitude. He will stop growling and relax. His back, which would have been straight and stiff, will slump, and he will begin to wag his tail. Throughout this episode, you are the object of the dog's attention, and the dog tracks you in the sense that his emotion is sustained or altered according as his perception of you remains steady or changes. And what remains steady or changes in his perception of you is his sense of the invasiveness of your behavior. That sense could become stronger as you encroach further on his territory, or it could disappear altogether as soon as he recognizes you. The question, then, is whether these two features of the perceptions that excite and sustain the dog's emotion, your being the object of his attention and his tracking you by virtue of his sensitivity to some property you have, are sufficient to constitute you as the object of that emotion. If they are, then the explanation is one the Darwinians should find congenial. For they could still conceive of the emotion, on this explanation, as a neurophysiological event. They would locate its object in the perceptions that excited and sustained that event, which is to say, in the sensory images that activated the neurophysiological mechanisms whose operations, on the Darwinians' view, it consisted of. Since the Darwinians do not expressly offer an explanation of the fact that emotions are intentional states, let us assume that they would endorse this one.

The most common objection to explanations like this one is that they confuse the cause of an emotion with its object. In the above example, you are both the cause and the object of the dog's emotion.[28] One can give other examples of emotions, however, in which the two are different, and the objection is that explanations like this one fail to capture that difference. I believe, though, that a little tinkering with the explanation can save it from this objec-

---

28. Some philosophers hold that the cause and the object of an emotion are always and necessarily distinct, and the reason they hold this position is that they understand the thought in virtue of which an emotion is an intentional state as having indirect rather than direct (in Frege's sense) reference to the world. My view is different. On my view, some emotions are intentional states, even though the thought in virtue of which they are intentional states makes direct reference to the world. The difference between the two views raises issues outside the scope of this essay and does not affect the argument I am making here. For a statement and defense of the position that the cause and the object of an emotion are always and necessarily different, see Robert C. Solomon, *The Passions: The Myth and Nature of Human Emotion* (Garden City, NY: Anchor Press, 1977), pp. 172–185.

tion. Consider an example of Norman Malcolm's. Imagining his dog chasing a neighbor's cat, Malcolm writes, "[The cat] runs full tilt toward an oak tree, but suddenly swerves at the last moment and disappears up a nearby maple. The dog doesn't see this maneuver, and on arriving at the oak tree, he rears up on his hind legs, paws the trunk, and barks excitedly into the branches above."[29] The dog, we might say, is barking at a cat he thinks is up the tree.[30] And if we further suppose that rustling leaves due to movements of a small bird that the dog doesn't see, or perhaps just the wind, cause the dog to continue to bark, then the object of the dog's excitement, the cat, is no longer its cause. In this case, although the dog can no longer be said to be tracking the cat, he can still be said to be responding to a sensory image of the cat that is sustained in his mind by the sound of rustling leaves. Accordingly, the cat is still the object of the dog's thought, and the dog is still responsive to the cat's image, and to changes therein, by virtue of his sensitivity to some apparent property of the cat presented in the image. Hence, by replacing the notion of tracking with that of responsiveness to an image, in the explanation of how certain features of the perceptions that excite and sustain an emotion constitute the emotion's object, we can preserve in this explanation the distinction between an emotion's cause and its object.

The real problem with the explanation lies elsewhere. When the neighbor's dog growls at you as you approach the gate, he senses something invasive about your behavior. This is something about you he doesn't like. If there were nothing about you he didn't like, then we could make no sense of his growling *at you* or the anger it expresses. In other words, the dog could not be angry *at you* unless there were something about you or, more exactly, unless there were something about the way you appeared to him that made him angry, and it must be something, like invasiveness, to which anger is an intelligible response. Indeed, by identifying the emotion as anger and the dog's growling as its expression we make intelligible behavior that would otherwise be no more intelligible than a fit of hiccups. And we do so because, in identifying the emotion as anger, we identify how its object appears to

<hr/>

29. Norman Malcolm, "Thoughtless Brutes," in *Thought and Knowledge* (Ithaca, NY: Cornell University Press, 1977), p. 49.

30. This remark, of course, requires some gloss to avoid taking it as implying that the dog is capable of propositional thought. What we must mean, then, when we say the dog thinks the cat is up the tree—and we say such things all the time—is something like the dog has been impressed with images of the cat's going up the tree and these images are guiding his behavior. Malcolm's response to the issue is to distinguish between saying the dog thinks such-and-such and saying the dog has the thought that such-and-such. According to Malcolm, the latter implies propositional thought but the former does not. See Malcolm, "Thoughtless Brutes," pp. 50–51.

the dog and not simply that its object is the object of the dog's attention and is being tracked by him. Hence, for something to be the object of an emotion, whether the emotion is anger, disgust, pity, embarrassment, shame, or what have you, it must appear to the subject in a way that makes his feeling an emotion of that type intelligible or it must be thought by him to have a property whose possession by the object makes his feeling an emotion of that type intelligible. To be the object of anger, for instance, something must appear or be thought to be invasive, injurious, offensive, or the like. To be the object of disgust, something must appear or be thought to be foul or rotten or putrid. To be the object of pity, something must appear or be thought to be in some sorry or wretched condition. The real problem, then, with the explanation that we are assuming the Darwinians would endorse is that it misses this intelligibility condition on something's being the object of an emotion. As far as the explanation goes, you could be the object of someone's attention, that person could be tracking you, and these features could be features of perceptions that activated neurophysiological mechanisms whose operations produced the facial movements that were the true facial expressions of a certain type of emotion, and yet you might still not be the object of an emotion of that type. For it might still be the case that you do not appear to its subject in any way that makes his feeling an emotion of that type intelligible.

This problem, unlike the last, defeats the attempt to come up with an explanation of the intentionality of emotions that the Darwinians would find congenial. One could, to be sure, revise the explanation again to resolve the problem. But one could not do so and still maintain the Darwinians' conception of emotions. And this gets to the heart of the trouble the Darwinians have in trying to accommodate the fact that emotions are intentional states. Because they conceive of an emotion as a neurophysiological event whose type is determined by certain facial movements, namely, those that are produced by the operations of the neurophysiological mechanisms that the emotion consists of, they have to allow, as a conceptual possibility, that those operations and the facial movements they produce can occur, and occur in response to perceptions of a particular object, even though the object does not appear to the subject in any way that makes his feeling the emotion intelligible. For they cannot deny this possibility without also denying the possibility that the facial expressions defining one of the basic categories into which they divide the emotions occur on some occasion as the true expressions of an emotion that belongs to some other basic category. And this surely can happen. That it can happen, moreover, confounds the Darwinians' theory. For when it happens, the object of the emotion appears to the subject in a way that makes his feeling that emotion intelligible but that does not make

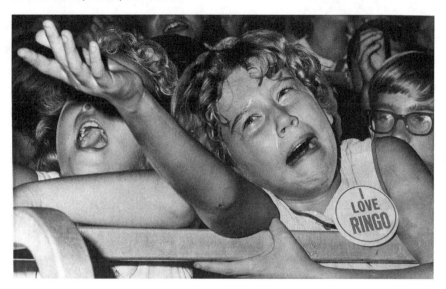

FIGURE 2.1   © AP/WIDE WORLD PHOTOS.

intelligible his feeling any of the emotions that, according to the Darwinians' scheme, belong in the category defined by his facial expressions. When it happens, in other words, the Darwinians must insist on his feeling some emotion that he is in fact not feeling.

Consider, as an example, the phenomenon known as Beatlemania. It has been wonderfully captured in a video of the Beatles 1965 concert at Shea Stadium.[31] Here is a brief description. The Beatles suddenly appear from a tunnel and run across the field directly to the stage on which they will play. At their appearance, thousands of teenage girls in the stands begin to scream and then to shriek. The noise is deafening. The girls continue to scream and shriek as the Beatles start to play, and their screaming never stops. Many of the girls, at some point, break down into tears. When they do, the tears flow freely. The girls weep. They sob. Their bodies slump. Their faces lose all composure and become blubbery and slack. If one were presented with pictures of these girls' faces and did not know the context in which the pictures were taken, one would say they were the faces of great sorrow, anguish, or grief. Yet the girls are experiencing none of these emotions. The object of their emotions is the Beatles, and nothing about the Beatles on this occasion would make sorrow, anguish, or grief an intelligible response. For any of these emotions

31. *The Beatles Anthology* (a video history of the Beatles).

to be an intelligible response, one or more of the Beatles would have to have suffered some grave misfortune or at least to have appeared to have suffered such misfortune, and none of them obviously has. To the contrary, all of them appear to be having a great time, though they are rather perplexed by all the screaming. The girls' faces, then, are products of a different emotion. It is ecstasy or rapturous joy at seeing and being near the objects of their most ardent devotion. On the Darwinians' theory, however, there is no basis for attributing ecstasy or joy to these girls. On their theory, whatever emotion the girls are experiencing, it must belong either to the category of sadness or to the category of distress.[32] Their theory, because it excludes considerations of intelligibility from its definitions of the basic categories of emotions, cannot correctly identify the girls' emotions in this case.

Needless to say, it is crucial to this criticism that the expressions on the girls' faces are true expressions of their emotions in Darwin's sense. They must be true expressions and not conventional, for otherwise nothing in the Darwinians' theory would require identifying the girls' emotions as belonging to either the category of sadness or that of distress. If the girls' behavior were merely histrionic, for instance, then it would not confound the Darwinians' theory. But to contend that it was merely histrionic would be implausible. It is evident that there is no artifice in the girls' expressions of emotion. Indeed, it is hard to see how a defender of the Darwinians' theory could deny that the girls' expressions were true. A true expression of emotion, recall, is one that is instinctive in the sense that it manifests an inherited disposition to make the movements that the expression consists of, and the girls' weeping is as much a manifestation of such a disposition as weeping that expresses anguish or grief when it too is brought on by a screaming fit. In neither case of weeping that results from screaming is there any reason to think that the display of emotion is less true than in the other.

Darwin's account of such weeping makes this point clear.[33] According to Darwin, strong contraction of the muscles around the eyes produces tears as a result of its stimulating the lacrimal glands, and such contraction occurs when one screams. Indeed, as Darwin explained, any violent expiration of air, such as violent coughing, sneezing, or laughter, will cause these muscles to contract and bring tears as a result. Of course, people do not cough or sneeze or laugh when they suffer great pain or become aware of a grave personal loss. But they do scream. Screaming, after all, is the common and presumably

32. As noted above (fn. 21), there is some uncertainty among the Darwinians about whether and how to distinguish these two categories.

33. Darwin, *Expression of the Emotions*, pp. 146–175.

universal response to pain among infants even before their lacrimal glands develop to the point where they can shed tears. And while learning to control the impulse to scream is part of learning how to deal with pain, the impulse remains even after one has acquired some control over it, and it still produces screaming when the pain or the loss is great enough. Thus, weeping and sobbing, and the facial movements that occur when weeping results from prolonged and intense screaming, are widely recognized as expressions of anguish and grief. The phenomenon of Beatlemania, by contrast, and similar crowd phenomena in which prolonged and intense screaming occurs, not as the result of pain or grave personal loss, but as the result of the sudden appearance of the objects of ardent devotion, are too peculiar for the facial expressions of the emotions characteristic of them to be widely recognized outside of the contexts in which they occur as expressions of those emotions. Nevertheless, these expressions are the very same ones as the expressions that, presented out of context, people readily identify as expressions of anguish or grief. They result from the operations of the same neurophysiological mechanisms and are therefore no less true facial expressions of the emotions characteristic of Beatlemania, when they express those emotions, than they are true facial expressions of anguish and grief, when they express them.

This conclusion points up a significant confusion in the Darwinians' theory. The source of the confusion is the assumption behind the Darwinians' division of emotions into basic, general categories according to the true facial expressions of the emotions in those categories. For the assumption behind this division is that the facial expressions defining a basic category are not only true expressions of the emotions in that category but are also never true expressions of an emotion that belongs to a category defined by different facial expressions. And the example of Beatlemania shows that this assumption is false. In the same way, the example shows that the Darwinians' identification of each basic category with the neurophysiological mechanisms whose operations produce the facial expressions defining that category represents a misconception of the nature of the emotions belonging in that category. For it shows that the difference between such emotions as joy, delight, gladness, and elation and such emotions as sadness, sorrow, grief, and dejection cannot consist, not even in part, in their being different types of neurophysiological event whose differentiae are determined by the expressive behavior that manifest them. This misconception is most sharply realized in the Darwinians' ambitious hypothesis that each of the basic categories corresponds to an affect program whose activation produces the type of neurophysiological event that every emotion in that category consists in. If prolonged, intense screaming, whether initiated by the excitement of suddenly seeing the object of one's ardent devotion or the shock of suddenly getting news of a tragic and personal loss, activates the same affect program, then the Darwinians who advance this hypothesis have to hold that the emotion in either case belongs to the same basic category, and therefore two emotions as seemingly opposed to each other as rapturous joy and devastating grief are really generically the same. This result may, to be sure, leave our philosophical enthusiast for this hypothesis undeterred. He may just shrug it off with the remark, "Well, modern biology teaches us that birds and lizards are generically the same; so why think this result is any weirder."[34] But most of us would not be so sanguine. For most of us, the incoherence of the result is sufficient to warrant adding the hypothesis to the large class of failed theories in scientific psychology.

Elsewhere I have written that the great changes in our understanding of emotions that took place in the twentieth century are rooted in the ideas of William James and Sigmund Freud.[35] James's ideas are the source of the view that one can fruitfully study emotions by studying the neurophysiological processes that occur with experiences of them. Of course, James did not identify emotions with these neurophysiological processes. He identified them with feelings. His famous definition is that emotions are the feelings of the bodily changes that "follow directly the perception of an exciting object."[36] But on this definition, emotions become epiphenomena, and the proper object of study becomes the physiological processes the feelings of which are identified with emotions. Freud's ideas are the source of the view that emotions transmit meaning or purpose to the feelings and behavior that manifest them. Though Freud often described emotions as flows of nervous energy, his view of them as transmitters of meaning and purpose was nonetheless implicit in his notion of an unconscious emotion and in the way he used this notion to make sense of feelings, behavior, and physical maladies that seemed otherwise inexplicable. Widespread acceptance of his explanations has thus led to studying emotions for the ways they render feelings, behavior, and bodily conditions meaningful products of the mind. Theorists of emotion who develop their theories from an understanding of emotions as phenomena common to humans and beasts are readily drawn to the view of how to study them that comes from James, for the neurophysiological mechanisms in human beings on which such studies focus are homologous to neurophysiological mechanisms in other animals, and by appeal to these homologies

---

34. See Griffiths, *What Emotions Really Are*, pp. 77–79.

35. John Deigh, "Emotions: The Legacy of James and Freud," *International Journal of Psychoanalysis* 82 (2001): 1247–1256 (ch. 1, this volume).

36. William James, *The Principles of Psychology* (New York: Dover Press, 1950), vol. 2, p. 449.

they can then explain how humans and beasts are liable to many of the same emotions. Theorists of emotion who take as their leading idea that emotions are intentional states and develop cognivitist theories based on this idea accept the view that comes from Freud, for to make thought essential to emotions is to introduce an element in emotions that can explain how emotions give meaning to the feelings, behavior, and bodily conditions they produce. These two different programs have, relative to the chief fact about emotions each takes as central to understanding the phenomena, yielded powerful and illuminating theories. The main problem for the study of emotions now is how to develop a theory that reconciles these two facts.

3

Cognitivism in
the Theory of Emotions

Cognitivism now dominates the philosophical study of emotions. Its ascendancy in this area parallels the ascendancy of cognitivism in the philosophy of mind generally. Yet the two trends have independent sources. In the philosophy of mind, cognitivism arose from unhappiness with the various behaviorist programs that prevailed at midcentury in psychology and philosophy. In the philosophical study of emotions, it arose from unhappiness with affective conceptions of the phenomenon that had been a staple of British empiricism for more than two centuries. The change of orthodoxy in the first case meant replacing conditioning, as the model of explanation, with computation. It also meant abandoning operationalist translation schemes and embracing functionalist ones instead. The change of orthodoxy in the second case meant reconceptualization. Thought replaced feeling as the principal element in the general conception of emotion. This second change is the subject of this essay.

What interests me is the question of progress. Specifically, has this change brought about a significant improvement in our understanding of emotions? The question, however, is not intended to invite a return to earlier, feeling-centered conceptions of the phenomena. The criticisms of them that propagated the current wave of cognitivist theory were well aimed and wholly successful. The question, rather, is intended to initiate examination of the conversion from these old, now discredited conceptions to the new, now widely favored ones. I want to see whether the accounts of emotion that incorporate the latter and that developed from criticisms of the former represent advances in the theory of emotions. Cognitivism, one could say, is the lesson philosophers working in this theory have drawn from the criticisms to which the feeling-centered conceptions succumbed, and the question I want to examine is whether their work shows that they have drawn the right lesson.

Two criticisms are chiefly responsible for the demise of feeling-centered conceptions. These criticisms are well known, and I will present them with a minimum of fuss. One is that feeling-centered conceptions cannot satisfactorily account for the intentionality of emotions. The other is that they cannot satisfactorily represent emotions as proper objects of rational assessment. I will begin with the first. Consideration of various ways in which cognitivists have tried to work and rework the idea of intentionality into an argument for their conception will then lead to the second.

I. Intentionality

Any feeling-centered conception of emotion assimilates the phenomena to bodily sensations, particularly the sensations of pleasure and pain. That is, emotions are conceived of as having similar intrinsic properties to such sensations. At the same time, the conception distinguishes emotions from bodily sensations by locating them in a different place in the mind's machinery. Emotions, on this conception, thus differ from bodily sensations in the relations they bear to other states of mind and to states of the body. Locke's conception is typical. Emotions, in Locke's view, are "internal sensations" of pleasure and pain, which differ from bodily sensations in being produced by thoughts of something good or evil rather than by alterations of the body (Locke [1695] 1975, bk. 2, chap. 20, sec. 3, pp. 229–230). Being simple ideas, however, they no more contain any thought than do the bodily sensations that are their simple counterparts. Moreover, Locke was largely following Descartes, who had defined emotions as excitations that seem to come from within the soul itself rather than from any part of the body or from some object external to the body (Descartes [1649] 1989, pt. 1, art. 25, p. 32). And Locke's view was in turn taken over by Hume, whose conception of emotions as impressions of reflection matches Locke's notion of them as internal sensations (Hume [1739] 1978, bk. 2, pt. 1, sec. 1, p. 275). The feeling-centered conception was thus a fixture of early modern philosophy.

Indeed, it represents one of the many ways in which the moderns tried to distance their philosophical programs from their medieval predecessors. The older schools, particularly the Scholastics, used the notion of intentional being to understand various states of mind including especially emotions, and this notion is just the sort of Scholastic innovation that Descartes and his successors had the signal aim of eliminating from natural and moral philosophy. They conspicuously omitted it from their general definition of emotion and introduced mechanistic relations among distinct thoughts and feelings to describe what the notion was meant to capture. Their strategy falls short of its aim, however. Intentionality, as we now call it, cannot be so readily replaced. This point lies behind the first criticism of feeling-centered conceptions.

The criticism itself is easy to outline. Intentionality is a property of actions and mental states. It is the property of being directed at or toward something. Emotions typically have this property. When one is angry or afraid, for example, one is angry at someone or something, afraid of someone or something. This someone, this something is the emotion's intentional object, that at or toward which it is directed. By contrast, bodily sensations of pleasure and pain, the comforting feeling of a warm bath, say, or the aching feeling of sore muscles, are not directed at or toward anyone or anything. They are not intentional states. Hence, a conception of emotion that identifies the phenomenon with feelings like these misrepresents it. Here, then, is the first criticism of feeling-centered conceptions.

One obstacle to converting this criticism into an argument for cognitivism is that not all emotions have intentional objects, or at least it is hardly uncontroversial to claim otherwise (see, e.g., Alston 1967, p. 486). Common opinion holds that one can experience anxiety or depression, say, without being anxious or depressed about anything, and the existence of such "objectless" emotions makes a cognitivist conception of emotion an unpromising corrective for the misrepresentation the first criticism brings out in the feeling-centered conceptions. One can grant, in other words, that intentionality is typical of emotions without believing that it is essential to them. Consequently, cognitivists appear to be overcompensating when they take thought to be the phenomenon's principal element.

The usual replies from cognitivists to this objection consist in either excluding experiences of objectless emotions from the class of emotions proper and placing them in some distinct class of mental states, such as moods, or attributing to them a subtle or suppressed intentionality, which then explains away their apparent objectlessness.[1] The persuasiveness of these replies depends,

---

1. Green 1992, pp. 33–34. See also Broad 1971, pp. 286–287; and Kenny 1963, pp. 60–62.

of course, on one's willingness either to allow some adjusting of conceptual boundaries for theoretical purposes or to allow sufficient opacity of conscious states to make the distinction between apparent and real objectlessness possible. But neither allowance seems extravagant, and an unwillingness to make either would be hard to defend. Charity and just good sense advise us to let the problem of objectless emotions pass. We may assume that the more successful the cognitivist theory is generally, the more compelling will be its way of conceptualizing emotions and so the more acceptable its ways of handling this problem. And starting with this assumption, our task then lies in seeing how far the theory can go when funded by the thesis that intentionality is essential to emotions. Although the thesis overstates the results of the first criticism, it should be treated less as an overdraft than as a loan, a loan that the theory needs to get started and is certain to repay if it prospers.

The first thing to look at, then, is the transition from intentionality to thought. This transition would be immediate if 'intentionality' were coextensive with 'cognitive content' (or 'the content of thought') and, of course, trivial if the two terms were synonymous. But whether the two are even coextensional, let alone synonymous, depends on the concept of thought the cognitivist theory assumes. On the one hand, if the concept it assumes applies to every state of mind with objective content, which is to say, every state the realization of whose content implies the existence of some object, and to no other, then the two would be coextensional. On the other hand, if the concept the theory assumes has a narrower range of application, then the terms would not be coextensional, and consequently the transition would not be immediate. If, for instance, the concept it assumes applies only to what grammarians call complete thoughts and logicians, conceiving of thoughts in abstraction from any thinker, call propositions, that is, thoughts of the kind expressed by complete, declarative sentences, then the concept's range would be narrower than that of intentionality, and the transition from the latter to the former would therefore require additional premises to establish that such thoughts were essential to emotions. Accordingly, let us distinguish two cognitivist or thought-centered conceptions of emotion, one that entails a concept of thought broad enough to apply to all states of mind with objective content and another that entails the narrower concept whose application corresponds to that of the grammarians' 'complete thought' and the logicians' 'proposition'.

The latter is the conception of contemporary cognitivism. One can trace the current ascendancy of cognitivism in the theory of emotions to its appearance and increasing acceptance. The former is the conception of an earlier period. While we shall largely be concerned with the latter, it will nonetheless be instructive to consider the former. Would it represent an advance over feeling-centered conceptions?

II. Cognition

The cognitivist theory of emotion that assumes the broader concept of thought was prominent in works produced during the first half of this century by English psychologists and analytic philosophers.[2] In these works, to sense, to imagine, or to remember something is to be cognizant of it, and cognitions, which is to say, thoughts in the most general sense of that term, are the states of mind that result from these operations as well as from the intellectual operations of understanding and judgment. Emotions, then, are classified within this theory as cognitions, since the theory conceives of them as mental states in which the subject is cognizant of some object. At the same time, since the theory allows that in some emotions the constitutive cognition results from the operations of an external sense or those of imagination, it follows that the theory does not conceive of emotions as necessarily connected to the intellect. In this respect, its account of the emotions differs significantly from that of contemporary cognitivism. The latter is intellectualist, in the philosophical sense, while the former, which I'll call traditional cognitivism, is not.

Traditional cognitivism, without question, represents a significant advance over such theories of emotion as Hume's. On a theory like Hume's, emotions have no intrinsic relation to cognition and thus, in principle, can arise independently of all thought. To be sure, Hume made much of the way certain emotions, what he called the indirect passions, were conditioned on certain antecedent thoughts as well as on sensations of pleasure and pain. But with regard to other emotions, he held that sensations of pleasure and pain alone were sufficient for their occurrence, and even with regard to the indirect passions, he held that their relation to the antecedent thoughts on which they were conditioned was extrinsic (Hume [1739] 1978, bk. 2, passim). That is, nothing in these passions necessitated the prior occurrence of their antecedent thoughts. Hence, his general account of the emotions, his conception of them as impressions of reflection, was ill equipped to explain their intentionality. The variations on his theory that continued into the nineteenth century among the English exponents of associationism in psychology

2. See, e.g., Broad 1925, pp. 574–575, and 1971, p. 286; Stout 1929, pp. 363–364; and Price 1953, p. 152.

were therefore, in this respect, decidedly inferior to the theories of traditional cognitivism that succeeded them.

By the beginning of this century, however, subtler accounts of emotion incorporating a feeling-centered conception of the phenomenon, the James-Lange theory, in particular, were being advanced, and they did not run as counter to traditional cognitivism as Hume's theory did (Lange and James 1922; James 1950, vol. 2, pp. 442–485). James, for instance, takes emotion to be constituted by certain feelings that are aroused by the thought or, as he says, perception of an exciting object. The object excites in that perceiving it precipitates changes in the body, and "our feeling of the same changes as they occur is the emotion" (James 1950, vol. 2, p. 449). Thus, feeling hot and agitated, when identified with anger, are feelings of certain physiological disturbances—"boiling blood," a churning stomach—that the perception of someone insulting one or the mere thought of one's least favorite politician excites. The difference then between James's conception and that of traditional cognitivism lies in the relation to thought that emotion is understood to have. It is a causal relation on one theory, constitutive on the other. Since neither theory supposes that one can understand an emotion independently of thought, it is unclear whether either represents a significant advance over the other.

Consider C. D. Broad's account of the emotions, which falls within traditional cognitivism (1971, pp. 283–301). Broad defines a cognition as any experience that has "an epistemological object" and accordingly distinguishes it from a pure feeling, which lacks such an object. Emotions, on his view, are cognitions that have a felt quality or tone. Crudely put, he conceives of anger, when one is angry at P, as thinking angrily about P rather than, as James would put it, feeling hot and agitated in response to some thought about P. James, nevertheless, could agree with Broad that some thought must be present, for otherwise these feelings, on his account, would not amount to anger.[3] Similarly, Broad could agree with James that some feelings must be present, for otherwise the thought, on his account, would not have the requisite tone to constitute anger. The two ultimately disagree, then, only in what part of the overall experience they would label the emotion. The difference between their accounts thus appears to be largely verbal. There appears, in other words, to be little if anything of material importance in either to make one significantly better than the other.

The difference between the accounts results from each thinker's having fixed on a different property of emotions and constructed his account

---

3. James sometimes strays from his account, however. See 1950, pp. 458–459.

accordingly. On the one hand, emotions are turbulent states. To become emotional, to be filled with emotion, to experience a flutter or rush of emotion, is to be in some state of agitation, commotion, excitation, etc. Thus, it is easy to assume that turbulence of the mind is what we mean above all by emotion, and this assumption no doubt lay behind James's identifying emotions with certain feelings of bodily changes. On the other hand, emotions are intentional phenomena. In experiencing an emotion, something about our circumstances, our lives, or ourselves captures our attention, orients our thoughts, and touches our sensibilities. Thus, it is easy to assume that the central truth about emotion is that it is a state through which the world engages our thinking and elicits our pleasure or displeasure, and something like this assumption no doubt lay behind Broad's classifying emotions as cognitions in the general sense he meant. Neither assumption, however, excludes the other, and each account readily accommodates, although as a secondary thesis, the assumption that lies behind the other. The difference, then, between the two accounts is a difference of emphasis rather than substance.[4]

III. Introspectionism

Broad and James accepted introspection as the main way to gather facts about the mind. Accordingly, both men, in giving their accounts of emotion, took themselves to be looking at consciousness and describing what they saw. To

---

4. There is some experimental research aimed at deciding between James's theory and cognitivism. Schacter and Singer's well-known experiments, in particular, are taken (by, e.g., the experimenters) to yield results that support cognitivism as against James's theory. As several critics have pointed out, though, they do not in fact yield evidence one way or the other. Either theory accounts with equal plausibility for the emotions, anger and euphoria, that the subjects in the experimental groups experience and for the absence of these emotions among the subjects of the corresponding control groups. In other words, nothing in the difference between the experimental groups and the control groups rules out or makes less plausible using James's theory to explain the anger and euphoria that occurred more frequently in the former. Schacter and Singer infer otherwise chiefly because they attribute all of the bodily changes that the subjects in the experimental groups and the relevant control group feel to the drug that was administered to these subjects. This attribution then leads them to assume that they have controlled for bodily changes (i.e., that no difference in the bodily changes felt by the subjects in these groups exists). They then infer that the differences in emotional experience found among these groups consists entirely of cognitive states. Nothing in their procedure, however, warrants either this assumption or the attribution of all bodily changes to the drug they administered. Nothing, that is, rules out the possibility that among the cognitions the experimenters induce in their subjects are Jamesian perceptions of exciting facts. See Schacter and Singer 1962; de Sousa 1987, pp. 53–55; and Gordon 1986, pp. 94–109.

say, then, that the difference between their accounts is a difference in emphasis is to say that, while they both saw the same phenomenal facts, each highlighted different ones in his description. And it is reasonable to suppose that
James highlighted turbulence, Broad intentionality, because of preconcep-
tions about emotions that each man brought to his study. Be this as it may,
introspection is now a defunct method in Anglo-American philosophy. It was
replaced in the philosophy of mind by conceptual and linguistic analysis, and
within the philosophical study of emotions this change from empirical investigations of the phenomena to investigations of the concepts and words we
use in understanding and describing the phenomena brought about the shift
in the study from traditional to contemporary cognitivism. With this shift, all
support for feeling-centered conceptions of emotion collapsed.

It would be hard to see how the change from empirical investigations to
conceptual and linguistic ones could bring about such a shift—let alone the
collapse of support for feeling-centered conceptions—if the new subject of the
study were merely the general concept of emotion or the most general words
we use to describe emotional phenomena. Nothing in the general concept,
as we ordinarily understand it, entails thought in the narrower or intellectualist sense; nothing in our ordinary use of the words 'emotion', 'emotional',
'emote', or 'emotive' to describe a person's state of mind or behavior implies
that the person affirms or even just considers some proposition. This general concept, however, and these general words were not the subject of the
study once it became dominated by conceptual and linguistic investigations.
Rather, these investigations focused on more specific concepts and words,
and this move to a level of greater specificity is what brought about the shift.

Thus, the concepts of anger, fear, envy, shame, pity, and so forth became
the real subject of the study, and in analyzing these concepts philosophers
converged on the conclusion that each entailed thought in the intellectualist sense. The refrain typical of philosophers engaged in these investigations
went (and still goes) something like this: "There is a logic to the concept of x
such that to say that a person feels x toward z implies that the person believes
such and such about z." There is a logic, for example, to the concept of pity
such that to say that a person feels pity for z implies that the person believes z
to be in some distress. Thus, by a kind of Socratic induction over the range of
specific concepts investigated, the thesis that emotion entailed propositional
thought became orthodoxy in the philosophical study of emotions.

Of course, this thesis could not have attained orthodoxy as easily as it did
if the empirical investigations of the introspectionists had yielded accounts of
specific emotions that could rival the accounts that the conceptual and linguistic investigations produced. But the introspectionists, because they took

emotions to be states of consciousness, in fact had little of substance to say about specific emotions. And this is true of both introspectionists, like Broad, who assumed the traditional cognitivist conception and those, like James, who assumed a feeling-centered one. They had little of substance to say because once anger or pity is reduced to a kind of introspectible state, a state of consciousness, its distinctive properties must be phenomenal, and not much can be said about an emotion's distinctive phenomenal properties beyond what experiencing the emotion feels like. Indeed, often the introspectionist account came to no more than that every specific emotion had a distinctive quale. Thus, Broad distinguished specific kinds of emotions by their characteristic emotional tone ("To be fearing a snake, e.g., is to be cognizing something...as a snake, and for that cognition to be toned with fearfulness" [1971, p. 286]). And G. F. Stout, another traditional cognitivist, held that what ultimately differentiated each specific emotion from the others was "a unique kind of feeling-attitude toward an object...[a] peculiar colouring [that] cannot be resolved into mere pleasantness or unpleasantness" (1929, p. 371).

James, on the other hand, was actually hostile to the whole enterprise of describing the distinctive properties of specific emotions. "The merely descriptive literature of the emotions is one of the most tedious parts of psychology. And not only is it tedious, but you feel that its subdivisions are to a great extent either fictitious or unimportant, and that its pretences to accuracy are a sham. But unfortunately there is little psychological writing about the emotions that is not merely descriptive" (James 1950, vol. 2, p. 448). In addition, he saw in this enterprise the misguiding influence of Lockean simple ideas. To take the names for specific emotions such as pity and fear as Broad and Stout do, that is, as names for unanalyzable qualities of consciousness that recur in mental life and are the building blocks of more complex qualities, is to misconceive of our mental life as a series of discrete, repeatable states whose elements are unalloyed and can therefore be individuated absolutely. "The trouble with the emotions in psychology is that they are regarded too much as absolutely individual things. So long as they are set down as so many eternal and sacred psychic entities, like the old immutable species in natural history, so long all that *can* be done with them is reverently to catalogue their separate characters, points, and effects" (James 1950, vol. 2, p. 449). A truly scientific psychology, James believed, aims at determining the general causes of the phenomena and leaves taxonomic exercises to the amateurs. "But if we regard [the emotions] as products of more general causes (as 'species' are now regarded as products of heredity and variation), the mere distinguishing and cataloguing becomes of subsidiary importance" (James 1950, vol. 2, p. 449). Suffice it to say that James had even less to offer than traditional cognitivists on the subject of the nature and differentiae of specific emotions.

The upshot of this void in the introspectionists' studies was that the accounts of specific emotions that the conceptual and linguistic analysts advanced took over the field by default. Of course, those accounts had to be plausible; their way of distinguishing among specific emotions had to make sense. Passing this test was not a real problem, however. And in the absence of any other way of drawing these distinctions, their way, which turned on each emotion's thought content and assumed an intellectualist conception of thought, became dominant as quickly as introspectionism became defunct. The shift from traditional to contemporary cognitivism appears, then, to have come about as an incidental consequence of the change in the methods by which philosophers studied emotions.

Nevertheless, the shift can be justified in its own right. Introspectionism treated emotions as states whose intrinsic properties were all inwardly observable. It treated them, that is, as purely empirical states. To be sure, introspectionists also regarded emotions as signs of other mental states that were their typical causes or effects, and as correlates of neurophysiological states that were their physical underside, basis, or constant companions. But in themselves, as mental phenomena, emotions were not seen by the introspectionists as having any theoretical depth. By contrast, the conceptual and linguistic investigations that replaced introspectionism allowed for an understanding of emotions as having such depth. These investigations concentrated on clarifying the criteria by which we apply the concepts of specific emotions, and one can construe these criteria theoretically. That is, one can take our everyday thought and talk about psychology to contain a theory of the mind whose principles determine these criteria. Indeed, this idea has now become a standard view in philosophical psychology. The theory that, on this view, our everyday thought and talk contains typically goes by the name of commonsense or folk psychology, and its principles are understood as governing relations of interdependence among various mental states, including emotions. The shift from traditional to contemporary cognitivism can be justified then, given that there is such a theory and given that its principles are such as to define a conception of emotions according to which their intentionality implies thought in the intellectualist sense.[5]

---

5. This is not to say that the change to a new understanding of the kind of state an emotion is came about smoothly. To the contrary, it did produce some wrinkles, and attempts by conceptual and linguistic analysts to iron these out have been a regular feature in the subsequent philosophical literature. In particular, a fair amount of attention has been paid to the problem

In short, change in the methods of philosophical psychology brought about change in the understanding of the kind of state emotions are, and as a result one can look to this new understanding for a way to justify the replacement, in the cognitivist conception of emotion, of its traditionally broad concept of thought by a narrower, intellectualist one. Justification, however, is not immediate. One may accept the new understanding of emotions as having theoretical depth and so the idea of folk psychology and still query the contemporary cognitivists' conception of emotions. In particular, one can still ask, "How is it that propositional thought is essential to emotions, given their intentionality?" Hence, insofar as contemporary cognitivists take the first criticism of feeling-centered conceptions of emotion as bolstering their conception, an argument that justifies the transition they make from intentionality to propositional thought is still needed.

IV. Belief

The most influential argument is due to Kenny.[6] Its main thesis is that the concept of each emotion, be it that of fear, pity, envy, or what have you, restricts what can be its object. That is, the object must have a certain character, or at least the subject must see it as having that character. Thus, the

---

of fitting into this new understanding the idea that emotions are characteristically turbulent states of mind. No similar problem arose for introspectionists since for them turbulence and intentionality were both coincident, observable properties of emotional consciousness. On the new understanding, however, because intentionality is explained by reference to a thought found in the subject's mind, which is attributed to the subject in virtue of the kind of emotion he is experiencing (i.e., as a piece of theory) and regardless of whether he is conscious of the thought, intentionality and turbulence are not comparable properties. Consequently, what the relation is between the thought and the turbulence characteristic of emotional experiences and whether an emotion contains both thought and turbulent feeling as essential components or is to be identified with one of the two while the other is treated as an essential cause or a typical effect have become arguable questions, questions on which no consensus position has developed. See, e.g., Thalberg 1964, 1980; Neu 1977, pp. 88–89, 161; Rey 1980, pp. 188–190; Greenspan 1988, chap. 2, passim; Green 1992, pp. 96–100; and Stocker 1993, pp. 20–24. The problem, it is worth noting, is not original to this literature. Freud recognized it as a problem that resulted from attributing emotions to the unconscious, since attributing a mental state to the unconscious meant treating it as having theoretical depth. See Freud 1969, pp. 177–179.

6. Kenny 1963, pp. 187–194. See also Neu 1977, pp. 36–43; and de Sousa 1987, pp. 114–123. Kenny, at an earlier place in his book (1963, p. 75), also argues for attributing to the subject of an emotion a belief about its object on the grounds that the object is intentional. This earlier argument, though it may actually be less central to Kenny's account, has attracted much more criticism, which effectively showed it to be ill conceived. See, e.g., Gosling 1965, pp. 486–503; Wilson 1972, pp. 67–69; and Green 1972, pp. 28–30.

object of fear must be seen as something or someone who threatens harm; the object of pity must be seen as someone who has suffered misfortune; and the object of envy must be seen as someone who has an advantage one lacks. Indeed, a dangerous man would not be feared if he were not known or believed to be dangerous, and someone with a terminal disease would not be pitied if no one even suspected he was ill. Conversely, one need only believe that something is a threat to fear it or that someone is in misery to pity him. Thus, the belief that the snake one suddenly finds slithering across one's path is dangerous suffices to make it an object of fear even though the snake is actually harmless, and the belief in the miserable existence of the crippled beggar with the twisted lip suffices to make him an object of pity even though his hideous appearance is a disguise and he is in fact a well-to-do gent working a remunerative con.[7] From these considerations it should be clear that what qualifies something as the appropriate object of an emotion is the subject's belief that it has a certain character. Belief and so propositional thought are therefore essential to emotion. Hence, the familiar refrain, "There is a logic to the concept of x such that to say that a person feels x toward z implies that he believes such and such about z."

I have deliberately omitted from this statement of the argument the medieval mumbo jumbo about formal objects in which the argument is sometimes couched, as well as the unnecessary bits about the grammar of direct objects and transitive verbs that Kenny thought advanced it (see Kenny 1963, pp. 187–194). These decorations have helped the argument win more converts than it should by obscuring the large jump it makes when it concludes that something qualifies as the object of a specific emotion in virtue of the subject's beliefs about it. For something can be an intentional object even if the subject has no beliefs about it and even if the subject's state of mind is such that only certain things can be its object. When a baby or a cat stares at you, you are the object of its stare. Yet it does not follow that the baby or the cat has any beliefs about you. When a dog relishes a bone, the bone is the object of its delight. Yet it does not follow that the dog has any beliefs about the bone. So too, by the very concepts of staring and relishing, you must be visible to be the object of a stare, and a bone must be pleasing to be relished. Yet a cat or a baby can stare at you without believing you are visible, and a dog can relish a bone without believing that the bone is pleasing.

7. The example is from Arthur Conan Doyle's story "The Man with the Twisted Lip," in Doyle (1930, pp. 229–244).

Kenny's argument seems valid because the examples it adduces do support its conclusion. These examples, however, are skewed. In each one, there is a dissonance between the actual character of an object or potential object of emotion and the character the object has in the subject's mind, a dissonance for which belief is typically the best explanation. But as the examples of staring and relishing show, not every intentional state, or even every intentional state the character of whose object is restricted by its concept, creates the possibility of such dissonance. Not every object of an intentional state is such that the best explanation for the character it has in the subject's mind are beliefs that the subject holds about it.

V. Evaluation

Perhaps, though, there is something about the character of an emotion's object that is best explained by belief. Perhaps the objects of emotion have a special character that justifies the inference from their intentionality to propositional thought. While contemporary cognitivists who move effortlessly from one to the other have not explicitly advanced this idea as a way to ground the transition, many have held that evaluation is essential to emotion, and perhaps the character of an emotion's object implicit in this view supplies the grounds they need to justify the move.[8] This possibility, it would seem, is the best hope for justifying the transition. The question, then, is what addition to Kenny's argument cognitivists could make to realize it.

That evaluation is essential to emotion is reflected in the restrictions that, on the main thesis of Kenny's argument, the concepts of specific emotions place on what can be their objects. If the object of fear must be something that is seen to threaten harm, then fear entails an evaluation of its object as the potential source or agent of some bad effect. If the object of pity must be someone who is seen to have suffered misfortune, then pity entails an evaluation of its object's condition as bad and undeservedly so. And similarly for the restrictions that the concepts of other emotions place. Cognitivists might then argue as follows. The object of an emotion can have, in the subject's mind, its evaluative character only if the subject believes or judges it to have this character. For each evaluation implies that the object is in some way good or in some way bad, and being in some way good or in some way bad

8. Pitcher 1965, pp. 326–346; Alston 1967, p. 485; Solomon 1976, pp. 185–191; Lyons 1980, pp. 53–63; Taylor 1985, pp. 1–16; de Sousa 1987, pp. 184–186; Greenspan 1988, pp. 3–9; and Roberts 1988, pp. 183–209.

can be seen as a property of an object only if one attributes it to that object. The conclusion then follows, given the assumption that such attributions only come from belief or through judgment. This argument is not obviously unsound, and if sound, it shows that contemporary cognitivists can use a doctrine common to many of their theories to fill a hole in the foundation of their program.

Some cognitivists who advance such theories have gone so far as to identify emotions with evaluative judgments (see, e.g., Solomon 1976, pp. 185–187; Nussbaum 1990, p. 292). Others have been less bold. While they take such judgments to be among an emotion's essential components, they take other states and phenomena to be among them as well.[9] On their view, emotions essentially combine evaluative judgments with some or all of the following: agitated states of mind, autonomic behavior such as perspiration and goose flesh, and impulses to action. Still other cognitivists who accept the doctrine that emotions entail evaluations have denied that the evaluation an emotion entails is always a judgment or belief (see, e.g., Greenspan 1988, pp. 3–9; Roberts 1988, pp. 195–201). In other words, they deny the final assumption on which the argument sketched in the last paragraph reached its conclusion. They accept instead an assumption on which a weaker conclusion follows, one that makes propositional thought, whether or not it is given any credence, essential to emotion, and they mark their dissent from views that take belief or judgment to be essential by calling emotions by such names as "propositional feelings" (Greenspan 1988, p. 4) and "concern based construals" (Roberts 1988, p. 184).

Consideration of certain groundless emotions recommends this last view over the other two. A garter snake may fill one with fear, even when one knows that it is perfectly harmless. According to either of the first two views, one must in this case be making conflicting judgments or holding conflicting beliefs about the snake. Yet attributing such a conflict does not seem necessary to understanding the case. After all, it is one thing to have a thought and another to affirm or accept it. Thus, one might have the thought that the snake threatens harm — this thought might even be intractable — and yet one need not have affirmed or accepted it. Indeed, as long as one knows that the

---

9. See, e.g., Alston 1967, pp. 485–486; Lyons 1980, pp. 57–62; Taylor 1985, pp. 1–2; and Greenspan 1988, pp. 15–17. Both Alston and Taylor, it should be noted, allow for experiences of emotion that do not contain evaluative judgments, but they argue that these experiences are parasitic on those that do. See Alston 1967, p. 486, and Taylor 1985, p. 3, n. 3. Lyons's objection (1980, pp. 87–88) that this maneuver is nothing more than a methodological dodge of embarrassing counterinstances to the dodger's account seems to me well taken.

thought does not correspond to the way things really are, one may have no tendency toward affirmation or acceptance. The last view, then, makes room for what seem to be real possibilities that the first two views exclude.

At the same time, one might wonder whether there are cases of ground-less emotion in which the subject reacts to an object without evaluating it.[10] Couldn't a garter snake, for instance, fill one with fear without one even thinking that it threatens harm? Couldn't snakes be a kind of creature whose serpentine shape and movements innately excite fear, just as, so one might suppose, thunderclaps and other sudden loud noises innately excite fear? Per-haps, as children, we learn the connection between fear and danger when we are taught not to be afraid of certain things that instinctively frighten us: large or barking dogs, strangers (who are older and bigger), thunder and lightning, darkness. We see a large dog and are afraid, and then our parents try to calm us and show us that the dog is really friendly and not at all a threat. "Don't be afraid; the dog won't hurt you," they say, and so we learn that the appropri-ate objects of fear are things that can hurt us. If this account were accurate, then our earliest fears would not entail an evaluation of their objects, for we would not yet have learned the criteria by which to evaluate them. Later experiences of groundless fear might then be best understood, in some cases, as repetitions of these earliest experiences.

Cognitivists who hold that emotions entail evaluations—Socratic theo-rists, I'll call them, since the view originates with Socrates (see Plato 1976, 358d–e, pp. 52–53)—would, of course, reject this possibility. What makes the reaction to the snake one of fear, they would ask, if not the character of the subject's thought? What else could be the basis for ascribing fear and not some other emotion like horror or disgust? To suppose that the subject is experiencing a special feeling, a turbulence of mind with a distinctive tone, would be to fall back on the discredited views of introspectionism. And to suppose that the fear is a matter of sweating palms and a palpitating heart, or rapid movement away from its object, is no solution either. While these are among fear's natural expressions, one could hardly maintain that the sub-ject's reaction required such behavior. Here behaviorist accounts of emotion are as unhelpful as Cartesian ones. Contemporary cognitivism, as we noted earlier, gained advantage over its predecessors by focusing on specific emo-tions and offering a plausible way of differentiating them. That noncognitivist ways of differentiating them presuppose a discredited metaphysics or rely on a crude symptomatology highlights this advantage. It makes clear the difficulty

10. See Morreal (1993) for additional examples.

of assuming that the concept of an emotion like fear applies to an emotional state when no propositional thought is attributed to its subject. By taking evaluative thought to be the principal differentia of emotions, Socratic theorists avoid this difficulty. The accounts of specific emotions that these theorists have produced are decidedly more persuasive than the introspectionist and behaviorist accounts that preceded them.

Still, their assumption of strict criteria for distinguishing among the different emotions invites James's complaint against philosophers and psychologists who treat the emotions as if they were "absolutely individual things...eternal and sacred psychic entities, like the old immutable species in natural history" (1950, vol. 2, p. 449). It should remind us as well of Wittgenstein's objections to taking words like 'fear', 'anger', 'joy', 'pity', and the like to be names of inner states, for taking them, as the cognitivists do, to be names of theoretical states instead of introspectible, private ones circumvents only some of those objections (1953, secs. 308, 571). The common target of James's and Wittgenstein's criticisms was theories of the mind, like Locke's, that represent thinking and feeling as a series of discrete, recurrable states, either elementary or compound, a kind of theory whose dominant theme is so well captured in Hume's famous description of the mind as "a kind of theatre where several perceptions successively make their appearance, pass, repass, glide away, and mingle in an infinite variety of postures and situations" (1978, bk. 1, pt. 4, sec. 6, p. 253). To be sure, the cognitivists' assumption of strict criteria for distinguishing among different emotions does not commit them to a full-blown Lockean theory of the mind. Nonetheless, it may wed them to enough Lockeanism to put them within the range of James's and Wittgenstein's criticisms. If we granted the assumption the cognitivists make, their accounts of specific emotions would be significantly more illuminating than the ones introspectionists and behaviorists offered. But the question is whether we should grant it.

VI. Primitive Emotions

Let us examine this question by considering a thesis that the assumption implies, the thesis that all experiences of a given emotion have a property in common that identifies those experiences as experiences of that emotion and not some other. On the Socratic theory, this common property is the specific form of evaluative thought the emotion is said to entail. Plainly, there are emotions all of whose experiences have some such thought in common. Any experience of resentment, for instance, includes the thought that one has been treated unjustly. Furthermore, this thought identifies the experience as one of resentment rather than, say, embarrassment. There is no mystery, however, as to why all experiences of resentment share a specific form of evaluative thought. Resentment is a moral emotion. To be capable of it one must have acquired certain moral concepts and principles, and an experience of resentment then signifies that one has applied these concepts and principles to one's situation. Indeed, with regard to any emotion that marks an individual as socialized and the beneficiary of a moral education, it is safe to assume that all of its experiences share a specific form of evaluative thought that identifies them as experiences of that emotion and not some other. For an experience of such an emotion signifies the application of concepts and principles one acquires through socialization and moral education, and to apply these concepts and principles is just to have certain evaluative thoughts about one's situation.

Needless to say, not every emotion marks one as socialized or the beneficiary of a moral education. Some emotions are more natural or primitive. Many experiences of fear, anger, love, joy, and sorrow, for example, do not presuppose the cultural transmission of concepts and principles. These are emotions to which other animals, and not just human beings, are liable (Darwin 1965, pp. 83–145). Hence, one cannot appeal to the application of concepts and principles acquired through cultural transmission to establish, with respect to any of these emotions, that a specific form of evaluative thought is common to all of its experiences. To be sure, no one innocent of the relevant culture could experience fear over the downward plunge of a stock market or anger at an obscene gesture. But to experience fear of falling as one looks down from a precipice or anger at an intruder when one is enjoying a quiet moment does not require knowledge of one's culture or training in its practices. The question, then, if these latter experiences share the same forms of evaluative thought as the former, is how their subjects acquired the corresponding evaluative concepts and came to understand the criteria governing their application.

One answer Socratic theorists might give is that, just as the reactions in the latter cases are instinctive, so the concepts they imply are innate. If we are born with a capacity for fear, then we are born with the power of sensing danger. The other answer, of course, is that these reactions are learned rather than instinctive, and the concepts therefore are acquired through experience. Thus, we learn to fear those things that cause us pain, and the unpleasant memories of the experience give us a sense of danger when those things are in our vicinity. Prey that have a keen sense of when a predator is approaching, antelope that can sense the stalking lion, smell the danger, as we sometimes say, and flee. Thus, whether the requisite concept for experiencing fear is inborn or acquired through experience, these beasts clearly possess it, and it is equally clear that they possess it independently of any culture. The same thing then holds of the seemingly instinctive fears to which human beings are liable. Or so these contemporary cognitivists might argue.

The problem with this argument, however, is that it confuses being sensible of something with having a concept of it. Many people are sensible of sharps and flats, for instance, though they have no concept of half steps in a diatonic scale. Wild geese are no doubt sensible of changes in the weather, though they have no concept of seasons. To be sensible of a property is to be able to detect its presence and to discriminate between those things that have it and those that do not. To have a concept of a property, by contrast, is to be able to predicate it of some object and, hence, to locate it in a system of propositional thought. Predication, after all, as we learned from Neurath, presupposes some system of propositions. This system is realized in an organization of thought that having a concept of some property implies, and such organization of thought is unnecessary for detecting the property or discriminating between those things that do and those things that do not have it. Such organization constitutes a conceptual understanding of things, and the powers of detection and discrimination that a creature's sensory faculties include do not require conceptual understanding. Thus, that a creature can sense danger in certain circumstances does not imply that it has the concept of danger. One cannot, in other words, infer the kind of evaluative thought Socratic theorists require for an experience of fear from the supposition that its subject senses danger.

Of course, dangerousness is an abstract property and not a sensory one. Anything that threatens harm is dangerous, and there are indefinitely many ways of being harmed. One might then conclude that a creature who had an ability to sense danger must understand the many ways in which it could be harmed and so must have the concept of danger. But the more telling conclusion is that a liability to primitive experiences of fear, like the fear of falling or the fear that strikes prey when being stalked by a predator, does not entail this ability.[11] We say an antelope has a keen sense of danger because it reacts so quickly when a lion comes on the scene, but we do not mean to imply by this that the antelope would react as quickly or at all if it stumbled on a live grenade. The sensibilia to which it reacts when it becomes aware of a predator are fixed, it is reasonable to suppose, by natural selection and the narrow

11. Morreal (1993, pp. 359–366) argues for a similar point.

range of experience characteristic of life in the wild and do not generalize to other dangers.[12] Dangerousness, in other words, is not the property of which the antelope is sensible when it flees a predator in fear.

The same conclusion follows from reflection on primitive experiences of fear where the subject knows that he is perfectly safe. Fear upon looking down from a precipice, for example, is a common experience even when one knows that one is in no danger of falling.[13] One can feel fear in such circumstances without having a sense of danger. Thus, the experience is not comparable to seeing water on a distant surface that one knows is perfectly dry. Dangerousness, since it is not a sensory property, is not a property of which one can have an illusion. And it would also be a mistake to insist that one must at least be imagining that one is in danger. One may of course be imagining oneself falling and the unpleasant outcome at the end of the fall, but that is to imagine certain harm, not danger or the threat of harm. To imagine that one is in danger, one must imagine some such circumstance as that one's enemy is lurking in the bushes, waiting for the chance to push one over the cliff, or that a sudden gust of wind catches one off guard, making it very difficult to maintain one's balance. And one does not need to imagine such a threat to feel fear upon looking down from a precipice. It is not the dangerousness of one's circumstances, therefore, that one is sensible of when one feels such fear. The thought of danger, propositional or otherwise, is not a thread that runs through all experiences of fear.

What is one sensible of in these primitive experiences? What makes them experiences of fear rather than horror or disgust? A plausible answer to this second question draws on the aesthetics of these different emotions. Roughly speaking, one feels fear at what is scary, horror at what is gruesome, and disgust at what is foul. These properties characterize the way things look, sound, taste, and smell. A scary mask, for instance, will have certain exaggerated

---

12. Indeed, even wide and repeated experience of things that harm would only enhance the antelope's sensitivity to such things, and having an enhanced sensitivity is not the same as having a concept. Without the rudiments of language, it is hard to see how experience alone could be transformed into a conceptual understanding.

13. The example is Hume's, though his own attempt to make the experience intelligible is notable only for its uncharacteristic incoherence. "But they are not only possible evils, that cause fear, but even some allow'd to be *impossible*; as when we tremble on the brink of a precipice, tho' we know ourselves to be in perfect security, and have it in our choice whether we will advance a step farther. This proceeds from the immediate presence of the evil, which influences the imagination in the same manner as the certainty of it wou'd do; but being encounter'd by the reflection on our security, is immediately retracted, and causes the same kind of passion, as when from a contrariety of chances contrary passions are produced" (1978, bk. 2, pt. 3, sec. 9, p. 445).

features that are designed to alarm or frighten the innocent or unsuspecting viewer, and a scary voice will have a certain unusual cadence and pitch that unsettles the listener. What is scary may also be a property of something independently of the way it looks and sounds. A bat may be scary only because it can menace: alone in a dark, cavernous place, one would naturally be frightened by swooping bats. Alternatively, though, bats may be scary because they are large, nocturnal, dark, swiftly flying, shrieking creatures. Be this as it may, the important point is that the scary differs from the dangerous in being at least sometimes a true or direct property of the way something looks and sounds. Something that looks dangerous is something one can infer is dangerous from the way it looks, whereas one need make no inference to see that something looks scary. Hence, the answer is congenial to rejecting the view of emotions as immutable species.

It gives us as well an answer to the first question, the question of what one is sensible of in these primitive experiences. That answer is whatever properties make a thing scary. These properties are distinct from those that make something gruesome and those that make something foul. The latter, as we have already noted, are the properties one is sensible of in primitive experiences of horror and disgust. Consequently, one can cite the difference between the characters of these emotions' intentional objects to distinguish among primitive experiences of fear, horror, and disgust. One is not, in other words, forced by an understanding of emotions as intentional phenomena always to take forms of evaluative thought as their differentiae. The answers thus form a basis not only for rejecting the view of emotions as immutable species but also for denying the thesis that evaluative thought is essential to the phenomena.

VII. Davidsonian Theory

Not every cognitivist theory of emotions currently in play has this thesis as a central tenet, however. A different type of cognitivist theory takes its lead from Donald Davidson's work in philosophical psychology.[14] The main idea of this work is that one can use interlocking combinations of beliefs and desires to explain a range of psychological phenomena, including, in particular, intentional actions and emotions. The beliefs in these combinations are typically

---

14. See essays 1–5, 14, and 15 in Davidson 1980. The last of these, "Hume's Cognitive Theory of Pride," is Davidson's most extended effort at applying his general program to a certain class of emotions, which he calls propositional emotions.

perceptual beliefs or other factual beliefs one could arrive at by perception and inference. The desires are conative or affective states with thought content that meshes with the thought content of their complementary beliefs in a way exemplified by an Aristotelian practical syllogism, and to account for a broad range of emotions, they are explicitly assumed to include pro and con attitudes with no conative force or whose conative force is too weak to be that of desire according to its ordinary conception. The class of Davidsonian desires is thus larger than the class of desires on their ordinary conception. And to simplify the discussion I shall follow Davidson in using 'desire' to denote any member of this larger class and 'belief' to denote any propositional thought of the kind that combines with desires to explain intentional actions and emotions (see 1980, pp. 3–4).

Common to theories of the type that applies Davidson's main idea is a cognitivist analysis of emotion in which desire rather than evaluative thought is an essential component.[15] That is, instead of representing the cognitive core of an emotion as some combination of evaluative thought and factual belief, these theories restrict that core to factual belief and add as an essential component a complementary desire. Instead of taking pride, for example, to entail the thought that one is in some way commendable, these theories analyze it as essentially a combination of a belief that one has a certain feature and a pro attitude toward a person's having that feature. Davidson himself vacillates between taking declarative sentences of the form 'x is commendable (good, bad, praiseworthy, blameworthy, etc.)' to be expressions of belief and taking them to be expressions of pro and con attitudes, which is to say, he vacillates between classifying evaluative thought as a genuine kind of belief and classifying it as a kind of desire (1980, pp. 27, 86). The latter classification obviously blurs the line that I mean here to draw between two types of cognitivist theory. Still, since one can in principle distinguish between evaluative thought and desire, a line can be drawn. And while one may be unable to say definitively which side of that line Davidson falls on, others who have taken up his idea have removed this ambiguity from their views. In

---

15. See Rey 1980; Marks 1982; Searle 1983, pp. 29–36; Gordon 1987; Davis 1987; and Green 1992. There are, of course, significant differences among the views that share the Davidsonian approach. Like the divisions within Socratic theory, some Davidsonians (e.g., Marks and Green) identify emotions with belief-desire combinations, and others (e.g., Rey and Searle) hold that emotions are not reducible to the belief-desire combinations that explain them. Green thinks the model applies either straightforwardly or with some modification to all emotions; Gordon follows Davidson in taking it to apply to a restricted class of emotions. These differences, though, do not affect our discussion.

their work, a distinction between evaluative thought and desire is expressly noted or made so that no confusion arises over which is to be understood as an essential component of emotion (Green 1992, p. 78).

These views then define a type of cognitivist theory that represents an alternative to Socratic theory. They do not, however, contain or even suggest an alternative way to make the transition from intentionality to propositional thought. Rather the idea of an intentional object is demoted, if not excluded altogether, from their accounts of emotion on the grounds that talk of an emotion's object is loose, confused, vague, suspiciously metaphysical, or merely shorthand for the proposition that is the thought content of the emotion (see, e.g., Searle 1983, pp. 16–18; Gordon 1987, pp. 45–46, 65–66). Exponents of these theories nonetheless continue to speak of the intentionality of emotion, by which they understand its thought content. This understanding is importantly different from the traditional understanding of intentionality as the property of being directed at or toward some object, for it omits the notion of a relation between the mental state and an object.[16] And by adopting it, Davidsonians effectively obliterate the question of the transition from intentionality to propositional thought, since that question just is the question of what grounds the inference of such thought from the relation captured in the traditional understanding. Davidsonian theories, in other words, do not fashion their accounts of emotion to fit the intentionality of the phenomena, as traditionally understood. Rather, they change the understanding of intentionality to fit their accounts.

One consequence of this change is that these theories offer a conception of emotion that is no less vulnerable than feeling-centered conceptions to the charge of misrepresenting the relation between an emotion and its object. For if the charge is correct as applied to feeling-centered conceptions, then it applies with equal force to Davidsonian conceptions. And if it has no force against the latter because of the criticisms Davidsonians make of the idea of an intentional object, then those same criticisms either negate its force against feeling-centered conceptions or beg the question of which conception is correct. Specifically, criticizing talk of intentional objects as loose, confused, vague, or suspiciously metaphysical negates its force, and holding that such talk is shorthand for the proposition that is the emotion's thought content begs the question.

This last point is worth elaborating since the change Davidsonian theories make in the traditional understanding of intentionality generates a different

---

16. I owe this point to Meredith Williams. See Searle 1983, pp. 18–19.

charge against feeling-centered conceptions, a charge that may appear to be every bit as forceful a criticism of them as the original. The new charge is that feeling-centered conceptions misrepresent the intentionality of an emotion in the sense of its thought content, and it goes without saying that these conceptions are no better able to account for an emotion's thought content than they are its relation to an intentional object. This new charge, however, unlike the original, implies something about emotions that those who put forth feeling-centered conceptions simply deny, namely, that an emotion contains thought. For this reason, the charge begs the question. It merely repeats the opposition between thought-centered and feeling-centered conceptions and does not base its criticism of the latter on anything outside of the dispute.

By contrast, the original charge bases its criticism on the intentionality of emotions as it is traditionally understood, which is not something about emotions that those who put forth feeling-centered conceptions deny. To the contrary, they accept it as a datum of psychology that any theory of emotions must explain and that their theories explain by describing certain mechanistic relations between thoughts and feelings. The dispute then centers not on whether intentionality is a property of emotions but on how to explain it. Thus, consider how the dispute plays out in the controversy over the existence of genuinely objectless emotions. The exponents of feeling-centered conceptions, far from holding that all emotions are objectless, regard such emotions as atypical. At the same time, they maintain that the existence of such emotions argues for the mechanistic model they use to explain the relation between emotions and their objects because it shows that the relation is an external one. This argument then puts the exponents of cognitivist conceptions under pressure to explain away the existence of genuinely objectless emotions, which eliminative explanations I canvassed in Section I. Clearly, the controversy proceeds from agreement by both parties that emotions in general have objects. In other words, both parties accept the intentionality of emotions, traditionally understood, as a datum. This agreement then gives the original charge against feeling-centered conceptions the probative force that is lacking in the charge that Davidsonian theories generate.

Many contemporary cognitivists, I imagine, would balk at this result. "Emotions are propositional attitudes," they would argue, "and as such they are intentional states in the traditional sense. Consequently, one need not suppose that Davidsonian theories introduce a change in the understanding of intentionality. Rather, the change they introduce is in the kind of object emotions have." This argument, popular though it may be, should be resisted.[17] Its major premiss is faulty. Admittedly, the premiss seems unexceptional, for we frequently describe emotional states by using sentences with noun clauses as direct objects, and after all, if 'Henny Penny believes that the sky is falling' describes a propositional attitude, why not assume the same thing about 'Henny Penny is afraid that the end is near'? Russell's observations about sentences with nondenoting definite descriptions supply the answer: the grammar of a sentence is not a foolproof guide to the structure of the fact it describes (1971, pp. 167–180). Thus, although the grammar in the first sentence about Henny Penny does accurately reflect a relation between her and a proposition, it does not in the second. The reflection is accurate in the first sentence because belief is a propositional attitude in the requisite sense, as are certainty, doubt, and assumption. That is, we believe propositions, are certain of them, doubt them, and so forth. It is misleading in the second because fear is not a propositional attitude in this sense. Anyone who is afraid of propositions needs to have his head examined.[18]

VIII. Rationality

At the outset of this essay, I mentioned two criticisms of feeling-centered conceptions that were largely responsible for the current ascendancy of cognitivism in the philosophical study of the emotions. The first of these criticisms, as we have just seen, provides no encouragement for Davidsonian theories. The second, however, does. Briefly, this criticism is that feeling-centered conceptions, because they assimilate emotions to bodily sensations, cannot explain how an emotion can sometimes be unreasonable or irrational and so (by implication) at other times be reasonable or rational. For instance, anger can be unreasonable when it is misdirected; fear can be irrational when its object is innocuous. By contrast, it would be gibberish to describe a bodily sensation, a toothache, say, as unreasonable. The criticism thus highlights

17. The description of emotions as having propositions as their objects is now common, and sometimes it results from the characterization of emotions as propositional attitudes in the way the argument suggests. See, e.g., Nissenbaum 1985, pp. 10–11; de Sousa 1987, pp. 137–139; Davis 1987, pp. 287–289; and Greenspan 1988, pp. 15–16.

18. His fear perhaps is like that of the protagonist at the end of Woody Allen's short story "The Kugelmass Episode" who, fresh from having projected himself into *Emma Bovary*, tries to inhabit *Portnoy's Complaint* but winds up in a different sort of book. "Kugelmass...had been projected into an old textbook 'Remedial Spanish' and was running for his life over a barren rocky terrain as 'tener' ('to have')—a large and hairy irregular verb—raced after him on its spindly legs."

something about emotions that eludes feeling-centered conceptions of them. Call it their rationality. This is a feature any Davidsonian theory is well suited to explain, for the explanations it offers represent emotions as the logical outcomes of the desires and beliefs that combine to produce them, which means that they can be described as reasonable or unreasonable, rational or irrational, according as the beliefs and, more controversially, the desires that combine to produce them are reasonable or unreasonable, rational or irrational.[19] The second criticism, one could say, issues an invitation to account for the rationality of emotions, an invitation that Davidsonian theories are primed to answer.

Of course, Davidsonian theories are not the only type of cognitivist theory with a ready response to this invitation. To the contrary, any contemporary cognitivist theory should be well equipped to respond. For to conceive of emotions as containing propositional thought is to take them to have an essential element that is subject to assessments of rationality, and an emotion can then be understood to be reasonable or unreasonable, rational or irrational, according as the propositional thought it essentially contains is reasonable or unreasonable, rational or irrational. Hence, the second criticism, like the first, highlights a feature of emotions that promises to decide the dispute between feeling-centered and thought-centered conceptions of emotion in favor of the latter. The question, then, is whether the promise in this case can be fulfilled. Can contemporary cognitivists draw from this second criticism a sounder argument for their conception of emotions than can be drawn from the first?

The immediate difficulty in converting the second criticism into an argument for contemporary cognitivism is that not all experiences of emotion have the feature this criticism highlights. The emotions of animals that lack reason are obvious examples, for a state of mind is rational or reasonable either directly, that is, in virtue of the operations of reason that alone or in conjunction with the operations of other faculties produce it, or indirectly, that is, in virtue of all of its essential elements (or rather all that have rationality) being rational or reasonable. In any case, what makes the state rational or reasonable is the soundness of the relevant operation of reason, and what would then make it irrational or unreasonable is the failure of reason to operate as it should. Hence, if a creature lacks reason, it lacks the faculty whose operations are presupposed in descriptions of states of mind as rational or irrational, reasonable or unreasonable. Such descriptions do not hold of any

19. Green (1992, pp. 93–94), e.g., holds the more controversial thesis.

of its states. Thus, the emotions of wild animals and of small children, whose rational capacities have yet to develop, do not have the feature the second criticism highlights, from which it follows that the criticism cannot yield grounds sufficient for a general conception of emotion.

This limitation does not seem to have bothered contemporary cognitivists, however. Few even stop to comment on the emotions of creatures who lack reason, and the tendency among those who do is to wall them off from the phenomena their theories are meant to explain.[20] De Sousa, for instance, characterizes such emotions as "mere responses" that fall short of being "full-fledged" intentional states and for this reason denies that they are emotions.[21] Likewise, Gordon removes them from the objects of his study, which are emotions explicable by reference to propositional thought. He classifies them instead as syndromes consisting of transfixed attention, overt behavior, and autonomic changes in the subject's physiological condition. Thus, he distinguishes between "propositional fear" and "the state of fear," where the former is a type of emotion to which his analysis applies and the latter is "the flight-arousal syndrome" common to many species of mammal and "too special a phenomenon" to be caught in the net of his analysis (Gordon 1987, pp. 71–72). Both thinkers, then, argue in effect for excluding the experiences of beasts and babies from the study of emotions on the grounds that these experiences lack the requisite intentionality. This argument may well capture a view that contemporary cognitivists in general hold. And if it does, we need look no further for an explanation of their inattention to the emotions of creatures who lack reason and can quickly bring our inquiry to a close.

For the argument is merely a variation on the by now familiar fallacy of inferring propositional thought from intentionality. In this variation, it is a fallacy of equivocation. Intentionality, in the sense of being directed at an object, is a property of emotions whether or not their subjects possess reason. The emotions of antelope, for instance, though neither rational nor irrational, are not objectless states: bucks, when rutting, display anger toward their rivals; does, having given birth, show affection for their young; and the herd when under attack by some predator collectively bolts in fear of its attacker.

---

20. Greenspan (1988, pp. 48–49) and Davis (1987, p. 304) are exceptions. They hold that the emotions of beasts, like those of humans, entail evaluations. Greenspan offers her cat's anger at another cat as an example; Davis cites fear induced in a mouse by, e.g., a loud noise. Neither, however, explains how the animal in question came to have the operative concept. So the objections to such a view given in Sec. VI apply.

21. De Sousa 1987, p. 101 (see pp. 181–182 for characterization of primitive emotions as mere responses).

Similarly for babies delighted with new toys, afraid of large dogs, distressed at spilt milk. Hence, cognitivists must be using the word 'intentionality' in some altered sense when they exclude emotions like these from their studies on the grounds that they lack the necessary intentionality. In this altered sense, the word describes a property of mental states that only rational creatures can experience. It thus furnishes nominal grounds for omitting phenomena that do not fit the preferred analysis, but in the absence of a sound argument for taking intentionality in this sense to be a defining property of emotions, these grounds are only nominal. Intentionality, when reintroduced into the philosophy of mind in the late nineteenth century, was proposed as the mark of the mental (Brentano 1973, p. 88). To redeploy it, as these cognitivists now do, as the mark of the rational is either to change it into a different notion while illicitly retaining its application to a wider range of mental phenomena or to risk commitment to Descartes's preposterous thesis that only rational creatures have minds.

It would be ungenerous, though, to insist that cognitivist inattention to the emotions of beasts and babies is due to cognitivist confusion of a mark of the mental for a mark of the rational. An alternative explanation is that contemporary cognitivists see their study as falling within the field of human psychology, a field that, unlike the fields of animal and infant psychology, concerns the thoughts and feelings, powers and susceptibilities, of rational creatures. Consequently, one should not expect their accounts of various emotions to extend to the emotions of creatures who lack reason, and the failure of those accounts to be so extendable is therefore no threat to the soundness of their theories. According to this explanation, contemporary cognitivists understand the relevant dispute to be a dispute over different conceptions of human emotion, which is emotion of the sort to which normal, adult human beings are liable, and given this understanding, no fact about the emotions of beasts and babies can defeat the conversion of the second criticism into an argument for the contemporary cognitivists' conception.

Clearly, this alternative explanation justifies cognitivist inattention to the emotions of beasts and babies only if it does not derive from a distinction between human beings and other animals that is as implausible as Descartes's. It could not, for instance, rest on the supposition that the human soul was ontologically distinct from the souls of animals who lacked reason. The Aristotelianism implicit in this supposition would be no advance over the Cartesianism suggested by de Sousa's and Gordon's remarks. In general, the distinction from which the explanation derives must, to be plausible, be compatible with our understanding of human, animal, and infant psychology as branches of natural science. Whatever differences in psychological capacities exist between humans and beasts, or grown-ups and babies, they cannot, consistent with evolutionary biology and developmental psychology, imply that mature human thought and feeling are phenomena utterly incomparable to their bestial and infantile counterparts.

Of course, what marks human beings as rational creatures and sets them apart from other species and the very immature of their own species is the special importance of language in human life. Its pervasive impact on human thought and feeling is obvious to anyone upon self-reflection. Human beings, as they mature, learn to speak and to encode their thoughts in language.[22] As their facility for language improves and the store of their encoded thoughts enlarges, they develop an increasingly powerful system of beliefs on which they rely in negotiating their way through life. At some point, perhaps fairly early in this process, the system of beliefs a person develops becomes sufficiently influential in his or her life that it shapes and orients every experience beyond those of simple reflex. It makes sense, then, in studying the thoughts and feelings, powers and susceptibilities, of mature human beings to regard belief as a ubiquitous factor and to assume that transitions of thought in the human mind often track logical relations among beliefs. Thus, to the student of psychology, the contents and workings of the human mind are so infused with belief and rational process as to distinguish their study from that of the minds of beasts and babies. Here is a plausible distinction between human psychology, on the one hand, and animal and infant psychology, on the other, that warrants treating the former as a separate field from the latter. Here is a distinction that contemporary cognitivists could invoke to justify restricting the scope of their theory to human emotions.

Yet contemporary cognitivists would be no closer to converting the second criticism into an argument for their conception of emotion if they invoked this distinction to avoid the difficulty that the emotions of beasts and babies create for them. The difficulty would remain because the distinction, being based on the observation that belief is ubiquitous in human experience, implies only that belief is always present in experiences of human emotion and not that it is, in every case, an essential element of such experiences. Consequently, the distinction, when applied to emotions, does not yield an account of the rationality of human emotions that supports the contemporary cognitivists' conception of them. It yields, rather, an account that renders the rationality of human emotions insufficient as grounds for conceiving of them as containing propositional thought as an essential element.

---

22. I mean 'thoughts' in the broad sense here.

What creates the insufficiency is the fact that an emotion can be infused with belief and nonetheless be intelligible without regard to any of the beliefs that permeate it. Thus, while fear of a plummeting stock market, to recur to an earlier pair of examples, would be unintelligible without regard to the subject's beliefs about stock markets and finance, fear of falling as one looks down from a precipice is intelligible regardless of the beliefs the subject has as he contemplates the fall. And while the former fear would be reasonable or unreasonable, rational or irrational, according as the subject's beliefs about stock markets and finance were sound or faulty, which is to say, according as one attributes those beliefs to sound or faulty reasoning, the latter fear could not be reasonable or unreasonable, rational or irrational, in the same way. This point is best seen in cases of unreasonable fear of falling, where the subject feels the emotion upon looking down from a precipice despite knowing that he is perfectly safe. In such cases, what makes the fear unreasonable is not that it contains a faulty belief but rather that it is felt despite a sound belief that should have immunized its subject from feeling this fear. What makes it unreasonable, that is, is not faulty reasoning resulting in false thoughts but rather the persistence of a tropism that should have yielded to sound reasoning and firm belief. A person can be unreasonable when he fails to listen to reason as well as when he speaks nonsense. Likewise, an emotion can be unreasonable when it fails to respond to reason as well as when it contains false thoughts that are due to faulty reasoning. And when an emotion is unreasonable because it fails to respond to reason, one cannot infer from its being unreasonable that it contains propositional thought as an essential element.

Human emotions, on this account of their rationality, include some that are not originally responsive to reason. These, we may assume, are the primitive emotions discussed in section VI. A child's primitive emotions become responsive to reason, then, as the child learns to speak and begins to develop a system of beliefs that expands and alters its understanding of the world. Part of what the child learns is to recognize certain objective conditions, and to respond to them, as distinct from the merely sensory phenomena to which it responds instinctively. It learns, for instance, to distinguish what is harmful from what is merely scary, what is rotten from what is merely foul. Acquiring the concepts of these objective conditions and the understanding of the world that having these concepts entails weakens the impact of the sensory phenomena, the scary and the foul. Accordingly, the child's susceptibilities to fear and disgust change. While it may continue to feel uneasy in the presence of large dogs, say, it is no longer afraid of them and may at some point cease even to regard them as scary; while it may continue to dislike liver, it is no longer disgusted by it, and the dish may at some point cease even to taste foul. These emotions, in being educated, as it were, for governance by the conceptual understanding of the world one acquires, thus become responsive to reason.

To be sure, once this happens, their rationality will fit the contemporary cognitivists' account. But with some emotions, it may not happen. Some emotions may never become completely responsive to reason, for one's susceptibilities to them in certain circumstances may be so fixed that they do not change as one learns to speak and develops a system of beliefs. These emotions are to that extent ineducable. Accordingly, experiences of them in the relevant circumstances will be irrational or unreasonable in a way that eludes the contemporary cognitivists' account, though a better description of some would be that they lacked rationality altogether since their unresponsiveness to reason is normal whatever the subject's stage of development and socialization. In this case, they tell directly against the contemporary cognitivists' conception, for that conception implies that rationality is a universal feature of human emotion. In either case, then, the account of the rationality of emotions that a plausible distinction between human and animal psychology yields does not support the contemporary cognitivists' conception. Short of assuming an obsolete metaphysics of the soul like Descartes's or Aristotle's, contemporary cognitivists cannot find in the second criticism of feeling-centered conceptions a basis for the one they favor.

IX. Conclusion

Current philosophical writing on emotions regularly contains discussions of fear and anger. Discussions of hope, pride, compassion, envy, and grief are also common. Love too is frequently discussed. It is not always treated as an emotion, though, and when it is, it is usually conceived of as an emotion of friendship independent of romance or amorous feeling. Indeed, in the current literature, the latter forms of love, particularly sexual passion and erotic desire, are virtually ignored. This fact should not come as a surprise, however. Contemporary cognitivism dominates this literature, and it would be rather hard to keep these emotions before one's mind and at the same time expound this school's characteristic view of the rationality of emotions. It thus becomes necessary to forget the truism that sexual passion and erotic desire are unresponsive to reason.

The argument of the last section, by contrast, affords an explanation of this truism. Amorous feeling is normally excited by sensory experience or fantasy. The impact on our psyche of the sensory phenomena of male or female beauty, depending, as we now say, on our sexual preference, which is to say, depending on which sex attracts us, does not obviously weaken with the development of a conceptual understanding of the world. In some people, of course, the susceptibility to such emotion becomes severely repressed because the conceptual understanding they acquire includes beliefs intolerant of deviant sexual desire. And presumably the demands of monogamy and the beliefs that support them make some repression of sexual desire unavoidable in most people. Nonetheless, for many the development of a system of beliefs, rather than bring repression of or immunization from amorous feeling induced by the sight of human beauty, enriches and makes more articulate those experiences. No one has captured this phenomenon better than Proust. In a wonderfully observed passage, he first writes of the early stirrings in a teenage boy's soul brought by the sight of a girl, glimpsed momentarily from a carriage that is rapidly returning home at the end of the day. Then he generalizes.

> If our imagination is set going by the desire for what we may not possess, its flight is not limited by a reality completely perceived, in these casual encounters in which the charms of the passing stranger are generally in direct ratio to the swiftness of our passage. If only night is falling and the carriage is moving fast, whether in town or country, there is not a female torso, mutilated like an antique marble by the speed that tears us away and the dusk that drowns it, but aims at our heart, from every turning in the road, from the lighted interior of every shop, the arrows of Beauty, that Beauty of which we are sometimes tempted to ask ourselves whether it is, in this world, anything more than the complementary part that is added to a fragmentary and fugitive stranger by our imagination over stimulated by regret. (Proust 1934, vol. 1, p. 540)

What Proust describes is a paradigm of an experience of primitive emotion infused with and altered by belief but nonetheless intelligible without it. What he describes defies the various attempts surveyed in this article to represent all our emotions as civilized experiences, to render them all answerable to reason.

There has been plenty of movement in the philosophical study of emotions over the past thirty years. How much of it counts as progress, however, is hard to say.

REFERENCES

Allen, Woody. The Kugelmass Episode. *New Yorker* (May 2, 1977).

Alston, William P. 1967. Emotion and Feeling. In *The Encyclopedia of Philosophy*, ed. Paul Edwards, vol. 2. New York: Macmillan.

Brentano, Franz. (1874) 1973. *Psychology from an Empirical Standpoint*, ed. Linda L. McAlister. New York: Humanities Press.

Broad, C. D. 1925. *The Mind and Its Place in Nature*. New York: Harcourt Brace.

Broad, C. D. (1954) 1971. Emotion and Sentiment. In *Broad's Critical Essays in Moral Philosophy*, ed. David Cheney. London: Allen & Unwin.

Darwin, Charles. (1872) 1965. *The Expression of the Emotions in Man and Animal*. Chicago: University of Chicago Press.

Davidson, Donald. 1980. *Essays on Actions and Events*. Oxford: Clarendon.

Davis, Wayne A. 1987. The Varieties of Fear. *Philosophical Studies* 51:287–310.

Descartes, René. (1649) 1989. *The Passions of the Soul*, trans. Stephen H. Voss. Indianapolis: Hackett.

de Sousa, Ronald. 1987. *The Rationality of Emotion*. Cambridge, Mass.: MIT Press.

Doyle, Arthur Conan. 1930. *The Complete Sherlock Holmes*. Garden City, N.Y.: Doubleday.

Freud, Sigmund. (1915) 1969. The Unconscious. *The Standard Edition of the Complete Psychological Works of Sigmund Freud*, ed. James Strachey, vol. 14. London: Hogarth.

Gordon, Robert. 1987. *The Structure of Emotions: Investigations in Cognitive Philosophy*. Cambridge: Cambridge University Press.

Gosling, J. C. Emotion and Object. *Philosophical Review* 74:486–503.

Green, O. H. 1972. *Emotion and Belief*. American Philosophical Quarterly, monograph no. 6. Bowling Green, Ohio: Philosophy Documentation Center.

Green, O. H. 1992. *The Emotions: A Philosophical Theory*. Dordrecht: Kluwer Academic Publishers.

Greenspan, Patricia S. 1988. *Emotions and Reasons: An Inquiry into Emotional Justification*. London: Routledge.

Hume, David. (1739) 1978. *A Treatise of Human Nature*, ed. L. A. Selby Bigge. Oxford: Clarendon.

James, William. (1890) 1950. *The Principles of Psychology*. 2 vols. New York: Dover.

Kenny, Anthony. 1963. *Action, Emotion and Will*. London: Routledge & Kegan Paul.

Lange, Carl, and James, William. 1922. *The Emotions*, ed. Knight Dunlap. Baltimore: Williams & Wilkins.

Locke, John. (1695) 1975. *An Essay concerning Human Understanding*, ed. P. H. Nidditch. Oxford: Clarendon.

Lyons, William. 1980. *Emotion*. Cambridge: Cambridge University Press.

Marks, Joel. 1982. A Theory of Emotions. *Philosophical Studies* 42:227–42.

Morreal, John. 1993. Fear without Belief. *Journal of Philosophy* 90:359–66.

Neu, Jerome. 1977. *Emotion, Thought, and Therapy*. Berkeley: University of California Press.

Nissenbaum, Helen Fay. 1985. *Emotion and Focus*. Stanford, Calif.: Center for the Study of Language and Information, Stanford University.

Nussbaum, Martha. 1990. *Love's Knowledge*. New York: Oxford University Press.

Pitcher, George. 1965. Emotion. *Mind* 74:326–46.

Plato. 1976. *Protagoras*, trans. C. C. W. Taylor. Oxford: Clarendon.

Price, H. H. 1953. *Thinking and Experience*. Cambridge, Mass.: Harvard University Press.

Proust, Marcel. 1934. *Remembrance of Things Past*, 2 vols., trans. C. K. Scott Moncrieff. New York: Random House.

Rey, Georges. 1980. Functionalism and the Emotions. In *Explaining Emotions*, ed. A. Rorty. Berkeley: University of California Press.

Roberts, Robert C. 1988. What an Emotion Is: A Sketch. *Philosophical Review* 97: 183–209.

Russell, Bertrand. (1919) 1971. *Introduction to Mathematical Philosophy*. New York: Simon & Schuster.

Schacter, Stanley, and Singer, Jerome. 1962. Cognition, Social, and Physiological Determinants of Emotional State. *Psychological Review* 69:379–99.

Searle, John. 1983. *Intentionality: An Essay in the Philosophy of Mind*. Cambridge: Cambridge University Press.

Solomon, Robert C. 1976. *The Passions*. Garden City, N.Y.: Anchor/Doubleday.

Stocker, Michael. 1993. Valuing Emotions. Typescript.

Stout, G. F. 1929. *A Manual of Psychology*, 4th ed. London: University Tutorial Press.

Taylor, Gabriele. 1985. *Pride, Shame and Guilt: Emotions of Self-Assessment*. Oxford: Clarendon.

Thalberg, Irving. 1964. Emotion and Thought. *American Philosophical Quarterly* 1:45–55.

Thalberg, Irving. 1980. Avoiding the Emotion-Thought Conundrum. *Philosophy* 55: 396–402.

Wilson, J. R. S. 1972. *Emotion and Object*. Cambridge: Cambridge University Press.

Wittgenstein, Ludwig. 1953. *Philosophical Investigations*. New York: Macmillan.

4

Emotions and Values

In *Il Deserto Rosso*, Antonioni presents scenes of Italian landscapes and sea-scapes marred by industrial life.[1] The film is a two-hour-long commentary on alienation in European society as it existed roughly twenty years after World War II, and the bleak scenery as well as the vacancy and despair of the main characters conveys disconsolation and discomfort about a world everywhere dominated by heavy industry and its pollutant effluence. The film opens with long shots of a massive, pipelined industrial plant, whose turbines are producing a deafening roar and whose smokestacks fill the air with filthy gas. Later, the director shifts to shots of countrysides blotted by power poles and shorefronts made gunky by chemical waste. The industrial workers are on strike; the fish mongers sell poisoned fish; and the men and women of the managerial class, whose lives are the subject of this film, live without human connection. Their spiritless condition is correlated to the decay of their surroundings. Their estrangement from each other coincides with their estrangement from the earth.

1. *Il Deserto Rosso*, directed by Michelangelo Antonioni; screenplay by Michelangelo Antonioni and Tonino Guerra.

The images of industrial dominance and waste that Antonioni captures so well elicit from us both aesthetic and moral responses. These images are jarring to look at. Their striking forms arrest our attention, yet the events and conditions they portray also unsettle us. And these unpleasant feelings immediately grow into disapproval and perhaps also anger, contempt, sadness. Antonioni shows us the ugliness of industrialization and the spiritual decline it breeds, and our feelings register these perceptions. This essay is about those perceptions and the feelings that register them. I want to understand how they come to be part of human psychology, what enables us to have them. When we are revulsed by the sight of a gunky shorefront, is our revulsion an immediate, automatic reaction like that of the pain we experience when soap gets in our eyes? Or does it involve a cognition as well? And if it involves a cognition, is there then some fact that we apprehend in feeling revulsion? Is there a fact, for instance, of which our revulsion makes us aware, about the nastiness of gunk when it has seeped into seashores and wetlands? Is Antonioni disclosing to us, through our feelings, truths about the industrialized world perceived in his film, or is he merely inducing disagreeable feelings in us by artfully manipulating images?

Answers to these questions typically fall into either of two schools of thought. On the one hand, there are those thinkers who believe in the objectivity of aesthetics and ethics. They believe our capacity for aesthetic and moral feelings presupposes the existence of aesthetic and moral facts. Accordingly, they would maintain not only that our being revulsed by the sight of a gunky shorefront involves a cognition but also that the revulsion consists at least in part in the apprehension of some moral or aesthetic fact. On the other hand, there are those thinkers who believe that what are commonly thought to be aesthetic and moral facts originate in our capacity for aesthetic and moral feelings. Accordingly, they deny the existence of such facts. In their view, the common attribution of aesthetic and moral values to the events and objects that provoke these feelings is an error insofar as it signifies belief that those values exist as features of the world independently of the feelings that register our perceptions of them. Hence, the perennial dispute between these two schools of thought in the theory of value can be seen as a controversy about how to understand our aesthetic and moral responses to the world in relation to events and objects that provoke them. Both schools agree on what these are, at least in paradigm cases. Neither, for instance, would question our taking as paradigm the perceptions and feelings that a film like *Il Deserto Rosso* elicits. Where they disagree is in their analysis of the nature of these perceptions and feelings and of the conditions that make them possible. In seeking to understand how they become part of human psychology, I hope to make some headway toward settling this disagreement.

I cannot, of course, hope to end the disagreement. It encompasses too many outstanding issues for a final settlement to result from answering the question of how these perceptions and feelings come to be part of human psychology. What I do hope to do, however, is first to show the difficulties in sustaining the belief that aesthetic and moral values originate in our capacity for aesthetic and moral feelings and then to show that a certain answer to the question of how these feelings become part of human psychology allows one to avoid the ontological excesses that those who hold this belief commonly accuse their opponents of indulging. This accusation received its best known contemporary statement in J. L. Mackie's charge that "[i]f there were objective values, they would be entities or qualities or relations of a very strange sort, utterly different from anything else in the universe."[2] The charge in effect sets up a problem: how can one oppose the view that aesthetic and moral values originate in our capacity for aesthetic and moral feelings, how can one oppose what, following Mackie, I'll call subjectivism in the theory of values, without committing oneself to belief in a realm of metaphysically extravagant things like Platonic forms or properties that are supersensible or nonnatural. The headway I hope to make toward settling the disagreement between subjectivism and its opposition is to resolve this problem.

Let us begin with a critical discussion of subjectivism. Hume's ethics, being the source in Anglo-American philosophy of the main arguments for subjectivism, will be our guide.

1. Humean Subjectivism

On the empiricist theory of mind from which Hume drew arguments for subjectivism, perceptions and feelings are distinct mental occurrences, and the one gives rise to the other automatically.[3] The mind is so constituted, Hume liked to say, that it reacts with certain feelings when impressed with certain images. It is so constituted, for instance, that the image of gaiety at a dinner party will automatically give rise to pleasure, and that of solemnity on a similar occasion will automatically give rise to an opposite feeling. This sharp distinction between perceptions and feelings serves, within Hume's theory, as

2. J. L. Mackie, *Ethics: Inventing Right and Wrong* (London: Pelican Books, 1977), p. 38.
3. I am departing from Hume's terminology here. Hume uses the term 'perception' to cover both feelings and thoughts (i.e., impressions and ideas), and I mean it in the narrower sense in which perceptions are forms of thought. See Hume, *A Treatise of Human Nature*, 2nd ed., L. A. Selby-Bigge, ed., with text rev. by P. H. Nidditch (Oxford: Clarendon Press, 1978), pp. 1–2.

the platform on which its arguments for subjectivism are built. For the theory excludes from our sensory experiences any image of goodness. It denies, that is, that, strictly speaking, we ever see or hear goodness in the things to which we attribute it. It holds instead that when we think something good, we think this as a result of pleasant feelings the thing induces in us.[4] Thus, on Hume's theory, the values we attribute to things originate in our aesthetic and moral responses to them. Hume, in the following passage from his second *Enquiry*, gives a typically crisp statement of this view in the case of aesthetics.

> It is on the proportion, relation, and position of parts that all natural beauty depends; but it would be absurd thence to infer, that the perception of beauty, like that of truth in geometrical problems, consists wholly in the perception of relations, and was performed entirely by the understanding or intellectual faculties. In all the sciences, our mind from the known relations investigates the unknown. But in all decisions of taste or external beauty, all the relations are beforehand obvious to the eye; and we thence proceed to feel a sentiment of complacency or disgust, according to the nature of the object, and the disposition of our organs.[5]

Of course, not every pleasant feeling that follows upon the contemplation of some object validates the thought that the object is beautiful. The theory, to do justice to our aesthetic responses, must distinguish among types of pleasant feeling, else there would be no reason to discount, as we do, the pronouncements of parents on the beauty of their children and the excellence of their performances in school plays, gymnastics tournaments, and musical competitions. Parents regularly mistake the joys of watching their children perform for the pleasures of watching a beautiful performance, and no adequate theory of aesthetic responses can ignore this difference between types of pleasant feeling. Hume certainly recognized it and, to account for it, introduced into his theory a distinction between interested and disinterested standpoints from which events and objects are viewed and pleasant and unpleasant feelings experienced.[6]

Another difference that the Humean theory must account for, one that the distinction between interested and disinterested standpoints does not explain, is that between aesthetic and moral feelings. To be sure, the theory, as Hume developed it, assimilates the latter to the former, and one might then suppose that it could treat this difference as nominal rather than real.

---

4. Ibid., pp. 470–471. See also Hume, *Enquiries Concerning Human Understanding and Concerning Principles of Morals*, 3rd ed., L. A. Selby-Bigge, ed., with rev. by P. H. Nidditch (Oxford: Clarendon Press, 1975), p. 289.

5. Hume, *Enquiries*, p. 291.

6. Hume, *Treatise*, pp. 471–472.

To do so, however, would render the theory powerless to explain contempo-
raneous experiences of both types of feeling. Specifically, it would render
it powerless to explain how the same event or object can elicit distinct aesthetic and moral responses, how one can enjoy the balletic representation of
violence in Peckinpaugh's *The Wild Bunch* while being thoroughly repelled
by its inhumanity, and how a similar mix of responses is possible on view-
ing Riefenstahl's *Triumph of the Will*, at least if you're someone who loves
a parade.[7] The theory, therefore, must recognize something in or about the
pleasures of witnessing graceful actions that differentiates them from those
of witnessing humane ones, and the same goes for differentiating the distresses of witnessing awkward actions from those of witnessing brutal ones.
Moreover, it must recognize these differences even if it assimilates one type
of feeling to the other. Hume, I believe, signaled his understanding of this
point when he advanced the argument quoted above. For he advanced it
immediately after making a similar argument about moral assessments, and
for the purpose of reinforcing that argument. Yet at the same time, he was
careful to use different names for aesthetic feelings from those he had used
for moral ones. He was careful to call the former complacency and disgust,
having called the latter approbation and blame.[8]

How, then, can Hume's theory account for the difference between aesthetic and moral feelings? How can it account for the difference between
complacency and approbation, disgust and blame? Traditionally, within
empiricism at least, questions of this sort were answered by looking inward
and locating the difference between types of feeling in their intrinsic character.[9] Such recourse to the intrinsic character of feelings follows from the traditional empiricist conception of occurrent mental phenomena as discrete,
serially connected states that their subject can directly observe but that others can know about only indirectly. On this conception, then, the difference
between two types of feeling should be apparent to anyone who has experienced them. The theory thus calls on our familiarity with having experienced
both aesthetic and moral feelings to establish the difference between them.
In doing so, it assumes that anyone who has felt both is capable, on reflection, of recognizing this difference. It assumes, that is, that a person who
has felt both is capable of telling one from the other by some identifying
mark, a distinctive tone, say, or a distinctive quale. Such identifying marks

7. *The Wild Bunch*, directed by Sam Peckinpaugh; screenplay by Walon Green and Sam
Peckinpaugh. *Triumph of the Will*, directed by Leni Riefenstahl.
8. Hume, *Enquiries*, pp. 290–291.
9. Hume, *Treatise*, pp. 471–472.

are presupposed by the traditional empiricist conception of occurrent mental states and, usually as a way to end further inquiry, invoked in lieu of specifying criteria for the application of that conception in any particular case.[10]

For well-known reasons, however, the conception is untenable.[11] It is supposed to capture our shared understanding of occurrent mental states the vehicle for which is a common language like English. To have such an understanding, an understanding, for instance, of the distinction between disgust and blame, those who share it must agree on the criteria for drawing the distinction. Yet there can be no such agreement if the marks by which a person tells one feeling from the other are observable by him alone. To be sure, on the empiricist conception, there can be agreement in the sense of a fortuitous coincidence, when everyone just happens to use the same marks in drawing the distinction. But a fortuitous coincidence is not a shared understanding. A common language that denotes our thoughts, sensations, and feelings is thus inexplicable on the traditional empiricist conception of them. Or, in other words, the conception fails to capture what it is supposed to capture.

As a result, Hume's theory cannot locate the difference between aesthetic and moral feelings by looking inward. It must therefore look outward. It must look to their typical causes, circumstances, or effects to account for the difference between them. In this regard, the comparison Hume makes between aesthetic and moral feelings in the course of assimilating the latter to the former turns out to be instructive.[12] Consider for example how it applies in the case of an action that is at once graceful and humane. On Hume's view, the qualities of the action that make it graceful will inspire the pleasant feelings that Hume calls complacency and those that make it humane will inspire the pleasant feelings that he calls approbation. Accordingly, the complacency arises from the perception of the overt behavior the action consists in, specifically, the bodily movements that account for its gracefulness, whereas the approbation arises from the perception of the action's inner springs, specifically, the compassion or benevolence that accounts for its humanity. Moreover, Hume underscores this contrast between exterior and interior qualities by adverting to two types of beauty, natural and moral, to characterize how objects of complacency and approbation look to their subjects. Graceful

---

10. The problem is sensitively treated by Warren Quinn in "Moral and Other Realisms: Some Initial Difficulties," in his *Morality and Action* (Cambridge: Cambridge University Press, 1993), pp. 1–19, esp. 15–19

11. See Ludwig Wittgenstein, *Philosophical Investigations* §§243–270.

12. Hume, *Enquiries*, pp. 290–291.

actions reflect one type of beauty, humane ones the other, according as the qualities involved are external or mental. The contrast, then, clearly suggests that on Hume's theory, notwithstanding its traditional empiricist credentials, the difference between aesthetic and moral feelings can be located in their cause in lieu of locating it in their intrinsic character.

Locating the difference in their cause, however, opens a gap in the theory's argument for subjectivism. Specifically, since the difference between aesthetic and moral values does not ultimately reside in the difference between aesthetic and moral feelings, it is now uncertain what role, if any, the feelings have in the explanation of the values. How, for example, do complacency and approbation figure in the theory's explanation of the beauty of a graceful action or the goodness of a humane one? Why not suppose instead that the beauty or the goodness perceived in the action explains the feelings? To answer these questions, the theory needs a stronger argument for subjectivism than the one Hume generates from his sharp distinction between perceptions and feelings. The argument he generates from the distinction consists of making the distinction fundamental in psychology, mapping onto it an equally sharp distinction between facts and values, and then using this mapping to explicate the latter distinction as a function of the former. The argument's cogency therefore depends on the mapping's having explicatory force, which is to say, on one's being able to answer satisfactorily questions about elements in either the domain of facts or that of values by reference to the characteristics of the elements of the domain onto which it is mapped. And, as we've seen, no satisfactory answer to questions about the difference between aesthetic and moral values is obtainable from the domain of feelings. Consequently, the argument must be supplemented or replaced to resolve the uncertainty about how Hume's theory explains the beauty of graceful actions and the goodness of humane ones as being conditional on the feelings of complacency and approbation.

Again, Hume's own treatment of the issue is instructive. Drawing on his general theme of the mind's "great propensity to spread itself on external things,"[13] Hume maintains that, in either case, the beauty or goodness amounts to a glow that is cast on the actions by the pleasant feelings they inspire. The subject of these feelings, according to Hume, projects them onto the actions when he regards them as beautiful or good, much as one projects visual impressions of color onto objects when one perceives them as red, green, blue, etc. "Taste," Hume writes, using his favorite term for the sensibilities associated with our aesthetic and moral feelings, "[is a] productive

---

13. Hume, *Treatise*, p. 167.

faculty,...gilding or staining all natural objects with the colors, borrowed from internal sentiment."[14] Hume thus explains how values depend on feelings by appealing to an analogy between them and so-called secondary qualities, color, sound, texture, and the like.[15] The upshot is that the explanation amounts to a different argument for subjectivism from the one that is based on a sharp distinction between perceptions and feelings. This new argument presupposes a distinction between primary and secondary qualities, and this is a distinction within either domain rather than a distinction between the two.[16] Projecting forward to twentieth-century metaethics, one could say that this new argument corresponds to the arguments for anti-realism that prominently surfaced during the century's last twenty years, whereas the earlier argument corresponds to the arguments for emotivism and other forms of noncognitivism that prevailed at the century's midpoint and the decade that followed. Having seen that Hume's proto-noncognitivist argument is too weak to account for the difference between aesthetic and moral values, we must now consider the argument that anticipates contemporary anti-realism.[17]

While this argument does explain how values depend on feelings, it nevertheless provokes the same doubts about its soundness as those that led to the earlier argument's collapse once the necessity of looking beyond the intrinsic characters of aesthetic and moral feelings to account for the

14. Hume, *Enquiries*, p. 293.

15. Hume, *Treatise*, p. 469, where Hume writes, "Vice and virtue, therefore, may be compared to sounds, colours, heat and cold, which, according to modern philosophy, are not qualities in objects but perceptions in the mind." To avoid the complications that Hume's phenomenalism creates, I take Hume to have accepted the thesis of modern philosophy to which he refers in this passage, namely, that primary qualities inhere in the objects to which they are attributed but secondary qualities do not. That is, to simplify our study, I treat Hume's subjectivism about moral and aesthetic values as resting on this thesis, even though what Hume says earlier in the *Treatise* (pp. 226–231), when he criticizes the thesis, is at odds with his basing his theory on it. See also pp. 235–237. I owe this observation about the apparent inconsistency in Hume's use of the distinction between primary and secondary qualities to explain moral and aesthetic values to David Ballie.

16. I say a distinction within either domain since the distinction between primary and secondary qualities can be a distinction between simple sensations of color, texture, temperature, etc. and simple sensations of size, shape, motion, etc. or a distinction between their corresponding ideas. Note, here I am using the terminology I introduced to replace Hume's 'impressions' and 'ideas': i.e., sensations count as feelings and ideas as perceptions. See fn. 3 above.

17. It should not, then, be surprising that the same difficulty that is the undoing of Hume's proto-noncognitivist argument resurfaces as a major problem for twentieth-century noncognitivism. Thus, one major criticism of emotivism is that its appeal to all-purpose pro and con attitudes as what evaluative judgments express leaves it without resources for distinguishing among different types of moral judgment or between moral judgments and other evaluative judgments. See William Alston, "Moral Attitudes and Moral Judgments," *Nous* 2 (1963): 1–23.

differences between them was recognized. These doubts recur with respect to the second argument because the distinction between primary and secondary qualities that it presupposes is not unambiguous. One can certainly take it as Hume did, namely, as a distinction between qualities that truly inhere in an object and qualities whose inherence in an object is a figment of sensory experience. But one can also take it as a distinction between qualities whose character is not determined by any one mode of sensory experience and qualities whose character is.[18] On this alternative, a secondary quality is naturally understood to be a disposition of an object to produce certain sensory experiences in appropriately situated subjects. So understood, secondary qualities no less than primary ones may truly inhere in the objects to which they are ascribed. And this result means that, contrary to what Hume implied, the analogy between values and secondary qualities does not unequivocally support subjectivism.[19] Depending on how one understands secondary qualities, one can use the analogy, as Hume did, to explain an object's having aesthetic or moral values as being conditional on certain feelings, or one can use it to explain the occurrence of those feelings as being conditional on an object's having those values. The argument from the analogy, in other words, provokes the same uncertainty as the argument from the sharp distinction between perceptions and feelings.

2. Hume's Analogy Examined

It is possible, then, by seizing on this uncertainty and pointing out how one can understand secondary qualities as dispositions of objects, to solve the problem of how to oppose subjectivism without committing oneself to belief in metaphysically extravagant objects or properties. A solution along these lines has been given by several prominent philosophers, notably John McDowell and David Wiggins.[20] On their way of solving the problem, that

18. See Jonathan Bennett, *Locke, Berkeley, Hume: Central Themes* (Oxford: Oxford University Press, 1971), pp. 96–100. See also Colin McGinn, *The Subjective View* (Oxford: Oxford University Press, 1983), pp. 5–9.

19. The point has been forcefully made by John McDowell in "Values and Secondary Qualities," *Morality and Objectivity*, Ted Honderich, ed. (London: Routledge and Kegan Paul, 1985), pp. 110–129.

20. See McDowell, "Values and Secondary Qualities"; and "Aesthetic Value, Objectivity, and the Fabric of the World," in *Pleasure, Preference and Value*, Eva Schaper, ed. (Cambridge: Cambridge University Press, 1983); and David Wiggins, "A Sensible Subjectivism," in *Needs, Values, Truth*, 2nd ed. (Oxford: Blackwell, 1991), pp. 185–211.

is, aesthetic and moral values are understood as dispositions of the objects to which we attribute those values. Specifically, just as colors, on this way of understanding secondary qualities, are dispositions of objects to produce certain visual sensations in appropriately situated subjects, so too aesthetic and moral values are dispositions of objects to excite certain feelings in appropriately situated subjects. When aesthetic and moral values are so understood, belief in them is no more of a metaphysical extravagance than the corresponding belief in colors.

Yet this way of solving the problem is not entirely satisfactory. Accepting Hume's analogy, as the proponents of this solution do, has a serious drawback. For there seems to be little to choose from between the two conceptions of secondary quality. Whether one understands secondary qualities as qualities of sensations that the mind spreads onto objects or as dispositions of objects to produce certain sensations in the right circumstances seems to be nothing more than ontological bookkeeping. Consequently, the tighter one takes the analogy to be, the more one will be driven to concede that aesthetic and moral values might just as well be figments of our affective experiences; whereas the looser one takes it to be, the more vulnerable the solution becomes to the very charge of metaphysical extravagance that its proponents maintained one could avoid by drawing the analogy. In the end, it seems that a successful challenge to Hume's second argument for subjectivism requires raising different doubts about its soundness. One must question the analogy itself.

To do this, let us press it a bit further. Specifically, let us suppose that the relation of values to feelings is as tight as the relation between secondary qualities and the sensory experiences through which they are known. The latter relation, being definitional or conceptual, is as tight as it could be. For a secondary quality is defined by the appearances that the objects it characterizes have by virtue of their possessing that quality. Consider, for instance, the standard definition of an object's being red. On this definition, an object is red if it appears red to qualified observers in circumstances conducive to their seeing true colors. Similarly, the standard definition of an object's being sweet is that an object is sweet if it appears sweet to qualified observers in circumstances conducive to their detecting true tastes. Hence, one cannot conceive of a given secondary quality apart from the appearances the objects it characterizes have by virtue of their possessing that quality. One cannot, that is, conceive of it apart from the sensory experiences through which it is known. At the same time, one cannot conceive of those experiences apart from that quality, since they are essentially experiences of an object as possessing that quality. This interdependence between the concepts of the quality and the experiences through which it is known thus makes it impossible to pry the two apart. The relation between them could not be any tighter.

So too, then, if we press Hume's analogy, the relation between values and feelings is equally tight. That is to say, the value of an object is defined by the appearances it has by virtue of its possessing that value. Consequently, one cannot conceive of the value apart from the feelings that the objects possessing it excite, and conversely, one cannot conceive of those feelings apart from the value of those objects, since they are essentially feelings one has toward the objects as the possessors of such value. These affective experiences are therefore as tightly related to the values one knows through them as sensory experiences are related to the secondary qualities one knows through them.

In either case, then, the property in question—be it redness, sweetness, goodness, or the like—is defined by reference to a qualified observer's experience of an object's having that property in circumstances conducive to his truly observing properties of that sort. The experience, let us say, has *objective content* in the sense that the content's realization implies the existence of an object with that property. And this objective content is what defines the property. Accordingly, the analogy holds on the assumption that the objective content of the affective experiences through which values are known is as free of conceptual elements as the objective content of the sensory experiences through which secondary qualities are known. More exactly, it holds on the assumption that the affective experiences through which values are known imply no greater conceptual understanding of their objects than the sensory experiences through which secondary qualities are known imply of theirs. The reason is that if any of the former implied a greater conceptual understanding of its object than the latter implied of theirs, then an object's possessing a certain value—its being good, say, or beautiful—could not be defined by its having the appearance it has owing to its possessing that value. Hence, the analogy weakens considerably if one can cast doubt on the assumption of parity between the two kinds of experience on which it rests. By showing that the affective experiences through which values are known contain more conceptual thought than the sensory experiences through which secondary qualities are known, one can effectively challenge the analogy.[21]

---

21. See Crispin Wright, "Moral Values, Projection, and Secondary Qualities," *Proceedings of the Aristotelian Society*, supp. vol. 62 (1988): 1–26, esp. pp. 12–13. McDowell, to be sure, acknowledges disanalogies between values and secondary qualities. He notes, e.g., that values, unlike colors, are conceived of not merely as eliciters of appropriate attitudes but also as meriting those attitudes. (See "Values and Secondary Qualities," p. 118.) The question, however, is whether he recognizes the disanalogy to which I am here adverting. As I argue below, this

3. A Refutation of Hume's Analogy

The strongest argument for there being more conceptual thought in the affective experiences through which values are known than in the sensory experiences through which secondary qualities are known is that learning is necessary to a child's developing the moral and aesthetic sensibilities that make it capable of having such experiences but unnecessary to its developing the sensory powers that make it capable of having experiences of secondary qualities. A child, it is safe to say, does not enter the world already equipped with moral and aesthetic sensibilities and does not soon come to have them just through the physiological developments of infancy. Children must receive some instruction before they can tell good from bad, right from wrong, and beauty from deformity. By contrast, no instruction is necessary for children to acquire the power to see different colors, hear different tones, or feel different textures. Rather, they acquire these powers early in life through the normal physiological development of their sensory organs. To be sure, a newborn may first need to be exposed to light, sound, and solid surfaces before it is able to detect differences in color, tone, and texture. That is, some exposure to visual, auditory, and tactile stimuli may be necessary for the relevant sensory organs to develop normally. But such exposure is not the same thing as instruction. Adaptation is not learning. The Wild Boy of Aveyron, to take a famous case of a grown but uninstructed child, showed no awareness of values. He was utterly uncivilized at the time of his capture, and the description of him as completely ignorant of values does not seem farfetched. Nothing, however, in his behavior ever suggested to his custodians or anyone else that he was completely ignorant of secondary qualities.[22]

Admittedly, no conclusion about the conceptual thought contained in an experience of value directly follows from the fact that learning is necessary to a child's developing moral and aesthetic sensibilities. Not all learning, after all, involves the acquisition of concepts or the enlargement of one's understanding of the world. Some consists in habituation in which the learner acquires no concepts or beliefs or at least none essential to the learning in question. And if the learning that is necessary to a child's developing moral and

---

disanalogy shows Hume's analogy to be inapt for understanding the relation of values to feelings and is thus fatal to McDowell's program. So either he does not recognize it, or he has not fully taken in its implications.

22. Jean-Marc-Gaspard Itard, *The Wild Boy of Aveyron*, George and Muriel Humphrey, trans. (New York: Appleton-Century-Crofts, 1962). See also Michael Stocker with Elizabeth Hegeman, *Valuing Emotions* (Cambridge: Cambridge University Press, 1996), pp. 68–69.

aesthetic sensibilities were of this sort, then it would not represent any threat to Hume's analogy. For if it were of this sort, then one could acknowledge that learning was a precondition of the affective experiences through which values are known but not of the sensory experiences through which secondary qualities are known without having to admit that there was more conceptual thought in the former than in the latter. Hence, to overturn Hume's analogy, one must show that the learning necessary to the development of moral and aesthetic sensibilities does not consist in mere habituation.[23]

The issue, in brief, is what goes on when a child develops moral and aesthetic sensibilities. What sort of learning is involved? Since it is a pre-condition of the affective experiences of which those sensibilities make one capable and since, on Hume's analogy, such experiences are certain feelings that objects excite in appropriately situated subjects, the learning must result in a capacity for those feelings. Accordingly, if it consists in habituation, then it consists in the acquisition of habits of feeling, and the feelings the habits of which the child acquires are, needless to say, the same as the feelings that, on Hume's analogy, objects excite in appropriately situated subjects when the subjects regard those objects as possessing value. The question, then, is whether the child could acquire these habits without also acquiring some concepts or beliefs. Pavlovian conditioning supplies, perhaps, the best model of such habituation, and its use in changing behavior through the formation of habits of feeling is well established. So examining whether it could be used to instill habits of feeling of the relevant sort should help to answer this question.

Consider, for instance, how Pavlovian conditioning is used by psychother-apists to treat alcoholism. By pairing a nauseant with drinking and repeating this pairing according to the program of conditioning Pavlov developed, a psychotherapist can bring an alcoholic patient to feel nausea whenever he is presented with an alcoholic beverage. The conditioning is successful if the habit it instills is strong enough to create in the patient an inhibition to drink. Its success, however, does not mean that the patient has learned to regard alcoholic beverages as having negative value. For it implies only that

---

23. In this section, I assume that the thesis that learning is necessary for the development of moral and aesthetic sensibilities will go unchallenged. One might say that I am here offering the thesis as a gambit and assuming that a defender of Humean subjectivism will accept it. He could, of course, decline the gambit by arguing against the thesis. I take up this possibility in section 5. The reason for postponing consideration of it for two sections is that I cannot show that defending the analogy against my challenge by denying the thesis fails without having an account of emotions as intentional states. I give this account in section 4.

the patient will experience a specific feeling, a wave of nausea, when presented with an alcoholic beverage, and not that he will experience the feeling toward that beverage. It does not imply, in other words, that the patient has some thought about or attitude toward the beverage. It no more implies that the patient finds the beverage nauseating than the success of Pavlov's original experiments implies that the dog Pavlov conditioned to salivate at the sound of a bell found the bell (or its sound) mouth-watering.

It follows, then, that Pavlovian conditioning alone is not sufficient to explain how a child develops moral and aesthetic sensibilities from the primitive feelings that define the child's original emotional range. The reason why is clear. If the affective experiences through which values are known are certain feelings that objects having those values excite in appropriately situated subjects, then the feelings must be directed at the objects. One's merely having the feelings in the presence of those objects would not be sufficient for one's having the relevant experiences. And Pavlovian conditioning cannot by itself explain how a feeling comes to be directed at an object. Perhaps, though, we can remove this deficiency by adding a hypothesis of projection. So let us suppose that projecting a feeling onto an object is a natural consequence of one's regularly experiencing the feeling in the presence of that object. Is this consequence sufficient for having the relevant experience? Is it sufficient for showing that one regards the object as having value, positive or negative according to the type of feeling one projects?

Again consider the example of the alcoholic patient who has been conditioned to feel nausea in the presence of alcoholic beverages. On the above hypothesis, he will project this feeling onto a glass of scotch, say, when one is offered to him, and as a result the scotch will appear nauseating to him. Yet it still does not follow that he regards the scotch as having negative value. Indeed, since he knows that the feeling is a consequence of his having been conditioned to experience it, then presumably whatever inclination he might have to regard the scotch as having negative value on account of its nauseating appearance would be undone by some such thought as, "There's nothing actually bad about the scotch; it just appears nauseating because of the treatment I've received." Consequently, even allowing that the projection of a feeling onto an object is a natural consequence of one's regularly experiencing that feeling in the presence of the object, Pavlovian conditioning still falls short of explaining how one becomes capable of the affective experiences through which values are known.

To be sure, this conclusion would not obtain if the point of the patient's thought were that the feeling of nausea induced by the scotch should be discounted on the grounds that the treatment had made him a deviant perceiver of alcoholic beverages.[24] For if this were its point, then the patient's not regarding the scotch as having negative value, despite its nauseating appearance, would have no bearing on whether mere habituation suffices for the development of moral and aesthetic sensibilities. It would have no bearing, that is, on whether mere habituation suffices for acquiring capacities for affective experiences through which values are known. It would have no bearing just as someone's not regarding a room as yellow, despite its yellowish appearance, because he knows he has jaundice has no bearing on whether human neurophysiological development suffices for acquiring capacities for visual experiences through which colors are known. But the point of the thought is not to discount the feeling on these grounds. One would discount it even if one had no reason to regard oneself as a deviant perceiver. Examples of what may be called provincial nausea make this clear.

Suppose, for instance, you felt nausea upon discovering, during a meal at a Chinese restaurant, that the dish known as roasted sea cucumbers from which you have sampled is actually a plate of cooked sea slugs. Even though the dish now appears nauseating to you, you might nevertheless refrain from regarding it as having negative value. For you might think, "There's nothing actually bad about eating sea slugs; it's just my upbringing that makes me so squeamish about it," and this thought could then undo whatever inclination you might have to regard the dish of slugs as having negative value. In this case, you discount the feeling, but you don't do so on the grounds that you are a deviant perceiver of cooked sea slugs. Rather, you do so on the grounds that the feeling is an accident of your upbringing. It is an accident in that it comes from your having happened to be raised in a culture that doesn't fancy eating sea slugs. You therefore discount the feeling as signifying nothing about the slugs without at the same time assuming that there is anything abnormal in your reaction to them. After all, the bare fact of having been raised in a culture that does not feast on sea slugs gives you no reason to suppose that your culinary tastes are deviant.

Of course, the thought that your feeling was an accident of your upbringing might never have occurred to you. You might simply have thought, upon

---

24. Nor would it obtain if its point were to discount the feeling on the grounds that it wasn't experienced from a disinterested standpoint. But why suppose that the standpoint from which one experiences a feeling must be interested or biased just because the feeling is the product of Pavlovian conditioning? Why suppose that if the patient viewed the whiskey from a disinterested standpoint, he would lose his disposition to feel nausea? What's crucial is that the patient discounts the nausea because he recognizes that, as a product of Pavlovian conditioning, it signifies nothing about the whiskey. Whether he thinks the feeling is experienced from a disinterested or an interested standpoint is a separate matter.

discovering what roasted sea cucumbers actually are, "how vile," and this thought would express your feeling at the same time as it assigned negative value to the dish before you. In this case, you don't discount the feeling but rather treat it as signifying that there is something bad about eating sea slugs.[25] Their nauseating appearance, in other words, has a meaning for you, a meaning that it loses when you recognize it as a mere accident of your upbringing. It means that the slugs are putrid, pestilent, or noxious, which in the context of the meal implies sickening if ingested. Plainly, if it is to have this meaning, you must have learned to interpret your feeling as a sign of something bad about the slugs beyond their nauseating appearance, for what is sickening is bad, not because of its appearance, but because of what it can do to you. And to have learned so to interpret your feeling presupposes at least the acquisition of beliefs to the effect that sickness results from eating what turns your stomach.

The immediate implication of this account, then, is that nausea cannot be an affective experience through which values are known without one's having first acquired certain concepts or beliefs. Their acquisition is basic to one's learning to interpret the experience as signifying something bad about the object of nausea. Consequently, when one knows that one's experience of nausea is due to factors that do not fulfill those concepts or support those beliefs—factors such as the forces of Pavlovian conditioning or the accidents of one's upbringing—one disjoins the feeling from the negative value one has learned to interpret it as signifying. And what holds of nausea specifically holds generally of affective experiences through which values are known. One cannot develop capacities for such experiences without acquiring some concepts or beliefs. Their acquisition is basic to one's learning to interpret the feelings in which they consist as connoting specific values. The upshot of this conclusion is that mere habituation, in which no concept or belief is acquired, does not suffice for the learning necessary to develop such capacities. Values, therefore, must be misconceived on Hume's analogy.

4. Naturalism

We must now take up the issue of metaphysical extravagance. Can one reject Hume's analogy between values and secondary qualities without having to conceive of values as something like Platonic forms, supersensible properties,

---

25. See Charles Taylor, "Self-Interpreting Animals," in *Human Agency and Language: Philosophical Papers 1* (Cambridge: Cambridge University Press, 1985), pp. 45–76.

or nonnatural properties of yet some other kind? For convenience, I will call this the problem of Platonism in the theory of values, taking Platonism as a stand-in for all views of aesthetic and moral values on which they are understood as radically different from the objects and properties of the natural world. The question, then, is whether, having rejected Hume's analogy, one can avoid Platonism if one denies that aesthetic and moral values originate in our capacities for aesthetic and moral feelings. Because the argument against the analogy turns on the point that there is greater conceptual thought in the affective experiences through which values are known than in the sensory experiences through which secondary qualities are known, it would almost certainly lead back to Platonism if the greater conceptual thought that the former contained implied the kind of special intellectual faculty to which Platonists have traditionally appealed to explain our knowledge of values. For their appeal rests on an assumption that the concepts with which this special faculty operates, the concepts of goodness and beauty, say, are in an important sense *a priori*. They yield an understanding of things that is distinguishable from the understanding that comes through sensory experience. Consequently, one needs to show that the argument does not lead back to Platonism, and one can show that it does not if one can show that the greater conceptual thought implied in the affective experiences through which values are known does not entail such *a priori* concepts.

The question is again one of learning. For Platonism, the concepts of goodness and beauty are *a priori* in the sense that they are implicit in certain intellectual and emotional capacities that human beings possess innately. The learning necessary to the development of these capacities, according to the Platonist account, consists mainly in bringing the concepts implicit in them to conscious thought and feeling. Such learning, Platonism holds, transforms knowledge and belief that one tacitly possesses in virtue of having these capacities into knowledge and belief that one consciously applies in working out the puzzles and problems that inevitably arise as one advances through childhood to adolescence and adulthood. Indeed, the learning occurs essentially through the working out of these puzzles and problems, a process that Plato brilliantly illustrated with his example in the *Meno* of how to teach an uneducated child geometry.[26] Hence, it entails not the acquisition of concepts and beliefs, but rather the realization of powers, a special intellectual faculty, through the exercise of which concepts and beliefs one possesses innately and at first only latently are activated and consciously employed.

26. Plato, *Meno*, 82b–85e.

It follows, then, that Platonists conceive of the learning necessary to the development of capacities for feelings through which values are known as a process by which tacit and inchoate knowledge of values, which certain feelings imply, becomes expressly present and articulate in one's experience of those feelings. Thus, even the child's earliest experiences of nausea and fear, on the Platonists' account, imply knowledge of values. They indicate the child's tacit understanding of the objects of those feelings as sickening or dangerous. This understanding then changes and grows into a conscious and articulable aspect of the child's later experience of these feelings as the child's innate capacities for them develop.

Can we give an alternative account of learning by which a child develops capacities for feelings through which values are known? Specifically, is there a sustainable alternative account on which the child's earliest experiences of certain feelings imply no knowledge of values and on which such knowledge becomes part of its experience of those feelings through the acquisition of certain concepts and beliefs? If there is such an account, then one can avoid the recourse to the *a priori* concepts that Platonists assume in appealing to a special intellectual faculty to explain our knowledge of values. And in avoiding recourse to such concepts, one thus avoids Platonism.

The difficulty in sustaining such an account lies in explaining how a capacity for feelings that originally imply no knowledge of values develops into a capacity for feelings through which values are known. It lies, for instance, in explaining how fear can originally be a feeling that implies no thoughts of danger and subsequently becomes one in which such thoughts are implied. On the Platonist account, by contrast, fear is an emotion the experience of which necessarily contains the thought of danger, so even its earliest manifestations imply such thoughts. This view follows from a general, cognitivist theory of emotions according to which every emotion necessarily contains some thought, and the different emotions, hope, fear, joy, sadness, and so forth, are then distinguished from each other by the different forms of evaluative thought they contain. The theory, whose classical expositors were the ancient Greek and Roman Stoics, plainly supports the Platonist account, given that some capacities for emotion are innate, since on this theory the capacity for an emotion like fear implies a capacity for evaluative thought.[27] Consequently,

27. This is the theory I referred to in "Cognitivism in the Theory of Emotions" (ch. 3, this volume) as the Socratic theory. While the ancient Stoics are the most important classical exponents of this theory, they are not its inventors. That honor belongs to Socrates, which is why I initially tagged it the Socratic theory. See Plato, *Protagoras*, 358 d–e, where Socrates offers expectation of evil as a definition of fear. It has since been prominently linked to its Stoic

sustaining an opposing account requires finding an alternative to this cognitivist theory, the theory of the ancient Stoics, on which it can rest.

The traditional alternative, of course, is a theory that flatly denies that
emotions contain thought. Any such theory, however, has well-known problems accounting for the relation between an emotion and its intentional
object. It has problems, that is, explaining how emotions, given that they have
no thought content, are characteristically felt at or toward things.[28] These
problems argue for a different, less extreme alternative, one that denies the
Stoic theory's other tenet, that what distinguishes one emotion from another
is the form of the evaluative thought it contains. This is a less extreme alternative obviously, for it is consistent with affirming the stronger tenet that every
emotion necessarily contains some thought. What it denies, specifically, is
that every emotion contains evaluative thought. Because this less extreme
alternative supports opposition to the idea of evaluative thought as innate,
I will call it the environmentalist theory. The question, then, that adherents to the Stoic theory would press is what differentiates the emotions that,
according to the environmentalist theory, lack evaluative thought. What, for
instance, according to this theory, differentiates fear from disgust in cases in
which these emotions are experienced before their subjects have acquired
knowledge of values?

---

exponents, and consequently referring to it as the Stoic theory has become standard. Con-
temporary defenders of the Stoic theory include Robert Solomon, *The Passions* (New York:
Anchor/Doubleday, 1976); and Martha C. Nussbaum *The Therapy of Desire* (Princeton:
Princeton University Press, 1994) and *Upheavals of Thought* (Cambridge: Cambridge Uni-
versity Press, 2001). See also William Lyons, *Emotion* (Cambridge: Cambridge University
Press, 1980).

The theory, in treating evaluative thought as propositional or predicable thought, runs into
problems accounting for the emotions of infants and animals. Mindful of these problems,
Nussbaum explains some forms of evaluative thought as nonpropositional—see *Upheavals of
Thought*, ch. 2. It is open to question, however, whether thinking something dangerous, good,
bad, etc. is possible in nonpropositional form, whether, that is, one can have such thoughts
though one lacks the concepts of dangerousness, goodness, etc.

For critical discussion of the Stoic theory, see Jenefer Robinson, "Startle," *Journal of Philosophy* 92 (1995): 53–74, and my two essays, "Cognitivism in the Theory of Emotions" and
"Nussbaum's Defense of the Stoic Theory of Emotions," *Quinnipiac Law Review* 19 (2000):
293–307.

28. Defenders of the traditional alternative typically appeal to psychological mechanisms to
explain how emotions are directed at objects. The appeal to projection in the previous section
of this chapter is one example. These explanations have trouble, however, capturing our understanding of emotions as essentially intentional states of mind. Hume, *Treatise*, pp. 277–282 is
representative of this sort of explanation. For criticism, see Anthony Kenny, *Action, Emotion
and Will* (London: Routledge and Kegan Paul, 1963), pp. 23–25.

The most cogent answer a defender of the environmentalist theory could give starts by affirming the thesis that every emotion contains some thought.[29] It starts, that is, by agreeing with the Stoic theory in taking emotions to be intentional states whose objects are determined by the thoughts they contain. Accordingly, on this answer, just as on the Stoic theory, what distinguishes one emotion from another is the character of its intentional object. At the same time, since the environmentalist theory departs from the Stoic theory by holding that not every emotion contains evaluative thought, its defenders have the burden of explaining what determines the character of an emotion's intentional object in such a case. What, for instance, determines the character of fear's intentional object when fear is experienced before the subject has acquired knowledge of values?

Well, how do frightful things appear to small children before they have acquired the concept of danger? What is it about large or barking dogs, strangers (who are older and bigger), thunder and lightning, darkness that instinctively frightens small children? These things are scary, one might say, meaning that to a small child they have a kind of look or make a kind of sound that immediately elicits fear. Something, after all, can be scary and elicit fear even when one knows it isn't dangerous. Think of a scary mask, a creepy voice, a slithering garter snake. Thus, certain sensory properties define an object as scary independently of its being dangerous, and these properties determine the character of fear's intentional object when the emotion is experienced instinctively.

In the same way, one can determine the character of disgust's intentional object when that emotion is experienced instinctively. What disgust a small child are things that taste foreign, smell rancid, feel or look slimy. These are foul or nauseating things, which is to say that to a small child they have a kind of taste, smell, feel, or look that immediately elicits disgust. And because something can be foul and elicit disgust even when one knows it isn't spoiled or rotten, the disgust it elicits can be experienced independently of any knowledge of values. Like the object of primitive fear, the object of such disgust has a distinctive character determined by certain sensory properties. Moreover, because the sensory properties that define something as foul are not the same as those that define something as scary—just try imagining something that smells scary—the two emotions are differentiable according to the character of their intentional objects. Hence, fear can be differentiated from disgust in cases in which these emotions are experienced before their subjects have acquired knowledge of values.

---

29. The following is an elaboration of ideas in my "Cognitivism in the Theory of Emotions."

The key to this defense of the environmentalist theory is the distinction it makes between those emotions, the primitive ones, whose intentional objects are defined by sensory properties and those emotions, the tutored ones (i.e., those that are conditioned on their subjects' having acquired knowledge of values), whose intentional objects are defined by evaluative properties. Such a distinction is, of course, impossible on the Stoic theory since the Stoic theory assumes that the intentional object of every emotion, primitive or tutored, is defined by some evaluative property. It is defined, in other words, by the predicate of the evaluative thought the emotion contains, and accordingly, the only distinction the Stoic theory can allow between primitive and tutored emotions concerns the availability to consciousness of that predicate. Nonetheless, the distinction the environmentalist theory makes seems unassailable once the different objects of primitive and tutored fear or primitive and tutored disgust, as the environmentalist theory characterizes them, are compared. It seems unassailable, that is, once one reflects on the difference between what is scary and what is dangerous or what is foul and what is rotten.

Consider, for instance, the difference between a scary mask and a dangerous one. What defines the former is a certain look designed to alarm or frighten the unsuspecting viewer. It is the visual properties themselves that define a mask as scary. By contrast, what defines a mask as dangerous are properties that, regardless of their sensory aspect, can cause significant injury to the wearer or to others. A dangerous mask, after all, can look perfectly innocent, whereas a scary one cannot. And while a mask can also be said to look dangerous, what this means is that one can infer that the mask is dangerous from the way it looks, whereas to say that a mask looks scary is to describe the way it looks independently of what one can infer therefrom. Similar points also apply to the properties of being foul and being rotten, as consideration of the difference between saying that something smells foul and saying that it smells rotten makes clear. These reflections imply that the objects of primitive fear and primitive disgust are distinct from those of their tutored counterparts by virtue of a difference in kind between their defining properties. The former are sensory, and the latter evaluative.[30]

Of course, the important assumption here, the assumption without which the foregoing reflections would not support the environmentalist theory, is that the class of sensory properties defining an emotion's intentional object

---

30. See Robert C. Roberts, "Propositions and Animal Emotion" *Philosophy* 71 (1996): 147–156.

excludes the class of evaluative ones. Specifically, it is the assumption that if an emotion's intentional object is defined by sensory properties, then it is not defined by the predicate of any evaluative thought the emotion contains. That it is not defined by such a predicate, however, simply follows from its not being defined by any predicate. Not every intentional state, after all, is such that its object is determined by some predicable thought it contains. If you hear something creaking, for instance, the creaking noise is the object of your auditory experience, yet you do not need to have predicated creaking of the noise, or anything else for that matter, to be in such a state. Hearing something creaking is one thing, judging that it is creaking is another. This example points unmistakably to a general distinction between intentional objects that are wholly sensory and intentional objects that are at least partly notional, and the distinction that the environmentalist theory makes between the intentional objects of primitive and tutored emotions is just this general distinction applied to those emotions.

It should be clear, then, that the environmentalist theory is a viable alternative to the Stoic theory and one on which the account of learning proposed at the end of section 3 can rest. Its way of distinguishing primitive from tutored emotions supports that account in that it makes intelligible how a capacity for feelings that originally imply no knowledge of values can develop into a capacity for feelings through which values are known. It thus resolves the apparent difficulty of explaining this development. The difficulty disappears, that is, once one catches hold of the distinction between intentional objects that are wholly sensory and those that are partly notional and sees how it applies to emotions that have both primitive and tutored forms. For one then sees that the development can consist in replacing or supplementing sensory knowledge of an object with conceptual or propositional knowledge of it. The passage from the one type of knowledge to the other, from knowing the neighbor's jittery, growling, teeth-baring Doberman as a scary beast to knowing that it is a dangerous one, is the same as the passage, to use Descartes' propitious example, from knowing the sun as a small, yellowish ball in the sky, not that far away, to knowing that it is a body whose volume and mass are many thousands of times greater than the earth's and whose location is 93,000,000 miles away.[31] An account of the learning that effects this passage, in either case, corresponds to the account offered in the last section. In either case, the learning consists in the child's acquiring concepts and beliefs that give meaning to its sensations and feelings.

---

31. Descartes, *Meditations on First Philosophy*, meditation vi.

The account, therefore, contradicts and so excludes Platonist beliefs in *a priori* evaluative concepts. Through it and the environmentalist theory of emotions on which it rests, one can then explain the conceptual thought contained in the affective experiences through which values are known without falling back into Platonism. This means that the argument against Hume's analogy advanced in the last section is consistent with denying that knowledge of values comes through the exercise of a special intellectual faculty. On this account, knowing that the neighbor's Doberman is a menace is as consistent with this denial as knowing the sun's true volume and mass.

5. Hume's Rejoinder

Hume, in the *Treatise* and again in the second *Enquiry*, expressly opposed the environmentalist theory. He denied that our understanding of moral beauty and moral deformity, of virtue and vice, could come entirely from teaching. We could never, Hume argued, come to comprehend the terms by which we praise people for their virtues and blame them for their vices if we did not have an innate sense of good and evil, which is to say, a disposition inherent in human minds to experience feelings of approbation and blame. Here is the argument of the second *Enquiry* in its entirety.

> From the apparent usefulness of the social virtues, it has readily been inferred by sceptics, both ancient and modern, that all moral distinctions arise from education, and were, at first, invented, and afterwards encouraged, by the art of politicians, in order to render men tractable, and subdue their natural ferocity and selfishness, which incapacitated them for society. This principle, indeed, of precept and education, must so far be owned to have a powerful influence, that it may frequently increase or diminish, beyond their natural standard, the sentiments of approbation or dislike; and may even, in particular instances, create, without any natural principle, a new sentiment of this kind; as is evident in all superstitious practices and observances: But that *all* moral affection or dislike arises from this origin, will never surely be allowed by any judicious enquirer. Had nature made no such distinction, founded on the original constitution of the mind, the words *honourable* and *shameful*, *lovely* and *odious*, *noble* and *despicable*, had never had place in any language; nor could politicians, had they invented these terms, ever have been able to render them intelligible, or to make them convey any idea to the audience.[32]

32. Hume, *Enquiries*, p. 214 (emphasis in original). One finds the same argument in the *Treatise*. Hume, in the course of explaining the origin of the artificial virtues, writes, "If nature did not aid us in this particular, it would be in vain for politicians to talk of honourable and dishonourable, praiseworthy and blameable. Those words would be perfectly unintelligible, and would no more have any idea annexed to them, than if they were of a tongue perfectly

What are we to make of this strange argument? On what grounds does Hume think our moral vocabulary would be incomprehensible if we lacked an innate sense of good and evil? One can safely assume that Hume is here relying on a traditional empiricist semantics. On his version of that semantics, words have meaning when they convey ideas, and ideas are copies of sensations and feelings, which we retain in our memory and can recall in our imagination. We form these ideas before we understand the words that convey them, and the words are thus for us nothing but meaningless sounds and meaningless concatenations of letters until we learn which of our already formed ideas they signify. Consequently, it would be impossible to acquire a moral vocabulary and the concepts and beliefs that its mastery entailed without first having the capacities for those feelings the copies of which are the ideas the vocabulary signifies. It would be impossible, in other words, to acquire this vocabulary without first having the capacities for the affective experiences through which moral values are known. These are the experiences, in particular, of the sentiments of approbation and blame, and to have the ideas that our moral vocabulary signifies we must first experience these sentiments. Hence, Hume concludes, a disposition inherent in the mind to feel approbation and blame is a necessary precondition of the teaching of moral values.

The analogy between values and secondary qualities, while not expressly invoked in this argument, is no doubt behind it. Hume's adherence to traditional empiricist semantics includes adherence to the empiricist view of how we learn the words in our vocabulary, and on this view the model of such learning is our learning the vocabulary of secondary qualities, the words for different colors, sounds, tastes, etc. To learn these words, we need first to have had the sensory experiences through which these qualities are known. From the sensations of different colors, for instance, we form ideas of those colors and then learn the words 'red', 'blue', 'green', and so forth as the words one uses to communicate those ideas. Presumably, then, Hume thought learning the vocabulary of values was no different. From the feelings of approbation and blame that are naturally elicited in us by acts of kindness and cruelty, say, we form ideas of the relevant pleasantness or unpleasantness with which those acts appear infused, and we then learn words like 'nice' and 'naughty', 'good' and 'bad', as the words one uses to communicate these ideas. Hume

---

unknown to us. The utmost politicians can perform, is, to extend the natural sentiments beyond their original bounds; but still nature must furnish materials, and give us some notion of moral distinctions." (*Treatise*, pp. 500 and 578–579).

could thus draw on the opposition of traditional empiricist semantics to the thesis on which the argument of section 3 depends, the thesis that learning is necessary to the acquisition of moral and aesthetic sensibilities, to defend his analogy between values and secondary qualities. I advertised the argument as a refutation of Hume's analogy, and this defense, if sound, would prove my advertisement false.

There is no possibility of its doing so, however. Such a defense would be only as sound as the soundness of traditional empiricist semantics, and no version of this semantics is sound. Its underlying assumption is that words generally—that is, apart from those we use to talk about language itself—signify ideas and thoughts that in themselves have no linguistic character. They have no linguistic character because the sensations and feelings from which they originate and of which they are copies have no linguistic character. This assumption seems to fit well words for secondary qualities. This is because, as we noted in section 2, these qualities are defined by the sensory experiences through which they are known. Hence, the ideas of imagination and memory that Hume described as copies of these sensory experiences are easily identified with what the words for these qualities signify. One uses such a word as 'red', for example, to refer to the quality of being red, and in doing so one must be thinking of the color. Thus, one has and conveys the idea of this color when one so uses the word. In short, the word signifies the idea. Unfortunately for traditional empiricist semantics, this simple model of word-meaning breaks down as soon as one applies it to words for everyday objects. The assumption underlying this semantics is mistaken.[33]

Consider, as an example, the word 'collie'. On traditional empiricist semantics, it signifies an idea of a collie that people acquire by encountering collies, seeing pictures of them, watching movies or TV shows featuring collies, and so forth. Imagine, then, a man who has this idea seeing a Shetland sheepdog for the first time. His neighbors, the Turners, have just brought home a "sheltie" for their young daughter, and he sees them bringing the dog into their yard. "The Turners just got a small collie," he tells his wife. He thus misidentifies the Turners' new dog. Shetland sheepdogs, though they

---

33. The argument that follows is an adaptation of Hilary Putnam's seminal argument in "The Meaning of Meaning." See his *Mind, Language and Reality: Philosophical Papers, Vol. 2* (Cambridge: Cambridge University Press, 1975), pp. 215–271. The target of Putnam's argument is any semantic theory that identifies the meanings of words with psychological states. I have adapted his argument to apply to semantic theories that identify the meanings of words (apart from those we use to talk about language) with psychological states that have a nonlinguistic character.

look like miniature collies and are often mistaken for such, are not collies. To mistake them for collies is to have wrongly applied one's idea of a collie to them, and to inform one's spouse that the neighbors' new dog is a small collie when it is a sheltie is to convey the wrong idea for knowing its breed. But how, on traditional empiricist semantics, can one understand these errors? How, that is, can one understand the man in our example as misapplying his idea of a collie to his neighbors' new dog, and how too can one understand him as conveying the wrong idea to his wife if the word 'collie' signifies this idea? Plainly, one cannot. Nothing in the idea distinguishes a collie that is significantly smaller than the average collie from a Shetland sheepdog. Hence, on traditional empiricist semantics, he has not misapplied the idea. Similarly, given that the word 'collie' signifies the idea, he has also not misinformed his wife in conveying it to her. Traditional empiricist semantics can therefore neither explain the first error as one of misapplication nor explain the second as one of misconveyance. Indeed, it cannot in any way account for either error.

Perhaps, this seems too quick. Perhaps, the man's errors are due to his having misunderstood what the word 'collie' means. After all, if he used the word 'maroon' to describe his neighbors' new car when their new car is bright orange rather than dark red, one would have no difficulty, on traditional empiricist semantics, explaining his error. It would be a case of his misapplying the word 'maroon' as a result of his failing to understand that it refers to a shade of red. Accordingly, traditional empiricist semantics can explain his error as one of ignorance about what the word signifies. But a man who, having never before seen a Shetland sheepdog, thinks it's a small collie is not necessarily someone who fails to understand that the word 'collie' refers to collies. He is not necessarily ignorant of what the word signifies. To the contrary, he may understand perfectly well that the word refers to collies. For all we know, until the time of his first seeing his neighbors' new dog, his use of the word to convey his idea of a collie was entirely faultless. His error, when he misapplies the word 'collie', would not, then, consist in his having misunderstood what it means. It would consist, rather, in his extending his use of the word to a dog of a different breed because of the dog's misleading appearance. In so extending its use, he misapplies his idea of a collie, and this is an error of a different kind.

The problem for traditional empiricist semantics is that it cannot explain errors of this kind. The idea of a collie that the man misapplies to his neighbors' new dog is, according to the theory, what the word 'collie' signifies, so he cannot be faulted for conveying it. And a Shetland sheepdog fits the idea conveyed by the phrase 'small collie'. His idea of a small collie is one and the same as the idea he would convey by the name 'Shetland sheepdog' if his relations to the two breeds had been reversed, if, that is, he had grown up knowing only Shetland sheepdogs and had never seen a collie of the kind for which Shetland sheepdogs are commonly mistaken. In that case, he would be disposed to call such a collie a 'large Shetland sheepdog' the first time he saw one. In either case, he forms an idea of the kind of dog with which he is familiar and then, upon seeing what appears to him to be the same kind of dog but of a different size, he applies that idea to the dog he sees. He cannot, therefore, be faulted for applying it as he does since doing so accords with his understanding of the phrase that conveys that idea. Thus, when in the original case he uses the phrase 'small collie' to describe his neighbors' new dog, the idea he conveys, according to traditional empiricist semantics, both applies to the dog and is what this phrase signifies, for it is what a Shetland sheepdog appears to be. That he errs in so describing the dog completely eludes the theory.

There are, of course, other properties of Shetland sheepdogs besides their height that to an expert's eye distinguish Shetland sheepdogs from collies, particularly, collies of the kind for which shelties are commonly mistaken. These differentia will not be apparent to people who are not expert in the different breeds of dog. One might then suppose that traditional empiricist semantics goes wrong only in holding that words convey the personal or private ideas of the speaker rather than the ideas of those who are expert in the field or science in which the words in question are used. Arguably, Hume had some such public standard of meaning in mind in those passages in which he speaks of language correcting our thoughts.[34] Accordingly, let us make a simple revision to the traditional empiricist semantics. On this revision, the idea that a word signifies, whether or not the speaker has that idea in mind and intends to convey it when he uses the word, is the idea that those who are expert in the word's use convey when they use it in circumstances like those of the speaker. By making this revision, one could keep the theory from being defeated by counterexamples like the one we are considering and at the same time preserve its thesis that words have meaning by virtue of their conveying ideas in Hume's sense. Hence, one could preserve the thesis on which Hume's opposition to the environmentalist theory depends, since the ideas that words would convey, when they had meaning, would, as copies of sensations and feelings, still have a nonlinguistic character.

Yet the theory, even if so revised, remains unsound. Again consider the word 'collie'. The idea that those who are expert in the use of this word convey

---

34. See, e.g., Hume, *Treatise*, p. 582.

when they use it will be applicable to any dog that appears to be a collie, since the idea is formed from these experts' experiences of collies or their simulacra. Accordingly, the word too, on the revised empiricist semantics, will be applicable to such a dog. To see the flaw in the revised theory, then, we need only consider a dog that is not a collie but appears to be one even to an expert's eye. Thus imagine a Shetland sheepdog that, with the exception of its height, is indistinguishable in appearance from collies. Such a dog is surely possible. Breeders of shelties might, for instance, decide to breed such shelties and after many generations succeed. Not knowing of these efforts, an expert in the use of the word 'collie' might then, upon seeing such a sheltie for the first time, be fooled and declare, "How interesting, a small collie." The expert's error in this case would be the same as the error of the man in our earlier example who told his wife about their neighbors' new dog. Yet the revised theory, no less than the original, is unable to account for it. What makes collies different from Shetland sheepdogs is their ancestry, or to be more exact, their genotype, and this difference fails to register in the idea of a collie, as compared with that of a Shetland sheepdog, that traditional empiricist semantics identifies as the meaning of the word. And even if revised as proposed, the theory fails to explain the meaning of the word in a way that accounts for this difference. Indeed, it should be clear that no semantic theory that identifies the meanings of words with prelinguistic states of mind that present to their possessor the appearance of things can account for this difference.

Hume's argument against the thesis that learning is necessary for acquiring moral and aesthetic sensibilities therefore fails. Its main premiss, that the words of our moral vocabulary would be incomprehensible to us if we did not already have ideas that some of these words convey when we are first taught them, rests on traditional empirical semantics, and as we've seen, no version of this semantics is sound. There remains, to be sure, the possibility of removing Hume's argument from its empiricist context and placing it on a different footing. This possibility, however, comes to no more than reasserting the analogy between values and secondary qualities.

Thus, one could, while allowing that no version of traditional empiricist semantics is sound as a general theory of word-meaning, maintain that its account of the meanings of words for the qualities of our visual experiences, gustatory experiences, affective experiences, and the like—qualities like redness, sweetness, pleasantness, and so forth—is defensible. One could, that is, defend this account on the grounds that the arguments used to refute traditional empiricist semantics do not refute it. For those arguments depend on the possibility of disparity between the properties that determine the kind of thing something is and the properties that characterize how that thing appears to normal human observers, and there can be no such disparity between the properties that make the redness of a red sensation what it is and the properties that give red sensations the appearance they have to a normal human observer.[35] But plainly, since the point of maintaining this account is to preserve Hume's belief that the words of our moral vocabulary signify the ideas of pleasure and displeasure expressed in praise and blame, it amounts to maintaining Hume's analogy between values and secondary qualities. Hence, to save the argument in this way is to render it useless as a basis for defending Hume's analogy against the objection of section 3.

The only avenue left to a defender of Humean subjectivism for attacking the thesis that learning is necessary for acquiring moral and aesthetic sensibilities is to appeal to what the words of our moral vocabulary actually refer to rather than to their meaning. After all, one does not need to learn a language to have knowledge of the things to which many of the most common words of a language refer. For this appeal to succeed, however, the words of our moral vocabulary would have to refer to properties of things that one knew through sensory or affective experiences of which one was capable prior to learning a language. In other words, a defender of Humean subjectivism would have to maintain that the words of our moral vocabulary refer to properties one knows through one's untutored affective experiences, which is to say, one's primitive emotions, which means that he would have to fall back on the analogy between values and secondary qualities to make this appeal. Like the previous attempt to rebut the thesis, then, this appeal too amounts to no more than reasserting the analogy.

At this point, though, the analogy should appear to be an unpromising last hope for any defender of Humean subjectivism. Our observations about fear and disgust in section 4 have already thrown into doubt any general use of the analogy to explain the values that one knows through affective experience. For to use the analogy to explain values one knows through experiences of fear and disgust would require taking the sensory properties characterizing the objects of primitive fear and primitive disgust as in each case a negative value. These properties are analogous to secondary qualities, if not identical with them, whereas the notional properties characterizing the objects

---

35. Putnam allows for this possibility when he notes, "Perhaps 'sense data' terms are not indexical…, if such there be." This is a possible account of these terms' meaning, however, only if they are understood as terms for "sense data." Thus, he continues, "[B]ut 'yellow' as a *thing* predicate is indexical for the same reason as 'tiger'; even if something looks yellow it may not be yellow." *Mind, Language and Reality*, p. 266.

of tutored fear and tutored disgust are neither. Yet if the sensory property characterizing the objects of primitive fear, say, is a negative value, it cannot be that of being dangerous or threatening harm, for these are the notional properties that characterize the objects of tutored fear. These are the properties parents teach their children to recognize when they teach them to be afraid of things that they believe will harm their children and worry that their children will not fear these things without instruction. The sensory property characterizing the objects of primitive fear is that of being scary, but this property, while the things it characterizes may be positively correlated to some degree with things that are dangerous or threaten harm, is far from perfectly correlated with them and, in any case, does not make any of the things it characterizes a bad or evil thing. If it did, then parents would not, as they do, teach their children to get over fears their children experience of things that are not dangerous or harmful, though to a small child they may still be scary. Being scary, the sensory property characterizing the objects of primitive fear, is not, then, a negative value. In short, what one knows through experiences of fear that is analogous to secondary qualities is not a value, and the value one knows through experiences of fear is not analogous to secondary qualities. Hume's analogy, as we should now expect, fails in this case.

The same argument applies *mutatis mutandis* in the case of disgust. Indeed, there is no reason to suppose that this argument does not apply generally. That is, lacking reasons to the contrary, we may suppose that moral and aesthetic values, like the negative values of danger and putridity or their opposites, safety and wholesomeness, are known through affective experiences that are tutored. Thus, goodness and beauty, no less than safety and wholesomeness, are properties children learn to discern, and part of the learning consists in their acquiring new objects of desire and admiration. What children first and instinctively desire are things that give them pleasure, and they then learn to desire things that are good even though these things would not, prior to their acquiring these desires, give them pleasure. They learn about the goodness of such things by learning how they contribute to living well and to succeeding in the activities that a well-lived life comprises. Such learning comes through instruction in distinguishing what is good from what merely gives pleasure and what is bad from what is merely foreign, and in so instructing a child one teaches it the concepts of good and bad the mastery of which enlarges the child's understanding of the world and its place in it. In this way, children come to be pleased at what benefits them or those whose lives matter to them or with whom they have sympathy. Likewise, they come to be displeased at what injures them or those whose lives matter to them or with whom they have sympathy. It is through such tutored experiences of pleasure and displeasure that we come to know moral values, both positive and negative, and the conceptual thought contained in the experiences, the conceptual thought that results from the learning necessary for our developing a capacity for them, entails that the moral values we know are not analogous to secondary qualities.

So too with our knowledge of aesthetic values.

6. Conclusion

Toward the end of *Il Deserto Rosso*, Antonioni inserts a scene of striking contrast to the desolate and cheerless imagery that dominates the film. Through the device of a story told by the lead character to her child, the director transports us to a secluded beach, uncultivated and serene, where a young teenage girl is swimming in the adjoining bay. The water is a transparent blue; the sand a roseate white; and the surroundings of tall, dark green trees and bright, sandstone rock show no sign of human enterprise. Our spirits, depressed and cramped throughout the film, suddenly lift. The scene is a breath of fresh air, and one realizes, in retrospect, how Antonioni has been using color to convey his ideas about the corrosive effects of industrialization on human relations and human life. The strong, sharp colors in this scene are pleasing and even invigorating. The pleasure we experience communicates the beauty of this unspoiled, natural setting. We would no doubt enjoy the visual experience even without the understanding we have of the scene and its symbols of purity and innocence. But such enjoyment would not imply knowledge of the values the scene exhibits. It would not communicate to us the purity of the setting or the goodness of life in a pristine environment. For it to do this, we must be able to interpret the sensations and feelings the film elicits, and such interpretations depend on our having acquired the concepts and beliefs that give them meaning. The power of a film like *Il Deserto Rosso* lies not in the filmmaker's skill at inducing feelings by manipulating images but in his skill at using feelings induced by those images to enlarge our aesthetic and moral understanding of the world as perceived in his film.

5

The Politics of Disgust and Shame

I

Upheavals of Thought, Martha Nussbaum's landmark book in moral psychology, opened with a powerful exposition of a general theory of the emotions.[1] The theory, which descends from the ideas of the Greek and Roman Stoics, identifies emotions with judgments of a specific sort. Its core principle is to attribute to every emotion cognitive content, namely, the content of the judgment with which the theory identifies the emotion. In this way, the study of emotions becomes, in large part, the study of how emotions acquire their content and how its transmission determines the actions that spring from them. It is, in other words, the study of certain cognitive states and how those states, in conjunction with other cognitive states, constitute the thought processes by which intelligent beings conduct their lives.

Such a study is remote from the way emotions are often studied in experimental psychology and neuroscience. The positivism of these disciplines demands that emotions be defined by empirically measurable indicators, and

1. Martha Nussbaum, *Upheavals of Thought: The Intelligence of Emotions* (Cambridge: Cambridge University Press, 2001).

103

consequently, orthodox work in them, by virtue of the protocols of the science, omits content from the very understanding of the phenomena they study. Cognitive content, needless to say, is not a measurable indicator. Physiological arousal of the kind that characterizes violent emotional reactions is, and as a result, because it is the most salient, quantifiable manifestation of emotions, the study of emotions in these sciences becomes the study of what causes such arousal and what parts of the brain explain its character. It is decidedly not a study of emotions as cognitive states. It does not regard them as ingredients in the production of intelligent conduct. Indeed, because physiological arousal tends to impede and disrupt thinking, the study encourages the time-worn view of emotions as episodes in the mind that are hostile to clear thinking and sound judgment. Someone whose idea of emotions matched this way of conceiving of them would have trouble comprehending how emotions give meaning to simple human actions, much less the workings and products of complex institutions like law and politics. By contrast, someone armed with the understanding of emotions that Nussbaum's theory supplies can easily see how emotions contribute to intelligent conduct and comprehend the work they do in shaping society's customs and institutions. Her theory equips one with ideas that not only yield understanding of the rich emotional ingredients in intelligent thought and action but also support trenchant critical study of the extent to which society's institutions are the work of human emotion.

Hiding from Humanity, Nussbaum's new book in legal and political theory, is just such a study.[2] Its chief object is law, particularly criminal law, in modern liberal democracies. Chapter 1, drawn from the pioneering law review article Nussbaum co-authored with Dan Kahan, shows how an understanding of emotions of the kind Nussbaum's theory supplies, a cognitivist understanding, is deeply embedded in Anglo-American criminal law.[3] Nussbaum points out how a cognitivist understanding is implicit in legal doctrines that concern the workings of various emotions—fear and anger, in particular—in many of the violent actions the criminal law regulates. Similarly, she describes how other emotions—compassion, in particular—have important roles in operations of the criminal law, such as sentencing, and how making sense of these roles requires a cognitivist understanding of the emotions

    2. Martha Nussbaum, Hiding from Humanity: Disgust, Shame and the Law (Princeton: Princeton University Press, 2004).
    3. Dan Kahan and Martha Nussbaum, "Two Conceptions of Emotion in Criminal Law," Columbia Law Review 96 (1996): 269–374.

that have them. The subsequent chapters, 2 through 7, concentrate on the emotions of disgust and shame. Nussbaum, in these chapters, considers how the criminal law should treat the workings of these emotions in the actions it regulates and whether either emotion should have an important role in the criminal law's operations. Nussbaum sees both disgust and shame as having had a pernicious influence on the law as it pertains to the regulation of sexual conduct, reproductive decisions, family life, and the relations between the sexes. And she sees them as having the same influence in legal regimes that reinforce the social stigmatization of minorities and other disadvantaged groups. Her main thesis is that laws catering to these emotions, are, with rare exception, inimical to the liberal ideal of a democratic society in which the law recognizes and respects equally the humanity of all members. Disgust and shame, she argues, are emotions to which certain conservative programs appeal, specifically those promoting the preservation of existing hierarchies within society. But it is not just these programs that Nussbaum sees as threatening this liberal ideal through the promotion of laws that cater to disgust and shame. Progressive programs too threaten it when they call for enforcing through such laws the egalitarian values of a democratic community. For such enforcement, Nussbaum argues, unavoidably demeans and humiliates those on whom the laws impose burdens, and such treatment of people is inconsistent with this ideal.

Her argument demonstrates the power of social criticism that focuses on the workings of emotion in law and politics. In this essay, I will examine the degree to which her critique of disgust and shame is successful. I believe there is good reason why conservative political theory would be friendlier to political and legal uses of these emotions in maintaining social order, and accordingly, I will explore and assess a conservative defense of them against Nussbaum's critique. To do so will require, first, setting out the general theory of emotions from which Nussbaum's critique of disgust and shame issues and then presenting the accounts of disgust and shame that Nussbaum develops out of this theory.

II

The theory, as I said, follows the one put forth by the ancient Stoics. Its chief idea, like that of its forerunner, is that emotions are evaluative judgments of a specific sort. Nussbaum, however, departs from the classical Stoic theory in two related ways. First, she modifies the Stoic conception of such judgments by broadening it so that it covers the emotions of nonhuman animals and human infants (or as I will say, beasts and babies). The ancient Stoics denied that beasts and babies were capable of emotions, for they conceived of the judgments they identified with emotions as affirmations of propositions, and they denied that beasts and babies had the linguistic capacities necessary for propositional thought. Consequently, if you're drawn to the Stoic theory but believe that animals other than humans experience emotions or that humans before the age of toddling experience them, you must either modify the Stoic conception of judgment or attribute linguistic abilities to beasts and babies. Nussbaum does the former.

Second, Nussbaum makes essential to our understanding of emotions their developmental histories beginning in infancy. Emotions, as she puts it, have a narrative structure in virtue of these histories. The classical Stoic theory ignored this structure, and as a result, it offers at best an inadequate understanding of its subject. The deficiency consists in treating emotions as if their cognitive content were independent of their root causes and conditions. When scientific psychology was largely a taxonomic enterprise, such treatment was standard. But since Freud's work on infantile sexuality, it has been largely abandoned. Freud, by tracing the emotional problems of his patients back to formative events in their early childhood, gave explanatory depth to the understanding of emotions that the taxonomic psychology of his time could not supply. And Nussbaum, who incorporates ideas of Freud's disciples into her theory, does the same by attributing narrative structure to emotions. Her version of the Stoic theory thus has explanatory depth that its classical statement lacks. And because the attribution of narrative structure requires an understanding of emotions as states to which babies as well as grown human beings are susceptible, we can see her modification of the ancient Stoic's conception of evaluative judgment as having a twofold purpose. It not only saves the theory from being anachronistic but also makes possible the introduction of the idea of an emotion's having narrative structure.

How, then, on Nussbaum's theory, is this narrative structure to be understood? The answer follows from the sort of judgment with which the theory identifies every emotion. Nussbaum characterizes this sort of judgment as eudaimonistic. What she means by a eudaimonistic judgment is an evaluative judgment that one makes relative to one's ends and interests. It is a judgment, that is, that something is good or bad because it serves or frustrates one's ends and interests. For example, I might think it's good that a department meeting was cancelled because cancellation serves my interest in having more time to work on an urgent piece of business. Coincidentally, a colleague might think it's bad that the meeting was cancelled because the cancellation frustrates her interest in having the department act on an item she had put on the agenda. These judgments would then constitute opposing emotions, according to the Stoic theory, namely, my pleasure and my colleague's displeasure at the same state of affairs. But though the emotions oppose each other, the evaluative judgments they consist in are not contradictory, since each is made relative to a different set of ends and interests. They are judgments of what is good or bad for the person making them and not judgments of what is good or bad absolutely. They are therefore conceived of as interested rather than disinterested judgments, for they are conditioned on the interest the person invests in the people and things that favorably or adversely affect his or her well-being. Accordingly, the history of one's investment and withdrawal of interest in such people and things, going back to infancy, defines the narrative structure of one's emotions.

Nussbaum, drawing on the works of several child psychologists, schematizes this history for both normal and abnormal emotional development in early childhood. She then uses the complex schemes she constructs to exhibit various general patterns of narrative structure that emotions can have. The schematization is more or less the same in both *Upheavals of Thought* and *Hiding from Humanity*. In brief and with omission of many complexities and variations, the schematic history she constructs goes as follows. Humans are born needy, and their primitive needs explain their initial investments of interest in objects in their environment. Accordingly, their earliest emotions concern the objects that they see as important to the satisfaction of the desires to which these needs give rise. Delight and distress, excitement and fear, happiness and sadness are the first emotions of human life. Subsequently, as the child acquires an increasingly distinct sense of itself as a unified being separate from other beings, it comes to feel love toward those who provide the objects that satisfy its desires, but it comes also to feel anger at them when they act to thwart those desires and to control its behavior contrary to its inclinations. At first, the child does not realize that the targets of its anger are the same as the objects of its love. But in time it does, and at this point its emotional life becomes acutely conflicted. It seeks a way out of this conflict by moderating its demands and learning to accept postponement of their satisfaction. This resolution does not come easily, however, and much growth in and transformation of the child's emotional capacities take place in the process. In the end, the child reaches a compromise with the world, so to speak, that represents a fair balance of its needs against those of the significant figures in its life on whom it depends for nourishment and protection and of those others, typically siblings, with whom it shares this dependency. It acquires, as a result, a rudimentary sense of fairness and, in virtue of this acquisition, capacities for distinctively moral emotions. These too fall within the Stoic theory. For the child, in acquiring a sense of fairness, acquires a primitive view of the world as structured by a moral order on which its well-being depends, and accordingly, it invests a strong interest in preserving this order. This interest anchors the evaluative judgments with which the Stoic theory identifies these emotions and so explains them as eudaimonistic.

III

Nussbaum's accounts of disgust and shame nicely exemplify the fertility of the Stoic theory she advances. She identifies disgust with a judgment about contamination. "The ideational content of disgust," she writes, "is that the self will become base or contaminated by ingestion of the substance that is viewed as offensive."[4] To be disgusted by something, then, is to find it offensive and to judge that ingestion of it would contaminate one. A child becomes susceptible to disgust, Nussbaum argues, when its parents begin to teach it about such contaminants.

> Disgust appears not to be present in infants during the first three years of life. Infants reject bitter tastes from birth, making the gaping facial expression that is later characteristic of disgust. But at this point disgust has not broken off from mere distaste; nor has danger even appeared on the scene. The danger category seems to emerge in the first few years of life, and full blown disgust is present only from around four years of age onward.[5]

Thus, for Nussbaum, disgust is not an instinctive or primitive emotion. It is not among the emotions the experience of which occurs early and naturally in infancy or the susceptibility to which humans share with other animals. While its precursor, mere distaste, may be primitive in this sense, one should not identify mere distaste with disgust if the judgments the two emotions consist in are different. And from the passage just quoted, it is plain that Nussbaum thinks they are. It is plain, that is, that she thinks the judgment mere distaste consists in concerns the offensiveness of an object without the more specific idea of its being contaminating. A child, then, comes to have this more specific idea and thus develops susceptibility to disgust through instruction about what things it must not come in contact with, and in particular must not ingest, to remain free of the taint or rot that contact would bring.

Disgust, in Nussbaum's view, is therefore unlike fear, say, which is a paradigmatic primitive emotion. Fear, on her theory, is identified with a judgment

4. Nussbaum, *Hiding from Humanity*, p. 88.
5. Ibid., p. 94.

concerning danger, and children have the capacity for making such judgments long before they receive instruction about what things are dangerous.
They begin, that is, with an innate sense of danger, which operates in their
earliest fears. Later they receive instruction about what things are dangerous
and, as a result, come to judge some things dangerous that they previously
didn't regard as dangerous and stop regarding as dangerous things that had
previously frightened them. Hence, the range of objects toward which they
experience fear changes. The sort of judgment Nussbaum identifies with disgust, by contrast, can only be made once the child receives instruction about
contamination. Children, in other words, have no innate sense of contamination on Nussbaum's view, and they can make the sort of judgment disgust
consists in only after they have acquired the relevant notion. Consequently,
while Nussbaum allows that susceptibility to the emotion may be an inherited trait, what would be inherited in that event are the mechanisms by which
the emotion manifests itself and not any sensitivity to features in the world
that elicit it. Such sensitivity, rather, is the product of parental and social
teaching.

Nussbaum further characterizes the judgment of contamination that she
identifies with disgust as being a reminder of one's vulnerability to decay. It is a
reminder, that is, of one's having an animal body whose integrity is liable over
time to weaken, degenerate, and ultimately collapse. This characterization of
the judgment reflects the influence on her account of Paul Rozin's experimental work on disgust.[6] Rozin and his colleagues reached a similar conclusion about disgust's having as its focus one's animal nature and the liability
to decay that it entails. The basis for this conclusion is somewhat obscure,
but one possibility is that themes of animality and decay are somehow supposed to emerge from a survey of the common objects of disgust: human and
animal excrement, other products of bodily functions like phlegm, semen,
and pus, various animals such as slugs, salamanders, cockroaches, and other
insects, decomposing corpses, and regurgitated food. Disgust, then, on this
view, is an emotion the susceptibility to which signals a "problematic relationship with our own animality."[7] Nussbaum has some reservations about
the view as Rozin articulates it, and accordingly she revises it in a way that
brings it more into line with her general account. So revised, the view is that

6. See Paul Rozin and April E. Fallon, "A Perspective on Disgust," *Psychological Review* 94
(1987): 23–41, and Paul Rozin, Jonathan Haidt, and Clark R. McCauley, "Disgust," *Handbook
of Emotions*, 2nd ed., M. Lewis and J. M. Haviland-Jones, eds. (New York: Guilford Press,
2000), pp. 637–653.
7. Nussbaum, *Hiding from Humanity*, p. 89.

the concern with contamination that the judgment disgust consists in implies a concern with one's own mortality and particularly with the decay of one's body due to its animal nature. The view, even given Nussbaum's helpful revision, does not strike me as especially compelling. Some insects, such as potato bugs, predictably provoke disgust. Others, such as caterpillars, do not. Neither, however, seems to be a greater contaminant than the other, and I can't see that the thought of ingesting either is more of a reminder of our vulnerability to decay due to our animal nature than the thought of ingesting the other. I will return to this point in the next section.

Shame, in contrast to disgust, on Nussbaum's account, is experienced by infants early in their lives. Nussbaum identifies shame with a judgment of inadequacy or failure. "[S]hame involves the realization that one is weak and inadequate in some way in which one expects oneself to be adequate."[8] Infants, she believes, acquire a sense of their own inadequacy and so a susceptibility to shame soon after they enter the world. For they come into the world from an environment, their mother's womb, in which all their needs have been met, and consequently, they have no sense of their being utterly dependent on external providers. Even after birth, they are the focus of attention and care, and from the experience of being catered to, they come to an exaggerated sense of themselves as all-important and all-powerful. Part of what goes into their coming to see themselves as distinct, finite beings, then, is their experiencing occasions when their needs go unmet and they are powerless to do anything about it. The frustration, anger, and despair they feel on these occasions induce in them a strong a sense of themselves as dependent and helpless, a sense that is directly at odds with their prior condition of self-satisfaction to which they still cling as the ideal that is their due. And now recognizing their weakness and inadequacy, they experience a kind of shame, which Nussbaum calls "primitive shame."[9] This primitive shame precedes any parental teaching of standards and ideals that the infant is expected to live up to. It precedes as well the incorporation into the personality of ideal traits to which the child aspires. Both developments serve to enlarge the range of inadequacies and failures over which a person feels shame, and in doing so, they further entrench the child's liability to primitive shame and promote its manifestation in an array of activities and endeavors beyond those in infancy that triggered the emotion.

To overcome this liability, Nussbaum argues, one must acquire ideals whose fulfillment requires seeing oneself as less important and less central

8. Nussbaum, *Hiding from Humanity*, p. 183.
9. Ibid., pp. 183–184.

to what matters in life. As she puts it, people must acquire ideals whose fulfillment opposes the primary narcissism manifested in primitive shame if shame is to become a constructive emotion in social life. The ideals she has in mind are, for example, ones that orient a person toward promotion of the common good in his community and toward regard for other human beings as his equals. In this respect, shame differs from disgust, for a sense of shame that the attachment to such ideals creates will be an important element in the kind of personality that befits liberal democratic institutions. The experience of such shame will, consequently, serve to reaffirm that attachment at times when one realizes that one has failed to measure up to those ideals, and in this way it has a constructive place in liberal democracy. Disgust, by contrast, in Nussbaum's view, has no constructive place in liberal democracy. It is not, in any case, a constructive emotion, and susceptibility to it therefore does not serve to maintain fidelity to the ideals of liberal democracy.

This difference between the two emotions complicates somewhat Nussbaum's critique of their place in the criminal law. Since she allows that shame, when constructive, is an emotion whose cultivation can have social benefits, she cannot hold of it, as she does of disgust, that it is, across the board, a dangerous emotion for society to enlist. Disgust, in her view, is inherently problematic as an emotion society might cultivate to help maintain its customs and institutions or advance its ideals. It is, she says, "a deeply and . . . an inherently self-deceptive emotion" that invites one to deny one's vulnerability as an animal and, in the service of that denial, to target those less privileged than one, especially the weak and the marginal, as objects of disgust.[10] In other words, it invites treatment of the weak and the marginal as undeserving of equal respect and concern and is, therefore, an enemy of the ideals of liberal democracy. But because shame, on Nussbaum's account, is only sometimes a threat to these ideals, she must distinguish its destructive instances from its constructive ones. She does this by explaining how the emotion, by virtue of its origins in the primary narcissism of primitive shame, can be like disgust in being self-deceptive and in leading to abusing those less privileged than one. It does so by encouraging people to aspire to being 'normal', a fictitious state the felt achievement of which gives them a sense of safety and comfort, and consequently to look for ways of distinguishing themselves from others

---

10. Ibid., p. 206. See also p. 102. Nussbaum further declares (p. 107), "So powerful is the desire to cordon ourselves off from our animality that we often don't stop at feces, cockroaches, and slimy animals. We need a group of humans to bound ourselves against, who will come to exemplify the boundary line between the truly human and the basely animal."

whose differences they can then regard as marks of deviance or abnormality.[11] Hence, shame is destructive of the ideals of liberal democracy when it is elicited in the service of enforcing standards that represent what it is to be 'normal' and thus stigmatizing those who depart from these standards.

IV

What political programs would treat either disgust or shame as an emotion to which the criminal law should cater? In the case of disgust, Nussbaum identifies several thinkers who believe that the emotion has an important role in determining the kinds of conduct the criminal law should prohibit. They are Leon Kass, Patrick Devlin, William Miller, and Dan Kahan. I will concentrate exclusively on Devlin's views. They are by far the best known and most influential. Devlin's case for the legal enforcement of morality is generally thought to be the most serious challenge to Mill's argument against such enforcement in *On Liberty* since James Fitzjames Stephen's famous attack on it.[12] Both Devlin's and Stephen's criticisms fall within the tradition of British conservative thought that Burke's *Reflections on the Revolution in France* began, and one can, with the help of Devlin's criticisms, see how the political program of this tradition supports the idea that disgust has an important role in determining what kinds of conduct society should tolerate and what kinds it should criminalize. To understand this role, however, it will be necessary first to revisit Nussbaum's account of the emotion and then to offer an alternative.

Let us return, then, to the reservations I had about Nussbaum's characterization of the judgment that she identifies with disgust. These did not concern her general characterization of this judgment as a judgment about contamination. Rather, they concern her specific characterization of the judgment as a reminder of one's mortality and vulnerability to decay in virtue of one's having an animal body. Nussbaum, as I mentioned, relies on the work of Paul Rozin in putting forth this specific characterization.[13] Prior to this work, there had been, in experimental psychology, only an occasional study or two focusing on disgust. There were also studies of it as part of the

---

11. See ibid., pp. 218–219.

12. James Fitzjames Stephen, *Liberty, Equality, Fraternity*. For a recent edition, see *Liberty, Equality, Fraternity and Three Brief Essays*, with a foreword by Richard Posner (Chicago: University of Chicago Press, 1991).

13. See Rozin and Fallon, "A Perspective on Disgust."

more general program of studying the emotions that comes out of Darwin's work, but these did not go significantly beyond Darwin's own observations. Rozin's research, which he has conducted with various colleagues over the past quarter century, represents, then, the first sustained study of the emotion within this field. Rozin (et al.), under the influence of his predecessors, defines disgust narrowly as a "food related" emotion. It is revulsion at the prospect of ingesting a contaminating object. While he acknowledges that this definition is "circumscribed" and does not cover instances of disgust that fall within more traditional definitions, he nonetheless believes it captures "the core and origins of the emotion." He finds support for this belief in the etymology of 'disgust', in the emotion's characteristic facial expression, the closing of the nostrils and the opening of the mouth, and in its most characteristic feeling, nausea. Rozin further narrows his subject by distinguishing disgust from distaste, a distinction that, as we noted earlier, Nussbaum accepts. It is these two restrictions, the definition of disgust as food related and the distinction between distaste and disgust, that jointly enable Rozin to make a seemingly plausible case for the thesis that disgust concerns the problematic relationship we have to our animal nature.

Briefly, Rozin's case is this.[14] There is a tendency in human psychology to regard what one eats as affecting one's very nature. The tendency is reflected in the slogan "We are what we eat." Disgust, as Rozin defines it, is an emotion of food rejection, and hence it serves to protect one from eating things whose ingestion one regards as changing one's nature for the worse. The objects of such disgust, in other words, are regarded as contaminants, and the contamination they threaten is regarded as debasing. These objects are either animals, their parts, or their waste. Indeed, there are relatively few animals, as compared with plants, that human beings are willing to eat, and to eat even these, the animals must be prepared in ways that disguise their origins. They must be cut up into pieces, for instance, or mixed with other foods as in stews and casseroles. Plants, by contrast, are frequently eaten without such preparation. This, along with the great number of plants human beings are willing

---

14. Ibid. In the later article cited above, Rozin acknowledges other aspects of human life besides eating and food in which disgust operates to protect people from things they judge to be contaminants. And as a result, he gives a different argument for his thesis that disgust concerns the problematic relationship we have to our animal nature. This later argument amounts to his making a sweeping generalization that anything that is a reminder of our animal nature can provoke disgust. But this generalization, Nussbaum herself observes, is hopeless. Human athleticism, she points out, may remind us of our animal nature, but it does not provoke disgust. One could say the same thing about sleep. See Rozin, Haidt, and McCauley, "Disgust."

to eat, implies that human beings are unconcerned about having their nature affected by eating plants, whereas their disgust at eating most animals, animal parts, and animal waste implies, to the contrary, that they are concerned about the effect on their nature of eating animals. The explanation, it is safe to surmise, is that humans are animals who, because they generally regard themselves as not only superior to all other animals but different from them in kind, are anxious about being animals. Hence, disgust, as a food-related emotion, signifies our problematic relationship with our animal nature.

One might naturally object to this argument that it ignores the disgust that many people, especially small children, feel at the prospect of eating certain vegetables like broccoli. Such disgust is obviously food related, yet it has no bearing on our animal nature. Rozin, though, anticipates such objections. He relies on his distinction between distaste and disgust to answer them. Thus, Rozin maintains, while the involuntary facial movements expressing the revulsion that children, say, experience when they are made to eat some vegetable they detest are the same as the involuntary facial expressions characteristic of disgust, these children are directly responding to the bitter taste of the vegetable. They are not responding to the thought of the vegetable as a contaminant. In other words, if one identifies disgust with a certain judgment—if the emotion must have a certain ideational content, to use Rozin's expression—then the revulsion children experience on eating vegetables they detest, or at the prospect of eating them, is not disgust but rather mere distaste.

Rozin's case, however, even on its own terms, is unpersuasive. A common object of disgust is spoiled or rotten food, including rotten fruits and vegetables. Someone who is revulsed by a pear that has turned into a heap of mold or a rotten tomato that he finds at the back of his refrigerator is no less responding to the thought of contamination than someone who feels disgust at thoroughly moldy cheese or rotten meat. Yet there is no reason to think his revulsion at the pear or tomato signifies a concern with his animal nature.

This observation may alone be sufficient to refute Rozin's case. Yet the real problem with his case is that its terms are too limiting. Potato bugs, as I mentioned earlier, predictably excite disgust (see fig. 5.1). Caterpillars do not. The reason, however, is found in their appearance. Potato bugs are hideous. Looking at them makes one's flesh crawl. Caterpillars, by comparison, are not particularly repellent to look at. Some, in fact, are attractive. Plainly, if what explains why one type of insect excites disgust and another does not is the difference in their visual appearance, that one is extremely ugly and the other is not, then the disgust that the ugly insect excites is not food related and therefore cannot be interpreted, as Rozin does, as signaling our problematic relationship with our animal nature.

FIGURE 5.1   Potato bug. Photo by Dr. Lloyd Glenn Ingles, © California
Academy of Sciences. To view this image in color, go to www.utexas.edu/law/
faculty/jdeigh/potatobug.jpg.

Of course, Rozin could declare that the emotion in this example is distaste
and not disgust, since the emotion seems to be a direct response to the potato
bug's visual appearance and does not seem to include a judgment that the bug
is contaminating. But there are too many such examples of disgust excited by
the sensory properties of its object to be plausibly put into a separate category,
distaste, that is distinct from disgust. At some point, doing so becomes merely
the act of subdividing experiences of disgust into those that are direct responses
to their object's sensory properties and those that include a judgment that their
object is contaminating. In other words, denying that the former are instances
of disgust becomes ad hoc. Surely, hideousness alone is sufficient to excite
disgust, a fact that the makers of horror movies understand very well.[15]

Indeed, the description of the response as making one's flesh crawl should
remind us that the characteristic physical symptoms of disgust are not confined
to the facial expressions that Rozin invokes to justify his conception of disgust
as a food-related emotion. Disgust is commonly aroused when one comes into

15. Horror is a combination of fear and disgust. See Nöel Carroll, "Horror and Humor,"
in *Beyond Aesthetics: Philosophical Essays* (Cambridge: Cambridge University Press, 2001),
pp. 235–254. Originally published in *Journal of Aesthetics and Art Criticism* 57 (1999): 145–160.

contact with slimy things or when creeping animals, like insects, amphibians, or small reptiles, crawl on one's body. Prolonged contact with something slimy or the discovery of a creeper crawling on one produces shivers and perhaps the violent reaction of shaking or brushing off the offending creature. Such behavior expresses disgust without any suggestion that the object of the emotion is being rejected as food. Nor must the object even be an animal. Disgust at having to wade barefooted through a swamp whose bottom is covered with muck or to swim in a pond whose surface is covered with scum lacks an animal object. The swamp bottom's muck or the pond's scum excites disgust, it would seem, apart from any concern about one's animal nature.

Finally, a further problem for Rozin's case is that immoral conduct often provokes disgust. This fact is, of course, central to Devlin's account of how to determine what conduct society should not tolerate. And although Devlin's account chiefly concerns conduct that transgresses traditional Christian limits on acceptable sexual practices, sexual transgression is not the only kind of immoral conduct that provokes disgust. Obviously, if it were, then disgust felt in response to immoral conduct would not be problematic for Rozin's case, since human sexuality is one of the chief foci of our anxieties about our animal nature. But disgust is also felt in response to moral corruption that has nothing to do with our sexuality or the other typical foci of the anxieties about our animal nature that we tend to suppress through moral customs. Corrupt public officials and the political practices that offer those officials opportunities for achieving riches or greater power through deceit and fraud are, for example, common objects of disgust. 'Disgusting' is a common epithet used to describe them. And it is also common to describe such officials metaphorically as bad apples or sewer rats whose behavior is filthy and stinks. Similar responses are no doubt frequent within private organizations whose leaders are discovered to have acted corruptly. Rozin, in one of his later collaborations, concedes this point about "sleazy politicians," and he acknowledges that his thesis that disgust concerns the problematic relationship we have with our animal nature does not extend to moral disgust, as he calls it. What he fails to appreciate, though, is the implication the point has for the viability of this thesis.[16]

---

16. See Rozin, Haidt, and McCauley, "Disgust," pp. 637–653. Thus, Rozin and his co-authors speculate that such disgust is a response to immoral conduct that is seen as "inhuman and revolting," such as betrayal of friends or cold-blooded killing, rather than springing from normal human motives as, they suppose, is the case with bank robbery. From this speculation, they infer, "This kind of disgust may represent a more abstract set of concerns about the human-animal distinction" (pp. 643–644). But such speculation is further evidence of Rozin's original mistake of thinking that the concept of disgust is at its core that of a food-related emotion. There is nothing abnormal about the motives of corrupt officials. Taking a bribe and robbing a bank are just two different ways of criminally enriching oneself.

V

Rozin's failure to make a convincing case for his thesis means that we need to consider an alternative to Nussbaum's account of disgust. We need, that is, to consider an account that is neither tied to Rozin's thesis nor focused on food rejection as the core theme in disgust. Elsewhere I have sketched such an alternative in the course of arguing for seeing some emotions, including disgust, as having two forms, which I call primitive and tutored.[17] The primitive forms are direct responses to certain objects in virtue of their sensory properties. The subject's discernment of these properties, when he experiences a primitive emotion, supplies the emotion's cognitive content and determines its object. The tutored forms of these emotions develop out of their primitive forms through socialization. Specifically, children are taught, with respect to each primitive emotion, what things are the appropriate objects of that emotion and what things are not, and in the course of this teaching they acquire evaluative concepts that enlarge their understanding of the world and alter the range of things to which they respond with that emotion. In general, then, as a result of this teaching, children become liable to experience emotions whose cognitive content consists in evaluative thoughts formed through the application of these concepts to the world. They become liable, in other words, to tutored forms of emotions that, prior to the acquisition of these concepts, were felt exclusively in response to objects by virtue of those objects' sensory properties.

Consider, for example, fear. In its primitive form, it is an emotion whose objects are defined by those sensory properties that make something scary. Children are then taught the concept of danger and to feel fear at what they recognize as dangerous. This teaching enlarges their understanding of the world by, among other things, bringing them to see that certain innocent-looking things can in fact harm them if they are not careful. Teaching children about danger thus gives them new objects of fear, and accordingly they become liable to the tutored form of the emotion. At the same time, the teaching may make them less prone to fear scary things that they have learned are not dangerous. Indeed, as they become more familiar with those things and confident that they will not harm them, these things may cease to be scary. Consequently, the range of objects to which they are liable to fear in its primitive form is reduced.

A parallel account of disgust is also possible. On this account, disgust is initially an emotion whose objects are defined by those sensory properties

---

17. See my "Emotions and Values" (ch. 4, this volume).

that make something foul. These are certain smells, tastes, sights, and tactile feelings that offend the senses. Children are then taught the concept of sickness and to feel disgust at things the ingestion of which or contact with which will make them sick. Presumably, then, the reason disgust focuses on what ought to be rejected as food is that small children are prone to eat things that will make them sick and therefore need to be taught to avoid such things and to eject them quickly if they are taken into their mouths. But things that make one sick if eaten are not the only things small children must learn to avoid and to remove quickly if they come into contact with them. They must also learn to avoid what is unclean or carries disease, for prolonged contact with these things may also cause one to become sick. Consequently, water or soil infested with decayed matter, rats, flies, the corpses of animals, squalid conditions, and so forth become objects of disgust apart from their foul smell or slimy texture or the possibility of their being eaten. Generally, then, teaching children about what causes sickness gives them new objects of disgust, and accordingly they become liable to the tutored form of the emotion. At the same time, the teaching may help them become less disgusted at things whose properties offend their senses but that are not otherwise causes of sickness. After all, eventually many of us come to enjoy eating raw oysters.

The teaching through which children come to be capable of tutored disgust may initially consist chiefly in their acquiring a narrow concept of sickness, one that applies only to physical conditions. At some point, however, children either learn to apply the concept more broadly to cover unsound moral conditions and so come to understand depravity as a kind of sickness, or they acquire the concept of depravity from their teachers' comparing unsound moral conditions to sickness. They learn, that is, to distinguish between what is wholesome and what is depraved, and these notions are either understood as falling within those of health and sickness or acquired as their analogues in the mental and moral sphere. In either case, depravity and its sources become objects of disgust. Accordingly, children are taught to avoid actions and places that will corrupt their minds and character and to avoid as well people association with whom will have a similar effect. What Rozin calls moral disgust is thus a tutored form of disgust that is continuous with or a development out of the tutored form the capacity for which children develop through their acquiring the concept of sickness and their learning to avoid things that are sickening.

The objects of such disgust, moreover, are not restricted to actions, places, or people who would corrupt one if one didn't avoid them. They also include actions, places, and people with whom one has no direct involvement or contact as well as actions, places, and people involvement or contact with whom would not necessarily corrupt one even if one did. Rozin's example of "sleazy" politicians illustrates this point. A politician's corrupt actions may disgust one even if one is incorruptible. For it is enough that one regard oneself as somehow tainted by the politician's actions. The taint is a kind of moral contamination that is due to one's being associated in some way with this politician, and it is not unusual for people to regard themselves as tainted by the corrupt actions of others as long as there is some affiliation between them. Indeed, it is a well-known phenomenon of group psychology.

Specifically, if one belongs to a group and identifies strongly with it, one will be liable to feel certain emotions in response to the actions of other members, regardless of whether one bears any responsibility for those actions. The pride people take in the achievements of their countrymen, solely in view of their being the achievements of their countrymen—an important scientific discovery, say, an international award for literary work, victory in the Olympic games, etc.—is a familiar example. So too people can be ashamed of their countrymen's actions, despite having no responsibility for them, when those actions bring disgrace upon their country. War crimes, for example, are typically a source of shame not only for the soldiers who commit them and the military and political leaders who may be responsible for their commission but also generally for the citizens of the country whose soldiers committed them. Americans who traveled in Europe after the publication of news and photographs of American soldiers torturing Iraqi prisoners at Abu Ghraib prison and who were engaged by their hosts in conversation about the policies that led to such conduct know this feeling well. The feeling, moreover, would be palpable, notwithstanding their own opposition to those policies or the war in which they were implemented.

With regard to disgust, the phenomenon manifests itself in shared revulsion at actions and people who betray the beliefs, norms, and ideals of a group to which its subjects belong and with which they strongly identify. When people who belong to a group thereby share beliefs, norms, and ideals, when they subscribe to the same faith and support the same practices, then members who break faith with them or subvert their practices, have, if only symbolically, weakened the group. They have compromised, as it were, the group's integrity, and such compromises of integrity are seen as corruption and even defilement. Politicians in a representative democracy who abuse the public's trust by trading votes for personal gain subvert the democracy in which they serve. Athletes who cheat to gain an edge on their competition damage the integrity of the sports in which they compete. The corruption, in either case, makes them objects of disgust on the part of the members of the relevant community, fellow citizens in the case of the corrupt politicians, teammates and opponents, their assistants and fans, in the case of the corrupt athletes. For corruption sullies the values and ideals for which the group stands, and the judgment of being tainted in consequence gives rise to disgust at the offending actions and the offenders who did them.

VI

When Devlin appeals to the disgust of the common man, in making his case for the legal enforcement of morality, he takes the emotion to be an expression of common sense moral judgment. The common man, as Devlin likes to think of him, is "the man in the jury box," a representative of the community whose judgment, when it accords with that of like-minded jurors, expresses the moral judgment of society. So the common man's disgust at cruel or licentious actions is thus understood, on Devlin's view, to express moral disapproval that decent people share. Furthermore, Devlin characterizes the moral judgment the emotion expresses as one of common sense in order to distinguish it from a judgment that issues from reason, for in Devlin's view the morality that the criminal law may enforce is the morality of common sense and not the morality of rationalist philosophy. It is not, as it were, the one true morality that philosophers and theologians have propounded as a set of universal principles discoverable, through the exercise of reason and reflection, by any rational being. It is, rather, the morality that is commonly recognized in the society and embedded in the dominant practices and traditions, principally religious, to which that society adheres. Consequently, different societies may have different common moralities, which is to say, the common sense morality of one society may differ from that of another in virtue of the difference in the practices and traditions to which the society adheres. The actions the disapproval of which is registered through disgust are thus offenses against the moral beliefs, norms, and ideals that the members of the society share.

Devlin's chief interest is, of course, British society. He was concerned with the principal recommendations in the report of the Committee on Homosexual Offenses and Prostitution, which the British government set up in 1954 to study whether the criminal law as regards homosexual acts and prostitution needed reform. Those recommendations were to reform the law so that homosexual acts between consenting adults, if not engaged in publicly, were no longer criminal offenses and to resist calls for reforming the law so as to make prostitution a criminal offense. The committee based these recommendations on much the same general argument that Mill had advanced in *On Liberty* against the enforcement by society of morality. The argument in a nutshell is that the purposes of the criminal law are restricted to maintaining peace within society and ensuring that people treat each other decently. They do not, in other words, extend to preventing immorality as such or promoting moral virtue for its own sake. What goes on between consenting adults in private is therefore beyond the scope of the criminal law. It is this argument that Devlin opposes and criticizes. He believes it fails to take account of the vital importance to a society of a common morality, which is to say, shared moral beliefs, norms, and ideals. Society, he maintains, could not exist without these shared beliefs, norms, and ideals. They are among the "invisible bonds" that hold people together. Hence, Devlin argues, society must be prepared to defend its common morality and to use the criminal law, in particular, to enforce that morality when disobedience to it threatens to weaken the bonds it partly constitutes. For a society that fails to defend its shared beliefs, norms, and ideals will tend to disintegrate and its members to "drift apart."

The disgust of the common man enters Devlin's argument at the point where he asks how legislators should determine which kinds of immoral conduct society would be justified in making criminal. Not every kind, Devlin concedes, should be regulated by the criminal law. There are kinds that society can tolerate, in the interest of individual liberty, without seriously jeopardizing its cohesion, and that interest should in all such cases outweigh society's interest in promoting moral conduct. The limits of society's tolerance, Devlin believes, are reached when the conduct provokes not merely displeasure on the part of the majority in society but disgust. And the basis of this disgust, moreover, must be the immorality of the action. Disgust that does not have immorality as its object, disgust that is typically aroused just by the sight of other people's genitalia, say, or their engagement in sexual acts, does not imply moral disapproval and thus should not be confused with the disgust that Devlin regards as the proper indicator of conduct society should not tolerate. After all, even the most liberal-minded person might naturally feel some disgust at the nudity in Fellini's *Satyricon* without his thinking the film should be banned or that only the nudity of the young and the healthy should be tolerated.[18]

Plainly, then, the understanding of disgust that Devlin incorporates into his position is that of an emotion decent people have toward immorality

18. *Satyricon*, Culver City. MGM/UA Home Video, 1988. Directed by Federico Fellini; screenplay by Fellini and Bernadino Zapponi.

without regard to whether the immorality that disgusts them has any directly corrupting influence on them. What they experience, according to the account of such disgust given in the last section, is a shared revulsion at actions and individuals who betray the beliefs, norms, and ideals of a group to which they belong and with which they strongly identify. The account of the last section therefore supports Devlin's appeal to disgust, for it makes clear why the kind of conservative opposition to Mill's argument that Devlin's position exemplifies would use the disgust of decent people toward immorality as an indicator of conduct the society would be justified in suppressing. On that kind of conservatism, a well-functioning society is essential to human well-being, and to function well, a society requires a high degree of solidarity among its members.[19] Conversely, lowering the degree of solidarity in the society jeopardizes the members' well-being. Such solidarity consists, at least in part, in agreement among the members on boundaries to conduct and on persons and things (which typically include symbols or representatives of the society itself) whose worth is inviolable and to which honor must be paid. The agreement represents the social unity that is understood to be essential to the members' well-being, and as such it serves as a norm deviation from which loyal members will see as threatening the society's integrity. Consequently, disgust will have the kind of role in the legal and moral enforcement of that norm that Devlin assigned it.

Of course, conservative thinking of this stripe is no more than dogmatism without at least some explanation of the connection it draws between solidarity among the members of a society and their well-being. It must give some support for its theses that a society functions well only if it achieves a high degree of solidarity and that reducing the degree of solidarity in a society will jeopardize its members' well-being. These theses are the distinctive tenets of conservative thought, like Devlin's, that takes limiting individual liberty and promoting social inequality as sometimes necessary for the sake of maintaining or strengthening social unity. For it is the mark of such conservatism to oppose liberal and democratic programs of legal and social reform on the grounds that such reform will weaken and even destroy bonds among the members of society, and these theses underpin that opposition. The explanation lies in a conception of society that significantly differs from those of its opponents.

---

19. Devlin did not hold this thesis but rather maintained the stronger, ontological thesis that society's very existence depends on there being a high degree of solidarity among its members. It was this ontological thesis that H. L. A. Hart effectively attacked in *Law, Liberty, and Morality* (Stanford: Stanford University Press, 1963).

On this conception, human society is a natural phenomenon. It develops from primitive groups of human beings through a process of civilization. However one individuates the different societies that result from this process—the different societies, for instance, that Western civilization comprises—they are to be conceived of genealogically. All of them, that is, are to be understood as the branches of a family tree (just as the connections among Indo-European languages are commonly understood as branches of a tree whose trunk is their proto-language). The members of each society are members either by birth or by privileged admission, and the sense of belonging is a deep fact of social psychology. Those who belong by birth have been initiated from an early age into the society's traditions, and their social selves consist in large part in the habits of thought, feeling, and action that they acquire through that initiation. Those who belong by privileged admission are expected to assimilate to some degree and consequently face significant social pressure to acquire the same habits. The society's members are thus both products and keepers of its traditions. They are products in that initiation or assimilation into the traditions, when successful, determines in large part their personality and behavior. They are keepers in that their fidelity to these traditions is necessary to sustain them. And this symbiosis between the society's members and its traditions is the basis of the connection conservative thinkers like Devlin draw between social solidarity and human well-being.

Above all, according to these thinkers, the members of a society are not to be thought of as independent contractors (or their descendants) who have come together for mutual advantage through cooperation. They are inheritors of the practices and institutions that make social cooperation possible, to be sure, but not in a sense that gives them dominion over those practices and institutions. The liberal conception of society as a voluntary association of people who as individuals are free and equal and who as a collective have authority to determine the terms of their social life is thus anathema to such conservative thought. Society may be understood as a partnership among its members, but it is, in Burke's words, "a partnership in all science;…in all art;…in every virtue, and in all perfection. As the ends of such a partnership cannot be obtained in many generations, it becomes a partnership not only between those who are living but between those who are living, those who are dead, and those who are to be born."[20] To think of it instead as a

20. Edmund Burke, *Reflections on the Revolution in France*, J. G. A. Pocock, ed. (Indianapolis: Hackett, 1987), p. 85.

corporation organized to promote the personal ends of the partners who are its current owners and who as such can at any time revisit the terms of the agreement that binds them together is to invite the kind of social malaise that results from people's losing their moorings and drifting apart.

VII

Nussbaum, in one of the most compelling parts of her critique of disgust, explains the emotion's role in the social subordination of people who belong to religious and ethnic minorities or who lack the privileges that those who control the society's wealth and power have. Anti-Semitism and misogyny are her chief examples. Regarding the former, she describes how Jews were depicted in medieval representations so as to evoke disgust and how similar but more extreme depictions by notorious nineteenth- and twentieth-century German anti-Semites were used to promote an ideal of Aryan masculinity from which the German people were supposed to draw inspiration and strength. Thus, she writes,

> The stock image of the Jew, in anti-Semitic propaganda from the Middle Ages on, was that of a being disgustingly soft and porous, receptive of fluid and sticky, womanlike in its oozy sliminess. In the nineteenth and twentieth centuries such images were widespread and further elaborated, as the Jew came to be seen as a foul parasite inside the clean body of the German male self.[21]

And she goes on to describe how Jews were caricatured as having grotesque physical features, which were identified as distinctively Jewish—Jewish noses, Jewish feet, Jewish skin—and which were then used to represent Jews as more animal than human. "[I]t was because there was a need to associate Jews...with stereotypes of the animal, thus distancing them from the dominant group, that they were represented and talked about in such a way that they came to be found disgusting."[22] Misogyny too, Nussbaum observes, has been expressed in different cultures and at different times in depictions of women meant to evoke disgust. These depictions, she argues, typically manifest a reaction formation to female sexuality and to the threat to male domination that female sexuality represents. "One may find," Nussbaum writes, "variants on these themes in more or less all societies, as women become vehicles for the expression of male loathing of the physical and the potentially

---

21. Nussbaum, *Hiding from Humanity*, p. 108.
22. Ibid., p. 111.

decaying."[23] Women, Nussbaum argues, because of bodily functions that define them as child bearers, are seen in these misogynistic depictions to be closer to nature and so to our animality than men, and men's need to deny their vulnerability as animals to infirmity, disease, and death has made these functions and women as their site the objects of disgust.

Nussbaum intends these examples as corroboration of her thesis about disgust's being a reminder of our animal nature and the vulnerability to decay it entails. As such, they anticipate her later criticism of the American judiciary's Devlin-like appeals to the disgust of the common man in determining the limits of the law's tolerance of pornographic materials and to Devlin's own appeals to such disgust in his defense of the law's prohibition of homosexual sodomy. Yet on the analysis of disgust I have given, the disgust Nussbaum describes in these examples is not the kind that concerns Devlin. Anti-Semites, after all, regard Jews as people from whom they must keep their distance lest they become polluted by contact with them. And misogynists either regard women similarly or regard their intimate relations with them as a form of depravity that only the good of reproduction can redeem. The disgust of anti-Semites and misogynists, in other words, is not disgust of the kind that implies moral disapproval apart from personal concern about being corrupted by contact with the objects of the emotion. Consequently, the force of her later criticism comes into question.

At the same time, it is clear that Nussbaum is right to find in Devlin's appeal to disgust support for the emotion's role in the subordination of religious and ethnic groups and of people who lack privileges that those in control of a society's wealth and power have. Indeed, her examples of anti-Semitic and misogynistic disgust, while not of the kind of disgust that concerns Devlin, nonetheless call attention to an important aspect of that kind. For they highlight the role disgust can have in creating and sustaining solidarity within a group. And if the disgust that concerns Devlin has a similar role in creating and sustaining social solidarity, then it too is open to criticism in those cases in which the solidarity it helps to create and sustain derives from shared beliefs, norms, and ideals of a supremacist ideology.

Nor is it difficult to see how it could have this similar role. In these examples, disgust works to unite the members of a group through common hatred and contempt of outsiders or people regarded as inferior. The dynamic is as familiar as it is pervasive in modern life. Ethnic divisions in a pluralistic society (or across a small continent) are a common source of such groups. But

___

23. Ibid., p. 113.

even if we leave aside such ancestral divisions, we still find human beings, beginning with grade school and summer camp, forming gangs and cliques and coteries whose unity is strengthened by the members' seeing themselves as different from others and superior to at least some of them. Later in life similar divisions appear in exclusive clubs, secret or elite societies, and gated or otherwise closed neighborhoods. When some such division characterizes a whole society or large sections of it and when it becomes entrenched in that society's traditions, then disgust of the kind to which Devlin appeals serves to reinforce the subordination that the division represents and therefore the inferior status within the society that the members of the subordinate group have.

One might, of course, still question whether disgust in such cases is the same as the disgust to which Devlin appeals. For Devlin appeals to the disgust of the common man, "the man in the jury box," and the common man need not be a member of any dominant group within the society. The disgust of the common man, it might therefore seem, must be different from the disgust of those who belong to a dominant group regardless of whether or not the latter includes concern with being corrupted by direct contact with members of the subordinate group. The common man's disgust, on this thought, must be neutral with regard to the customs of any of society's subgroups and likewise neutral with regard to physical features or the characteristic conduct of any of their members. And so one might conclude that the disgust to which Devlin appeals is not implicated in the oppression of subordinate groups.

But this line of reasoning is specious. The common man's disgust in Devlin's theory is not necessarily neutral, and in a society in which division between a dominant group and a subordinate one is entrenched in the society's traditions, it is bound to figure in the general social attitudes that maintain the dominance. This is because the members of a society, barring cultural isolation from the society's traditions, will internalize the beliefs, norms, and ideals that constitute those traditions. Hence, in a society in which division between a dominant group and a subordinate group is entrenched in the society's traditions, disgust that members of the dominant groups feel at the conduct or physical features of the members of subordinate groups will not be limited to those who belong to a dominant group. It will also be part of the psychology of many who belong to subordinate groups. W. E. B. Du Bois's description of the double consciousness that African Americans, forty years freed from bondage and subject to a system of apartheid, experienced illustrates this point tellingly. It is, Du Bois wrote, "[the] sense of always looking at one's self through the eyes of others, of measuring one's soul by the tape of a world that looks on in amused contempt and pity."[24] Having constantly to face the dominant culture's prejudice against one's looks, one's manners, and indeed one's very being, one is brought, Du Bois declared, to the "inevitable self-questioning and self-disparagement and lowering of ideals which ever accompany repression and breed in an atmosphere of contempt and hate."[25] Devlin's common man, if he lives in such a society, will naturally express the social attitudes, including disgust, that castes and other oppressive hierarchical relations create, not only in the members of the higher orders toward those of the lower orders but also in those of lower orders toward themselves.

Nussbaum's objections to Devlin's appeal to the common man's disgust follow from her general critique of the emotion. Because on her account the emotion, when its objects are people or their actions, consists in judgments that invite regard for those people as less than human, one promotes dehumanizing and abusive treatment of some of them when one argues for the society's enlisting disgust in the service of maintaining the customs and traditions that bind its members. And Devlin's appeal is no exception. On the alternative account of disgust that I have proposed, by contrast, the emotion, when its objects are people or their actions, does not necessarily invite such treatment of those people, for the judgments in which it consists do not always serve as a reminder of our animal nature and vulnerability to decay. They are sometimes judgments about corruption that threatens the integrity of a group with which one identifies by betraying the group's shared beliefs, norms, and ideals. And if those beliefs, norms, and ideals are integral to just social institutions and humane moral practices, then the emotion has a salutary role in removing threats to those institutions and practices. A clear example is public disgust at widespread graft by elected officials, enriching themselves at the expense of those whom they are sworn to serve, when it leads to tightening laws and rules governing the relations between those officials and private parties and the gifts and favors that the latter can give to or do for the former.

Thus, replacing Nussbaum's account of disgust with the one I have proposed, we should conclude that the proper target of her criticism of Devlin's appeal to disgust is not the emotion per se but the conservative political thought that lies behind the appeal. It is, in particular, the premium that such thought gives to social solidarity and the corresponding calculation it accepts, a calculation that allows vast numbers of people in a society to suffer

24. W. E. B. Du Bois, *The Souls of Black Folk* (New York: New American Library, 1969), p. 45..
25. Ibid., p. 51.

the indignities and cruelties of subordination and second-class status and to live lives of crippling self-doubt and self-loathing so as to preserve the social order. And while we need not suppose that there is no limit to the amount of oppression and misery that conservative thinking of this stripe would allow in the interest of maintaining the practices and traditions that bind the members of a society together, it is certain to be significantly greater than that which political thinking whose calculus gives greater weight to considerations of equality and individual liberty than to those of social solidarity. At bottom, what matters to conservative thinkers like Devlin is not the quality of the individual lives of the members of a society but the orderly functioning of the whole. And it is this set of values that Nussbaum, in her objections to Devlin and, I suspect, the views of the other conservative thinkers whose appeals to disgust she discusses, so eloquently opposes.

VIII

Nussbaum's criticisms of programs that give shame a place in the criminal law focus first on the use of shame-inducing sanctions as punishment for certain criminal offenses. The imposition of such sanctions, Nussbaum observes, has been favored recently by judges and academic commentators who regard them as effective ways of both communicating society's intolerance of these crimes and deterring their perpetrators and others from repeating or committing the same offenses. Of course, even standard forms of punishment, like incarceration, are likely to induce shame in those on whom they are imposed, but their inducing shame is typically a byproduct of their imposition rather than an intended effect. Sanctions designed to induce shame, by contrast, are meant to make the offender an object of public attention on account of his offense and so to invite public disdain and contempt. They are modern day equivalents of putting criminals in stocks or making misbehaving children sit in corners wearing dunce caps. Common examples are drunk drivers who are made to drive for a fixed period of time with a license plate that advertises their crime, customers of prostitutes whose names are published in local newspapers as having been convicted of unlawful solicitation of sex, shoplifters who are required to stand outside the shops from which they stole holding signs that say "I stole," and other thieves who are required to wear shirts that identify them as pickpockets, purse snatchers, embezzlers, etc. The appeal of these sanctions is economic: they create unpleasant circumstances for an offender that appear to serve the normal expressive and deterrent purposes of punishment at a cost to the state that is far less than the cost of incarcerating the offender.

Nussbaum sees in these sanctions the same social pathology that occurs when public officials use the criminal law to degrade people whose "crimes" consist mostly in conduct that offends conventional sensibilities or violates conventional norms defining personal space. In these cases, Nussbaum notes, the processes of the criminal law are used first to alienate those convicted of these crimes from society and then to brand them and the groups or types to which they belong as deviant and a danger to public health or safety. Typically, when public officials undertake campaigns to clean up the streets or rid neighborhoods of bad elements, they target groups or types of people whom they identify as troublemakers and undesirables, and they use arrest, trial, criminal conviction, and punishment to vilify the members of these groups or types. Despised and feared minorities are especially vulnerable to such treatment. But vagrants and pan handlers are also natural targets. One may think, in this regard, of Rudolph Giuliani's campaign in the 1990s to remove "squeegee men" from New York City streets or the efforts of municipalities generally to remove the homeless from their sidewalks, parks, and plazas. Nussbaum traces the pathology in these cases to the reaction formation that she earlier explained as the product of primitive shame. Like the reaction formation disgust produces, this one too creates a disposition to aggress against people whom one can treat as inferior to oneself. Primitive shame, because it consists in a deep-seated sense of one's own weakness and inadequacy, produces anxiety about one's own worth relief from which comes from seeing others as having less worth. And treating them as inferior reinforces one's perception of them as inferior. Hence, acts that deliberately and systematically denigrate others, especially when they are undertaken for a "moral" cause, are symptomatic of this pathology. They signify, in Nussbaum's words, a fragile ego that finds affirmation of its own precarious sense of worth in the humiliation and dehumanization of others.

Similarly, then, Nussbaum argues, there is reason to think that sanctions designed to induce shame, because they are commonly used publicly to humiliate those on whom they are imposed, often manifest the same pathology. Indeed, part of their appeal, at least to their leading academic supporters, is their capacity to humiliate those on whom they are imposed.[26] For this feature, their supporters maintain, makes them more fitting, as alternatives to incarceration, than fines and community service. The argument, in short,

---

26. See Dan Kahan, "What Do Alternative Sanctions Mean?" *University of Chicago Law Review* 63 (1996): 591–653, and Amitai Etzioni, *The Monochrome Society* (Princeton: Princeton University Press, 2001), pp. 37–47.

is this. One of the principal purposes of punishment is the censure of the offender for his offense, and sanctions designed to induce shame fulfill this purpose more successfully than either fines or community service.[27] They do so because in humiliating the offender, they not only effectively convey society's reprehension of his offense but also its scorn for him. Fines, by contrast, can too easily be regarded as fees the state charges for committing the offense, and community service is an even less reliable vehicle of censure, since it can be regarded positively as an opportunity to do something good for the community. Thus, the very feature to which the supporters of these sanctions appeal in recommending them over other alternatives to incarceration makes them a kind of sanction that would also, on Nussbaum's developmental hypothesis, better feed the need that comes from primitive shame to aggress against people whom one can treat as inferior. Consequently, to promote the use of these sanctions as suitable alternatives to incarceration is to invite the abusive treatment of convicted criminals toward which this need impels. And in a system of criminal justice that is already hard-pressed to recognize the humanity of many of those who fall into its clutches, the adoption of these sanctions would therefore tend more to aggravate this problem than diminish it.

Nussbaum cites the potential for abuse that sanctions designed to induce shame have to support her general thesis about the dangers to a just society of enlisting shame in the service of the criminal law. She makes other objections to these sanctions as well, but none of the drawbacks she attributes to the sanctions in making these objections is due to the workings of shame in either those who receive or those who mete out the sanctions. That is, neither the emotion itself nor behavior it can excite is the object of Nussbaum's criticisms in these objections. So her case against enlisting shame to forward the aims of the criminal law turns on her account of the emotion as, in its primitive form, the source of hostile and derogatory conduct toward those who are easily treated as low. The use of sanctions designed to induce shame incites in the officials responsible for imposing such sanctions and in the public generally this primitive shame, to which we are all liable, and abuse of those convicted of criminal offenses is then a predictable outcome. The case, therefore, is like Nussbaum's case against the law's catering to disgust. Both emotions are sources of persecutory conduct toward the weaker and less

---

27. Kahan emphasizes this point in "What Do Alternative Sanctions Mean?" For discussion of the expressive purpose of punishment, see Joel Feinberg, "The Expressive Function of Punishment," in *Doing and Deserving: Essays in the Theory of Responsibility* (Princeton: Princeton University Press, 1970), pp. 95–118.

privileged members of society by the stronger and more privileged, and the criminal law ought not to encourage such conduct.

It is curious that Nussbaum's case against the criminal law's catering to shame does not depend on there being anything bad about the shame that the sanctions in fact induce in those on whom they are imposed. To be sure, Nussbaum criticizes the sanctions for having the capacity to humiliate those on whom they are imposed, but as she observes, a person can be publicly humiliated without experiencing shame.[28] So the emotion the sanctions are ostensibly designed to induce is not itself an object of this criticism. This suggests that we look into shame when it is induced in criminal offenders by imposing such sanctions to see why some political theories might favor sanctions designed to induce it. What we will find is that some political theories do favor these sanctions—and indeed the use of shame generally to forward the aims of the criminal law—that these theories include conservative theories, like Devlin's, that place a premium on social solidarity, and that support for using shame to forward the aims of the criminal law makes sense from these theories' perspective. Accordingly, we may conclude that, like her case against the use of disgust in the criminal law, the proper target of Nussbaum's case against practices in the criminal law that cater to shame is not the emotion itself but such theories as Devlin's that support these practices.

We need not look far to see why theories like Devlin's would support the use in the criminal law of sanctions designed to induce shame. As I noted earlier, when one belongs to a group and identifies strongly with it, there will be certain characteristically self-regarding emotions to which one is liable whose objects in some instances are the actions of other members of the group (or conditions in which they have fallen), actions (or conditions) for which one is not in the least responsible. Shame and pride are among these emotions. A measure, then, of a group's solidarity is how liable its members, on average, are to experience these emotions vicariously in response to each other's actions. This is a measure of solidarity, for it indicates how strongly the members identify with the group, and the strength of their identification corresponds to how strongly they have internalized the norms and ideals to which they, as members of the group, expect each other to conform.[29] It

28. Nussbaum, *Hiding from Humanity*, pp. 203–204.
29. Identification, in the sense I am using it here, implies an emotional attachment to that with which one identifies. See Freud, *Group Psychology and the Analysis of the Ego*, ch. 7, in *The Standard Edition of the Complete Psychological Works of Sigmund Freud*, James Strachey, trans. (London: Hogarth Press, 1953–1971), vol. 23, pp. 105–110.

represents, in other words, the extent to which the group is united by shared moral beliefs, norms, and ideals.

We can now give a general characterization of the experiences of shame the use of which to forward the aims of the criminal law political theories like Devlin's would favor. To feel such shame, whether vicariously or directly, over an action that either deviates from the norms of a group to which one belongs or abandons its ideals is to experience a blow to the sense of worth one has by virtue of one's identity as a member of the group.[30] When people strongly identify with a group to which they belong, be it their family or ancestry, their community, their ethnicity, their country, and so forth, their membership in that group becomes a part of their identity and a source of their sense of worth. The shame they then experience, when they act against the norms and ideals of the group, entails a painful recognition of their having acted beneath themselves, of their having betrayed an identity that is a source of their sense of worth. This complex experience thus implicitly includes an affirmation of their belonging to the group, an affirmation that may be further shown in efforts, typically expressive of shame, to cover up what is seen as shameful in what they have done. Hence, political thought that puts a premium on maintaining social solidarity would, in principle at least, favor imposing on criminal offenders sanctions designed to induce shame. Provided that the criminal offender is capable of feeling shame over his crime, such punishment, insofar as it is successful in inducing in him shame and so affirmation of his identity as a member of the society, would promote the offender's return to accepting and conforming to the social norms that he has violated. It would promote, that is, the strengthening of the "invisible bonds" that hold society together.

Why, then, do we not find the leading supporters of the law's use of sanctions designed to induce shame making arguments that appeal to these social benefits of inducing the emotion in criminal offenders?[31] Why does

---

30. I draw here on the account of shame I gave in "Shame and Self-Esteem: A Critique," *Ethics* 93 (1983): 225–245; also reprinted in John Deigh, *The Sources of Moral Agency* (Cambridge: Cambridge University Press, 1996), pp. 226–248. In speaking of a person's identity, I use a 'identity' in a sense that derives from the concept of identification specified in the previous footnote. In short, a person's identity in this sense is determined by the people, groups, institutions, etc. with whom or which he identifies.

31. An exception is John Braithwaite, whose theory of what he calls "reintegrative shaming" recognizes these benefits and distinguishes them from the effects of stigmatization. See his *Crime, Shame and Reintegration* (Cambridge: Cambridge University Press, 1989), and also E. Ahmed, N. Harris, J. Braithwaite, and V. Braithwaite, *Shame Management through Reintegration* (Cambridge: Cambridge University Press, 2001), pt. 1.

the debate between the friends and foes of such sanctions turn instead on other things, like how well the sanctions satisfy the expressive and deterrent aims of punishment and the extent to which the sanctions encourage abusive treatment of convicted criminals? The answer lies, I believe, in the common confusion of shame with humiliation. For each side makes its case by appealing to the sanctions' capacity to humiliate those on whom the sanctions are imposed, and this suggests that neither side sees any significant difference between humiliation and shame. It suggests that either is prone to mistake the former for the latter.[32] Consequently, both sides miss the features of shame that explain why a political program might promote sanctions that induce the emotion in criminal offenders.

It is necessary, therefore, to understanding the politics of shame to appreciate how the emotion differs from humiliation. We can best see this difference by comparing the characteristic experiences of each, which is to say, experiences that are self-regarding rather than vicarious. Accordingly, what principally distinguishes characteristic feelings of shame from characteristic feelings of humiliation is the thought of oneself as having done something shameful or of being in some shameful state. For one can feel humiliated without having this thought. When one feels humiliated, as the result, say, of being treated with blatant disrespect, one feels small, weak, or helpless. Another or others have treated one cruelly or insultingly and, in doing so, conveyed their view of one as someone whose interests do not matter and who has no claim on them for decent treatment. Yet one need not think there is anything about oneself that warrants such treatment or makes one deserving of it. One need not think there is anything about oneself that makes one unworthy of the respect or esteem of those who are humiliating one or the members of the group they represent. By contrast, when one feels shame, one recognizes something about oneself that is shameful, and to recognize such a feature in oneself is to recognize something that, relative to a component of one's identity, makes one unworthy of belonging to the group identification with whom (or with whose archetype) yields that component. When we say of a tennis player, for instance, that she suffered a humiliating defeat, we do not imply that she played badly or displayed incompetence on the court. Perhaps

---

32. Nussbaum, to her credit, sees that the two are different and offers a distinction between them. She writes, "We may also speak of feelings of humiliation, which will be very closely related to feelings of shame but with the added idea that something has been *done* to the person who feels it." *Hiding from Humanity*, p. 204. The distinction Nussbaum draws is apt but, as I argue below, an even sharper distinction is needed to understand why certain political programs would favor sanctions designed to induce shame.

she did. But alternatively she could be an excellent player for her age who, despite playing her best, was unfairly matched against an older and merciless opponent. On the other hand, when we say of a player that her defeat was shameful, we imply that she played badly, that her play was unworthy of her, given her talents, or unworthy of tennis players at her level. In this simple contrast, the difference between the two emotions should be clear.

It may now appear that Nussbaum's criticisms of sanctions designed to induce shame miss their mark. For her criticisms appeal to the tendency of these sanctions publicly to humiliate those on whom they are imposed and do not deal with the shame the sanctions are designed to induce. And once the difference between shame and humiliation is made clear, then it is easy to conclude that successful criticism of these sanctions requires finding fault with them in view of the shame, and not the humiliation, they cause. Yet to conclude this would be hasty. The criticisms undoubtedly miss their mark if the sanctions are conceived of abstractly as sanctions that induce shame in those on whom they are imposed without also humiliating them. But the sanctions Nussbaum criticizes are not mere abstractions. They are sanctions that judges have recently imposed and whose imposition academic commentators have subsequently promoted. That these sanctions have the capacity to humiliate those on whom they are imposed is not in dispute. Indeed, as we have seen, both their supporters and their opponents acknowledge the importance of this feature, and in any case it would be difficult to imagine concretely sanctions used in the criminal law with the aim of inducing shame in those on whom they were imposed that did not have the capacity to humiliate their recipients. Consequently, it would be a mistake to think that such sanctions, because they were designed to induce shame in those on whom they were imposed, were immune from criticisms like Nussbaum's.

Accordingly, Nussbaum's criticisms could be successful if either these sanctions, though designed to induce shame, typically failed to do so or the humiliation they caused overpowered whatever shame they typically induced. In either case, the social benefit the sanctions promise, the benefit, that is, of inducing in criminal offenders affirmation of their identity as members of society and so spurring them to reconnect with the social norms and ideals against which they have acted, will not result. Obviously, it will not result in the case in which the sanctions typically fail to induce shame. But it will also not result in the case in which humiliation overpowers whatever shame the sanctions induce. The reason is that humiliation, as Nussbaum and other critics of these sanctions have noted, tends to embitter and enrage those subjected to it and thus cause disaffection from and opposition to the norms and ideals against which they have acted.[33] Hence, the sanctions, even if they induce shame in the criminal offenders on whom they are imposed, may nonetheless be counterproductive. Clearly, then, supposing the sanctions did not produce the social benefit they promised, Nussbaum's criticisms would be successful if her claims about the severity and consequences of the humiliation that they did produce were sound.

Is shame too volatile an emotion for our society to attempt to enlist it in the service of the criminal law? Nussbaum's argument does not show that it is. Rather, it shows that the attempt itself, because it is liable to produce abusive and unjust treatment of those who are its targets, is dangerous. The attempt, Nussbaum argues, whether it is made by imposing sanctions specially designed to induce shame or by using other legal processes—criminalization, arrest, and trial—tends to stigmatize and humiliate those who are its targets, and such stigmata and humiliation represent use of the criminal law to denigrate those in society who are seen as outcasts or deviants. This danger, we can now see, is heightened when interest in enlisting shame in the service of the criminal law comes from a political program, like Devlin's, that seeks to promote social solidarity by legally enforcing the moral beliefs, norms, and values it identifies as the society's common morality. For such enforcement if carried out through, say, the use of sanctions designed to induce shame is liable to produce humiliation and not shame (or humiliation that overpowers whatever shame it does induce) when the sanctions are imposed on those who belong to a subculture of the society that dissents from what is identified as its common morality and whose dissent is the object of the enforcement. It is liable to have this effect because in such cases, the sanctions will be imposed on people whose identity is typically more strongly determined by their belonging to the subculture than it is by their belonging to the society generally, and consequently, the sanctions, being used to enforce some norm that is alien to these people's subculture, will have a greater tendency to cause them to feel humiliated than ashamed. Nussbaum's concern about the ease with which sanctions designed to induce shame can be used to persecute vulnerable minorities and others whose ways of life depart from that of the majority or dominant culture becomes particularly apt, then, when the sanctions are supported by conservative political theories, such as Devlin's, that allow for the subordination of some groups and the curtailment of their members' liberty in the interest of promoting social solidarity. Here too, I believe, it is these theories, rather than the emotion, that is the proper object of her criticism.

33. See Nussbaum, *Hiding from Humanity*, p. 236, and Ahmed, et al., *Shame Management through Reintegration*, pp. 5 ff.

6

Emotion and
the Authority of Law

Variation on Themes in
Bentham and Austin

Thinking about the authority of law can lead one to dizzying heights of wonder, like those reached in Ronald Dworkin's *Law's Empire*.[1] It can also lead to oppressive depths of despair, like those depicted in Franz Kafka's *The Trial*.[2] The stark contrast between the views of law found in these two works—one of fiction, the other of, well, legal fiction—illuminates old disputes over the nature of law and the grounds of its authority. Is law essentially anything more than a miscellany of imperatives and instructions issued by individuals or groups within a society who are specially designated to guide the society's members and by whom those members are disposed to be guided? And is its authority grounded in anything firmer or more certain than the existence of this general disposition in the membership? In particular, is its authority grounded in some moral property that law necessarily has?

Dworkin answers each of these questions with an unqualified yes. On his view, law is an enormously rich and complex intellectual object whose exposition requires a theoretical understanding of a very high order. The elements

---

1. (Cambridge: Harvard University Press, 1985).
2. Trans. Willa and Edwin Muir (New York: Random House, 1956).

of positive law—statutes, judicial decisions, written constitutions, and the like—are on his view merely evidence of what the real law is, and the judge's task in any particular case is to discern from an assemblage of such evidence the true law that underpins these surface phenomena and yields the correct decision. To do this, the judge must have a theory that enables him or her to understand these disparate elements as forming a coherent system of normative political thought. On the best theory, Dworkin maintains, the disparate elements of positive law are unified through a set of underlying principles, which includes the abstract principles of justice and fairness at the core of the society's political morality. It is the best theory, moreover, not only in virtue of the coherence and unity it brings to our understanding of the law but also in virtue of the accuracy it achieves in its representation of the law. Hence, law, on Dworkin's view, is essentially more than a miscellany of imperatives and instructions. It is a coherent system of normative thought organized by fundamental principles of justice and fairness and perhaps by other principles of political morality and wisdom. It thus draws its authority from the authority of these principles, and since they are moral principles, the law's authority is a form of moral authority.

What is striking about the legal world that Kafka describes in *The Trial*, when compared with this grand vision of law that Dworkin presents, is how it turns Dworkin's vision upside down. One would never for a moment think that law in the world Kafka described was a coherent system of normative thought or that it rested on fundamental principles of justice and fairness. The arbitrary legal decisions and actions that define the protagonist's case are the essence of Kafka's characterization of law, and one would have to be a singularly obtuse reader to regard them, instead, as mere surface phenomena behind which existed a coherent and just legal order. This is, after all, a Kafkaesque world. At the same time, the law's authority in this world is compellingly evident throughout the novel. Indeed, its authority seems to be enhanced by the very incomprehensibility of the legal regime in which the protagonist finds himself enmeshed.

Not that there should be anything surprising in this. An institution's authority will appear increasingly imperious to those subject to its governance as it makes them feel increasingly small, and an institution can make those subject to its governance feel small by preventing them from understanding how the decisions applying to them were reached, what methods or reasons were followed in reaching them, and what their consequences are. The principle is the same as one we teachers know well. Few things if any, I submit, can make one seem a more profound teacher to one's credulous students than mystification. Students are dependent on their teacher for instruction;

he or she is the authority under whose tutelage they have come; and by promoting their helplessness, a teacher can enlarge the authority he or she has
in their eyes. Likewise with legal authority: it too will appear grander to those
subject to it when it works to promote their helplessness.

To be sure, promoting the helplessness of those subject to one's authority
is not the only way one can make one's authority appear grander. Another is
to make the subjects feel more powerful, as we teachers do when we bring
our students to a significantly deeper understanding and greater mastery of
the material we're teaching and as governing authorities do when by the force
of their decisions their subjects feel collectively empowered. The mechanism
at work in this case is projection: the students or the governed feel more powerful as a result of successful teaching or popular governance, and they naturally project this feeling of greater power onto its source. Be this as it may, the
point is the same in either case. The dynamic in the relation of authority to
subject depends on an emotional bond between the bearer of authority and
those subject to it, and insofar as this dynamic is essential to the relation, it
follows that the relation itself entails this bond. Accordingly, the authority of
law, being a specific case of this general phenomenon, is conditioned on an
emotional bond between law and its subjects. The opposition, then, between
Dworkin's view of law and that represented in *The Trial* is fundamental. For
the idea implicit in Dworkin's view, that the law's authority derives from the
authority of the basic principles of justice and fairness at its foundation, is
directly contradicted by the possibility that the emotional bond between subjects and the law on which the dynamic of the relation between the two
depends can form in a legal system, like the one imagined in Kafka's novel,
that lacks such a foundation. My aim in this essay is to defend an idea of legal
authority consistent with that depicted in Kafka's novel. Specifically, it is to
defend the thesis that the authority of law is conditioned on an emotional
bond between the law and its subjects.

I

The thesis needs to be clarified if not qualified. Baldly stated, it invites immediate criticism. For one thing, it is easy to imagine people who have no emotional tie to the law in their community but who are nonetheless subject to
its authority. For another, one can also imagine the authority of law in the
person of someone, a bullying sheriff, say, or a hanging judge, to whom none
of those subject to his authority has an emotional bond. These cases may
appear to refute the thesis. Yet once the character of the law's authority is

understood, they will no longer seem incompatible with it. Two features, in particular, are important. First, the law's authority is authority with respect to a collective or community. Second, either the law's authority is sovereign, which is to say, paramount in that collective, or the law represents the will of the individual or assembly of individuals who is the sovereign, and thus its authority comes directly from the paramount authority in that collective. By drawing the implications of these two features, one can then see how, compatibly with both cases, the authority of law can be conditioned on an emotional bond between the law and its subjects.

Consider the first case. Plainly, in any civil society there will be some people who have no allegiance to the law. Outlaws, revolutionaries, and anarchists are examples that come immediately to mind. To explain their being subject to the law's authority, despite their lacking allegiance to it, one can point to the first feature, that legal authority is authority with respect to a collective. As such, the law has authority over each and every member of the collective. In this respect, the authority of law is like the authority a coach has over a team. Such authority depends on the team's having allegiance to the coach, and it has such allegiance just in case the bulk of the team's members have it. Accordingly, belonging to the team is sufficient for being under its coach's authority, given that enough of the team's members have an allegiance to her. Hence, even a rebellious member is subject to the coach's authority. Similarly, then, outlaws, revolutionaries, and anarchists come under the authority of law by virtue of their belonging to a society in which enough of the members have allegiance to law to secure its authority over the collective.

The second case is also common. Any legal system will have some officials who enforce the laws vigilantly, rigidly, and with a swagger, and officials of this sort invariably inspire fear and hatred among those subject to their authority. Indeed, where the official is the chief and most visible enforcer of the law, the sheriff of a small, rural town, say, or the marshal of some frontier territory, he may well be identified by those subject to his authority as "the law." In such cases especially, one might think, the fear and hatred the official inspires in the subjects are incompatible with their having allegiance to law, and therefore his authority could not be conditioned on such allegiance. Yet attention to the second feature shows that the subjects' fear and hatred of this official, even if universal, do not exclude their having allegiance to law. This is because the official's authority, like that of any magistrate or administrator, is delegated. In other words, however dominating he may be within his jurisdiction, he is not sovereign. His authority is not paramount. The subjects' fear and hatred of him do not therefore imply that they lack the emotional bond to law on which its authority is conditioned. For the emotional bond between the law and its subjects on which the law's authority is conditioned is a bond between the subjects and that which has paramount authority in the legal system. Consequently, the official's authority, being delegated, could be conditioned on such a bond despite the fear and hatred that the official inspires in those who fall within his jurisdiction.

II

These explanations, while they answer the initial criticisms of the thesis, that it cannot account for the law's authority over outlaws or its being administered by bullies, invite new ones, for it is evident that they echo ideas from the traditional positivist theory of law and consequently appear open to some of the same objections that showed that theory to be untenable. On the traditional theory, the theory developed by Jeremy Bentham and John Austin, law is a set of general commands that express the will of the sovereign, and the sovereign is that person or assembly of people whom the bulk of the subjects habitually obey and who habitually obeys no other person or assembly.[3] Accordingly, the law's authority is conditioned on a habit of obedience to the sovereign that those subject to the sovereign's authority have, and it represents the paramount authority in the legal system. The explanations of how it can be so conditioned compatibly with the law's having authority over outlaws and its being administered by bullies thus parallel the explanations of how it can be conditioned on an emotional bond between the law and its subjects compatibly with these two phenomena. And this parallel then suggests that some criticisms of the traditional positivist theory may well apply mutatis mutandis to the principal thesis of this paper.

Not all of these criticisms apply, however. Specifically, we can ignore those that fault the theory's doctrine that every legal system has a sovereign, a person or assembly of people whose general commands are the laws of that system.[4] These criticisms were perhaps the most damaging to the theory's

---

3. Jeremy Bentham, "Of Laws in General," H. L. A. Hart, ed. (London: Athlone, 1970), pp. 1, 10–13, 18–21, and A Fragment on Government (Cambridge: Cambridge University Press, 1988), pp. 39–43; and Austin, The Province of Jurisprudence Determined and the Uses of the Study of Jurisprudence (London: Weidenfeld and Nicolson, 1955), pp. 133–136, 193–196. For a comparative discussion of Bentham and Austin, see H. L. A. Hart, "Bentham's Of Laws in General," in his Essays on Bentham: Jurisprudence and Political Theory (Oxford: Oxford University Press, 1982), pp. 105–26.

4. See H. L. A. Hart, The Concept of Law (Oxford: Oxford University Press, 1961), pp. 70–76.

credibility since, as is clear on reflection, many modern legal systems are ill conceived of as the issue of a supreme legislator or legislative body. But the thesis of this paper corresponds only to the traditional positivist idea that the law's authority is conditioned on the subjects' habit of obedience, and that idea, though incorporated into the theory's doctrine about sovereignty, is separable from it. Once separated, it escapes the criticisms that showed the doctrine to be untenable. So too, then, does the thesis that the law's authority is conditioned on an emotional bond between the law and its subjects.

A different line of criticism concerns the failure of the traditional positivist theory to capture the difference between valid exercises of legal authority and exercises of brute force.[5] The use of threats and violence to coerce others to act as one demands exemplifies the latter. The issuance of directives in accordance with the criteria of an authoritative performance of one's office exemplifies the former. Traditional positivism could, to be sure, distinguish between valid and invalid exercises of legal authority by officials whose authority was delegated. Valid exercises truly represented the will of the sovereign; invalid exercises did not. But the theory lacked the conceptual resources for explaining what determined in the first instance authoritative expressions of the sovereign's will. Consequently, it could not explain the difference between the authoritative directives of a sovereign and mere demands backed by threats from a person or group used to having their way with those to whom the demands were issued.

The problem goes to the root of the traditional positivist program. The program originated in Bentham's opposition to the theory of natural rights (and natural law) on which Blackstone rested his exposition of English law.[6] On this theory, what explains the difference between the authoritative directives of a sovereign and mere coercive demands by some individual or group used to having their way is the consent to be governed that the subjects are supposed to have given the sovereign, at least tacitly. Bentham, impressed by Hume's critique of the idea that political authority derives from such consent, rejected this explanation.[7] He maintained, instead, that the subjects' habit of paying obedience to the sovereign and their continued disposition to obey were all the conditions necessary for establishing the sovereign's authority over the subjects. On this point, however, he was seriously mistaken. For to distinguish the sovereign's authoritative directives from mere coercive

---

5. The criticism is due to Hart, *The Concept of Law*, pp. 79–88.
6. Bentham, *A Fragment on Government*, pp. 93–95.
7. Ibid., p. 51. For Hume's critique, see *A Treatise of Human Nature*, bk. III, pt. 2, sec. 8.

demands by reference to the character of the subjects' responses to those directives, one must be able to explain the subjects' responses as rule-following behavior.[8] Otherwise, the relation of subjects to sovereign ceases to be political and becomes more like that of livestock to herdsman. Unfortunately for Bentham and the traditional positivist theory he developed, the concepts of habit and disposition are too thin to yield the needed explanation. One can use them to explain the subjects' responses as regular and predictable, but rule-following behavior is more than just regular and predictable behavior. It is conduct that flows from the reasons the rule being followed represents. It involves, then, the understanding of one's situation as calling, in virtue of the rule, for this conduct and thus making one liable to rebuke if one does not engage in it. Hence, to explain the subjects' responses as rule-following requires concepts whose import includes these cognitive states and liabilities. It requires concepts richer than those of habit and disposition.

The same line of criticism may then seem to apply to an account of the law's authority according to which it is conditioned on an emotional bond. It may seem to apply in this case because the concept of an emotional bond does not include, as part of its import, the cognitive states necessary to the production of rule-following behavior. Yet unlike the concept of habit, the concept of emotion, as is now widely recognized, includes cognition as part of its import. Emotions, that is, as is now widely recognized, are more than just inner sensations and pure feelings. Rather, they are intentional states of mind and as such contain thoughts.[9] Consequently, while the general concept of an emotional bond does not entail concepts of the cognitive states necessary to the production of rule-following behavior, one can assume that there are types of emotional bond whose concepts do. For example, while the type of emotional bond newborns form to their mothers soon after birth plainly does not imply such cognitive states, the type that children develop to their parents with the internalization of parental authority does. This latter type was

---

8. Hart, *The Concept of Law*, pp. 79–88.

9. Among the many works that have made and elaborated this point, see Anthony Kenny, *Action, Emotion and Will* (London: Routledge & Kegan Paul, 1963); Robert C. Solomon, *The Passions* (Garden City, N.Y.: Anchor/Doubleday, 1976); Jerome Neu, *Emotion, Thought and Therapy* (Berkeley: University of California Press, 1977); William Lyons, *Emotion* (Cambridge: Cambridge University Press, 1980); Ronald de Sousa, *The Rationality of Emotion* (Cambridge, MA: MIT Press, 1987); Patricia Greenspan, *Emotions and Reasons: An Inquiry into Emotional Justification* (London: Routledge, 1988); and O. H. Green, *The Emotions: A Philosophical Theory* (Dordrecht: Kluwer Academic Publishers, 1992). For a discussion of these and other cognitivist accounts of emotion, see my "Cognitivism in the Theory of Emotions," *Ethics* 104 (1994): 824–854, ch. 3 above.

brought to prominence by Freud through his theory of how a child acquires a conscience or superego, and it is assumed as well in other theories of moral development, such as Piaget's and Rawls's.[10] Thus, by specifying this type of emotional bond as the type between the subjects and the law on which the latter's authority is conditioned, one can make the thesis more definite so that it is free of whatever problems traditional positivism has in understanding the subjects' obedience to the sovereign as rule-following behavior. On this more definite formulation, then, the thesis avoids the line of criticism concerning traditional positivism's failure to capture the difference between authoritative expressions of sovereign will and mere coercive demands by a person or group whose power dominates all others in the community.

III

This line of criticism will be familiar to readers of H. L. A. Hart's *The Concept of Law*.[11] Hart advanced it by drawing attention to the difference between being obliged to do something and being obligated to do it. The former, Hart pointed out, is an apt expression for circumstances in which one is compelled or coerced to do the action, whereas the latter is an apt expression for circumstances that fall under a social rule requiring one to do that action, a rule that one cannot disregard without risking censure. Because traditional positivism lacked the conceptual resources for explaining the subject's obedience to the sovereign as rule-following behavior, Hart argued, the theory could not account for the subjects' obligation to obey the sovereign. What it offered as an account of this obligation was better understood as an account of the subjects' being obliged to obey the sovereign. Correspondingly, then, what it offered as an account of the sovereign's authority over the subjects was better understood as an account of mere domination by one person or group over a whole population. In other words, traditional positivism could not distinguish authoritative expressions of the sovereign's will from mere coercive demands by a person or group whose power dominates all others in the community. It could not account for sovereign authority.

10. See Sigmund Freud, *The Ego and the Id*, chs. 3 and 5, and *Civilization and Its Discontents*, chs. 7 and 8, in *The Standard Edition of the Complete Psychological Works of Sigmund Freud*, James Strachey, gen. ed. (London: Hogarth Press, 1969), v. 19, pp. 28–39, 48–59, and v. 21, pp. 123–145; Jean Piaget, *The Moral Judgment of the Child*, Marjorie Gabain, trans. (New York: Free Press, 1965); and John Rawls, *A Theory of Justice* (Cambridge, MA.: Belknap Press, 1971), ch. 8.

11. See especially Hart, *The Concept of Law*, pp. 79–88.

Hart then developed out of this criticism his own positivist theory of law.[12] On this theory, law is a complex system of social rules. At its foundation is a rule of recognition that officials in the system, particularly those who hold adjudicative office, use to determine the legal validity of the other rules. This rule of recognition is authoritative by virtue of its general acceptance by these officials. It defines their understanding of what in the system counts as law, and that they have this shared understanding is then sufficient, according to Hart, to give the rule its authority. Other rules are then authoritative by virtue of their meeting the criteria for validity specified in the rule of recognition at the foundation of the system. Thus, Hart's idea, so it appears, is to replace the traditional positivist notion of a sovereign as the fount in any legal system of the law's authority with the notion of a rule of recognition as, in virtue of its general acceptance by the officials of a legal system, the fount of that authority. Whether or not this idea represents Hart's considered view is uncertain. *The Concept of Law* contains conflicting passages.[13] But even if this idea weren't Hart's considered view, his theory certainly encourages it, and other prominent legal philosophers have endorsed it.[14]

The idea that the authority of law springs from the general acceptance of a rule of recognition by the officials who administer and adjudicate the law, an idea I'll call the mandarin-centered conception of legal authority, clearly excludes the thesis that the law's authority is conditioned on an emotional bond between law and its subjects. To be sure, the mandarin-centered conception presupposes an understanding of the subjects' obedience to law as rule-following behavior. For the conception is part of a jurisprudential theory that identifies law with a complex system of social rules, and this system comprises rules that the subjects follow. But a person can follow rules without having an emotional bond to them. Playing checkers, for instance, does not require any emotional attachment to the game: alphabetizing one's address book does not require any emotional attachment to the practice. Similarly, one can administer rules or adjudicate the conflicts they generate without having an emotional bond to them. So the opposition between the mandarin-centered conception and the principal thesis of this paper is more than just a matter of whether the primary conditions of the law's authority in a

12. See ibid., esp. pp. 97–120.
13. Ibid., p. 95; cf. p. 196.
14. See, e.g., Neil MacCormick, "The Concept of Law and *The Concept of Law*," in *The Autonomy of Law: Essays on Legal Positivism*, Robert P. George, ed. (Oxford: Clarendon Press, 1996), pp. 163–194; and Jules Coleman, "Authority and Reason," in *The Autonomy of Law: Essays on Legal Positivism*, Robert P. George, ed. (Oxford: Clarendon Press, 1996), pp. 287–319.

legal system consist of the attitudes and conduct of its officials or those of its subjects. It is also a matter of whether these conditions consist merely of a shared understanding of and disposition to apply the criteria determining what rules and actions count as legally valid in that system or include as well or instead an emotional bond to the law. The mandarin-centered conception of legal authority therefore challenges the very idea that an emotional bond to the law is necessary to the law's having authority over its subjects.

This challenge, however, can be met. While the mandarin-centered conception does capture a kind of authority with which law is invested, it is not a kind that is specific to law as a political institution. Rather, it is the kind that any system of social rules has for those who participate in the activity the system defines and regulates. The rules of competitive games, for instance, have such authority, which is typically manifested in the officiation of the games by umpires, referees, timekeepers, scorekeepers, and the like. The authority of the rules springs from a shared understanding these officials and the game's participants have of what the rules are or how they can be determined (e.g., by consulting Hoyle or an official rule book), and it does not depend on the officials' or the participants' having an emotional attachment to the game. Similarly, the authority of law that the mandarin-centered conception captures springs from a general acceptance of a rule of recognition by the officials responsible for administering and adjudicating the law and does not depend on either the officials' or the subjects' having an emotional attachment to the law. But to conceive of the law's authority in this way is to lose sight of its authority as or as part of a system of government. It is to ignore its essentially governmental character. In other words, the mandarin-centered conception fails to capture the kind of authority at issue in the dispute between traditional positivism and the natural rights/natural law theory in opposition to which traditional positivism developed. Once this equivocation on the kind of authority in question is shown, it then becomes clear that the mandarin-centered conception poses no real challenge to the idea that an emotional bond to the law is necessary to the law's having authority over its subjects.

The mistake in the mandarin-centered conception lies in its implicit assumption that law is no more than a system of social rules under which a form of human activity is organized and in which there are officials on whose judgments the felicity of the activity depends. Law, being essentially a system of government, is more than a system of such rules. Governing is more than officiating. The mistake in the conception thus consists in its using generic features of law to define one of its essential characteristics. What is more, this mistake is traceable to Hart's program of putting at the foundation of a legal system, in place of the sovereign of traditional positivism, the notion of which he had skewered, a rule of recognition commonly accepted by the officials who administer and adjudicate the law.[15] For this replacement presupposes that Hart's notion of such a rule and the traditional positivist notion of a sovereign are at the same theoretical level, that they yield alternative theoretical explanations of the same legal phenomena, and this presupposition is false. The former notion is in fact decidedly more abstract than the latter. In particular, there is nothing distinctively political in Hart's notion of a rule of recognition, whereas the traditional positivist notion of a sovereign is a distinctively political one. As a result, whereas the traditional positivist notion contains elements for explaining law as a system of government, Hart's notion does not.

On the traditional positivist notion, the sovereign is politically superior to the subjects in the sense that the sovereign's will, as it is expressed by the sovereign's general commands, dominates the will of each subject. Put differently, the sovereign's political superiority consists in the sovereign's setting ends for the subjects, through the laws the sovereign issues, that are superior to the ends the subjects set for themselves. In this way, traditional positivism explains government of the subjects by the sovereign and so law as a system of government. By contrast, the notion of a rule of recognition commonly accepted by officials responsible for administering and adjudicating the law contains nothing that implies the superiority of the ends set by laws to the ends that those subject to the laws set for themselves and hence contains nothing to explain law as a system of government. To be sure, the traditional positivist explanation of law as a system of government rests on a doctrine about sovereignty that cannot survive criticism, as we noted in section II.[16] But the point holds nonetheless: to understand law as a system of government requires that one understand it as setting ends for the subjects that are superior to the ends that they set for themselves, and traditional positivism would afford such an understanding if its explanation were sound, whereas there is not even the possibility of arriving at such an understanding by conceiving of law as founded on a rule of recognition. The authority of law, then, entails the authority to set ends for the subjects that they do not set for themselves and that dominate many of those ends that they do set for themselves. The law's authority in this respect is the authority it has as a system of government. Such authority, it is important to keep in mind, is distinct from the power of government to coerce obedience, for the same arguments that bring out the difference between being obligated and being obliged apply as well to the difference between having authority and having power. Consequently,

15. Hart, *The Concept of Law*, pp. 97–107.
16. See pp. 140–143.

while the power of government to coerce obedience is conditioned on the subjects' vulnerabilities to harm and capacities for fear, the authority of law must be conditioned on something more. This additional factor, moreover, as the argument of this section has shown, cannot be the acceptance of a rule of recognition by the officials responsible for administering and adjudicating the law. Rather, it must be the subjects' allegiance to the law, their willingness to be governed by the law apart from their being vulnerable to the punitive sanctions by which it is enforced and capable of fearing those sanctions. It must, in short, be the subjects' willingness to subordinate their own ends to the ends the law sets for them. Hence, a defense of the principal thesis of this paper becomes a defense of the view that what explains the subjects' willingness to subordinate their own ends to the ends that the law sets for them is an emotional bond between them and the law.

IV

Let us call this view the emotion-based account of the law's authority. Fully specified, it is the view that an emotional bond between the subjects and the law of the type exemplified by the bond children develop to their parents with the internalization of parental authority explains the subjects' willingness to subordinate their own ends to the ends the law sets for them. That such an emotional bond can explain this disposition is evident from the explanation its prototype supplies of a like disposition children acquire through socialization. For through socialization, specifically, the internalization of parental authority during the child's early years, the child becomes sensitive to the wrongfulness of disobeying its parents and liable to feelings of guilt and bad conscience over such disobedience, where before the process occurred, the child was merely cognizant of the dangers of disobedience and liable to anxieties about them and to fear of being found out when it did disobey. And similarly, through the same process, respect comes to characterize the child's attitude toward its parents and the rules and dictates they issue, where previously the principal motives of the child's obedience were wholly instrumental: a desire to receive praise and affection for being "good" and a fear of the anger, unpleasantness, and loss of love that come with being found "naughty."[17] These new motives of conscience and respect that the child

---

17. For further discussion of these aspects of moral development, see my "Love, Guilt, and the Sense of Justice" and "Remarks on Some Difficulties in Freud's Theory of Moral Development," both of which are reprinted in my *The Sources of Moral Agency: Essays in Moral Psychology and Freudian Theory* (Cambridge: Cambridge University Press, 1996), pp. 39–93.

thus acquires constitute a disposition on the child's part to do right even at the cost of forgoing pleasures it would otherwise have happily consumed or experiencing discomforts it would otherwise have instinctively avoided. This disposition is analogous to the disposition to obey the law that legal subjects must have as a condition of the law's authority, and hence one can plausibly suppose that the same type of emotional bond that explains the former explains the latter.

In addition, it is plausible to suppose that the former is not only an analogue of the latter but also its precursor. Socialization, after all, is a developmental process. Thus, the disposition to subordinate one's own ends to the ends the law sets for one arises out of precedent dispositions, the earliest of which is the disposition, acquired when very young, to respect the rules and dictates of one's parents and to feel guilt and bad conscience over disobeying them. In view of this plausible supposition, then, we can deepen the emotion-based account of the law's authority by embedding it within an overall account of this process that generalizes its chief idea. Accordingly, the process depends on the emotional bond one forms to one's parents with the internalization of their authority and on the subsequent bonds one forms to various other people and institutions as one gets older. These are, specifically, the people and institutions to whose authority one becomes subject as one moves from the context of one's family to those of school, church, work, and recreational and civic organizations. Hence, on this account of the socialization process in question, the emotional bonds one forms to one's parents and to the subsequent authorities and authoritative structures to which one becomes subject as one gets older explain the successively more mature dispositions to submit to the rules and dictates of these authorities and authoritative structures, including, in particular, the disposition to subordinate one's own ends to the ends the law sets.

This account squares with the theories of moral development noted earlier, Freud's and Rawls's, in particular, that identify the initial acquisition of conscience with the internalization of parental authority.[18] On Freud's theory, the emotional bond one develops to one's parents with this internalization is at the root of the subsequent bonds one forms to other authorities and authoritative structures and is therefore the ultimate explanation of all the dispositions to submit to the rules and dictates of authority one acquires. For on Freud's theory, the emotional bond to one's parents that develops in the formation of a conscience, a superego, survives intact in one's unconscious,

18. See n. 10 and also the essays cited in n. 17.

and it then influences significantly, though unconsciously, the attitudes one takes and the feelings one experiences toward later authorities such as teachers, pastors, bosses, public officials, and the institutions they represent. By contrast, Rawls's theory does not explain these dispositions as products of unconscious material and mechanisms or as rooted in the emotional bond one forms to one's parents with the internalization of their authority. Instead, it assumes that the same factors that produced this bond are present as well in the wider social contexts into which one is introduced as one gets older, and consequently, similar emotional bonds to the people and institutions who bear comparable authority in those contexts are formed as one comes to understand and appreciate their role in one's life. Each of these bonds then explains the corresponding disposition one acquires to submit to the rules and dictates of the relevant authority. Either of these two contrasting theories of moral development thus represents a substantial elaboration of the emotion-based account. Either provides substantial theoretical support for it.

V

However substantial this theoretical support, the account may still fall short when compared with alternatives. We must consider, then, how well it stacks up against the competition. It is not possible, however, to examine all of the leading alternatives. I will, instead, consider two. One is due to H. L. A. Hart, the other to Joseph Raz. Hart's represents a volition-based account. Raz's represents a reason-based one. While there might, of course, be some other volition-based or reason-based account that offers stiffer competition, this possibility should seem remote once Hart's and Raz's are presented and examined. Theirs are representative of the two classes, and examination of them, though insufficient as a complete defense of the emotion-based account, should be sufficient as a presumptive one.

To determine how well the emotion-based account stacks up against Hart's and Raz's, let us consider whether either of theirs better fits the main features of the law's authority. Four have surfaced in the course of our clarifying and expounding the emotion-based account. First, the law's authority is authority with respect to a community. Second, either the law has paramount authority in that community or it represents the will of the individual or assembly who has paramount authority. Third, the authority of law presupposes that the subjects' compliance with the law is rule-following behavior. And fourth, the authority of law is the authority of government and, as such, depends on the willingness of the subjects to subordinate their own ends to the ends the law sets for them. The emotion-based account will then prove to be the superior account if it can be shown that neither Hart's nor Raz's fits these four features as well as it does. And for this purpose, it will suffice to consider how well they fit the first and the fourth.

On the account due to Hart, which he gave in *The Concept of Law*, legal authority is conditioned on voluntary compliance by those subject to it, or at least enough of them to solidify its force.[19] Thus, he wrote in the penultimate chapter, "It is true, as we have already emphasized in discussing the need for and the possibility of sanctions, that if a system of rules is to be imposed by force on any, there must be a sufficient number who accept it voluntarily. Without their voluntary cooperation, thus creating authority, the coercive power of law and government cannot be established."[20] Clearly, the account fits the first of our test features well. Its explanation of the law's authority as authority with respect to a community is the same as the explanation an emotion-based account yields, except that it appeals to voluntary cooperation with law where the emotion-based account appeals to an emotional bond to law. If the bulk of the membership voluntarily cooperate with the law, then the law's authority over the community and so each of its members is secured.

Where Hart's account runs into trouble is in its explanation of the fourth feature. Because the voluntariness of an action does not depend on its motive, voluntary cooperation with the law by sufficiently many subjects can, on Hart's account, establish the law's authority regardless of the motives from which their cooperation springs, a point Hart himself makes a few paragraphs after the passage quoted above.[21] It follows, then, that, on his account, law would have authority over its subjects even if all those who cooperated voluntarily with it did so solely out of calculative self-interest, reckoning that the costs of noncooperation were not worth the benefits. But to act solely out of calculative self-interest means that one acts for one's own ends and does not subordinate them to ends that another or others have set for one. Hence, the fourth feature eludes Hart's account. This defect in the account is made apparent in a passing remark Hart makes, when he characterizes the voluntary cooperators on whose cooperation legal authority is conditioned as having allegiance to law and thus implies that their allegiance is the source

---

19. See Hart, *The Concept of Law*, pp. 196–197. Hart may have subsequently abandoned this account in view of Raz's criticisms. See "Commands and Authoritative Legal Reasons" in his *Essays on Bentham*, pp. 241–268.

20. Hart, *The Concept of Law*, p. 196; italics in original.

21. Ibid., pp. 198–199.

of law's authority.[22] Purely calculative cooperators do not have allegiance to anyone or anything save themselves.

Of course, traditionally, political philosophers have maintained that the subjects' voluntary cooperation with the law establishes its authority on the grounds that such cooperation implies their consent to being governed by law and that such consent confers authority on the law. Hobbes, for instance, cited voluntary submission to the sovereign as a sign of such consent: in virtue of such submission one becomes a subject of the sovereign's authority, whereas refusal to submit would leave one essentially a captive or slave.[23] And Locke took voluntary enjoyment of the law's protection and its other benefits as signifying tacit consent to its governance.[24] On these accounts, the subjects' voluntary cooperation with the law establishes their allegiance to it, for the accounts take voluntary cooperation with the law to imply consent to its governance regardless of the motives from which that cooperation springs, and the consent then establishes the subjects' allegiance in virtue of implying a willingness to subordinate their own ends to the ends the law sets for them. Hence, these traditional accounts, unlike Hart's, fit the fourth feature. But for well-known reasons they are untenable. In particular, the thesis that voluntary cooperation with law implies consent to the law's governance has been thoroughly thrashed.[25] Hart's account avoids this thrashing, but at the cost of being disabled from explaining the subjects' allegiance.

Let us turn, then, to Raz's account.[26] This account is much more complex than Hart's. Its basic idea is that legal authority is conditioned on an understanding of law as a system of norms that purports to supply those it governs with reasons for action. Raz divides reasons for action into two kinds: interest-dependent and interest-independent.[27] An interest-dependent reason is a fact that weighs in favor of a person's taking a certain course of action because doing so would, on account of this fact, promote his or her interests. An interest-independent reason is a fact that weighs in favor of a person's taking a certain course of action because doing so is, on account of this fact,

22. Ibid., p. 196.
23. Hobbes, *Leviathan*, ch. 22, pars. 10 and 14.
24. Locke, *The Second Treatise of Government*, §119.
25. For a clear and thorough statement of the case against taking the subjects' consent to be the basis for political authority, see A. John Simmons, *Moral Principles and Political Obligation* (Princeton: Princeton University Press, 1979), pp. 57–100.
26. Joseph Raz, *The Authority of Law: Essays on Law and Morality* (Oxford: Clarendon Press, 1979), pp. 3–33; and *The Morality of Freedom* (Oxford: Clarendon Press, 1986), pp. 23–69.
27. Joseph Raz, *Practical Reason and Norms* (Princeton: Princeton University Press, 1990; reprint from 1975), pp. 28–35.

rationally required independently of his or her interests. On Raz's view, all interest-independent reasons are moral reasons, and thus, in effect, he divides reasons for action into the prudential and the moral. We can ignore this thesis, however, the thesis that all interest-independent reasons are moral reasons. Its purpose is to show how legal authority makes a claim to moral authority and thus how Hart's famous thesis about the separability of law and morality can be challenged. We can thus regard it as a supplement to Raz's account of how the law's authority derives from its purporting to supply its subjects with certain interest-independent reasons for action. It is this account that we should examine.

Raz draws this account from his rather elaborate theory of reasons for action. An important element in this theory is the idea of second-order reasons for action. These fall into two types: reasons to act on certain reasons, and reasons to ignore certain reasons on which one has to act. Thus, if I offer to help you whenever you need it, as I might, say, if you were my neighbor and you or your wife had just given birth to triplets, then my offer is itself a reason for me to act on your requests for help, which is to say, a reason to act on the reasons your requests represent. And if I promise to drive you home right after a meeting, then I have reason to ignore the reasons I might come to have to do something else after the meeting—such as accepting a subsequent invitation to go to a movie—that would prevent me from doing what I promised. The promise, in fact, should be seen as generating both a first-order reason to drive you home and a second-order reason to ignore reasons to act in ways that would prevent me from driving you home. In this respect, it generates what Raz calls a protected reason for action. Raz then, with some additional complications, which need not concern us, explains having authority over someone as being in a position both to generate for that person protected reasons for action and to eliminate such reasons from the set of reasons that person has to act. Accordingly, the authority of law consists in law's being for its subjects both a generator of protected reasons for action and an eliminator of such reasons.

Raz's account clearly captures the fourth feature of the law's authority. To generate for someone a protected reason for some action Ø is to give that person both a first-order reason to Ø and a second-order reason to ignore reasons for doing things that would prevent him from Øing. In other words, it is to set a rationally required end for the person and to give him reason to subordinate his other ends to this end. Because the subjects are rational agents and therefore responsive to reasons, their recognition of the law as a generator of protected reasons for action amounts to a willingness to subordinate their ends to the ends the law sets for them. Thus, Raz's characterization of the law's authority as consisting in the law's generating for its subjects protected reasons for action fits the fourth feature well.

How well Raz's account fits the first feature, however, is another matter. Uncertainty lies in how it explains the law's authority over outlaws, revolutionaries, and anarchists. One possibility would be to follow the same pattern of explanation that the emotion-based account and Hart's account use. Accordingly, law would have authority over a community as a result of its generating protected reasons for the bulk of that community, and it would therefore have authority over outlaws, revolutionaries, and anarchists in virtue of their belonging to this community. Of course, the question would then arise, why does law generate protected reasons for most members of the community but not for these renegades? And a natural answer would be that the latter lacked the civic interests and public spiritedness that the former had and that disposed them to see the laws of their community as reasons for action. On this answer, however, facts about legislation—for example, that the legislature had banned private ownership of bazookas—would be protected reasons relative to the agent's interests, desires, and emotional dispositions. They would, that is, be interest-dependent reasons. Raz's reason-based account would, therefore, turn out to be merely an emotion-based account dressed up in an elaborate theory of reasons for action.

This, to be sure, is not what Raz intends. Rather, he sees these protected reasons as interest-independent and therefore as reasons for all subjects and not just for those who are civic minded. His view rests on two assumptions. First, Raz assumes that if law has authority over its subjects, then that authority is legitimate. Second, he assumes that reasons generated by the law in any legal system in which the law's authority is legitimate are interest-independent. Accordingly, he can explain the law's authority over outlaws, revolutionaries, and anarchists, for given these assumptions, if the law has authority over any of its subjects, then it has authority over all of them in virtue of the interest-independent reasons it generates. The legitimacy of the authority ensures this result.

These two assumptions thus form the backbone of Raz's account. Since neither is self-evident, their defense becomes crucial to its cogency. Raz defends the first on the grounds that the relevant notion of authority is essentially normative. To say that x has authority over y in normative discourse implies that y has an obligation to obey x, and to attribute an obligation to someone in such discourse is to say in effect that, other things equal, the person ought to do the act or acts that fulfillment of the obligation requires. So attributing authority over y to x in a normative sense implies that, other things equal, y ought to obey x. Yet this implication would not follow, Raz argues, unless one assumed in attributing authority to x that the authority was legiti-mate. As Raz sometimes puts it, to make a claim to authority over someone is to make a claim to legitimate authority. Thus, taking the notion of authority relevant to the philosophical question of the nature of the law's authority as normative, Raz concludes that the law's authority over its subjects is legiti-mate if it indeed has authority over them.

Raz defends the second assumption on the ground that what qualifies the authority of someone or some institution as legitimate is the person's or insti-tution's fulfilling well the purposes for which they have authority. In the area of government, Raz maintains, the purpose for having authority is to generate for the governed certain kinds of reasons for action that in a population of rational agents would help significantly to reduce conflict among them and to facilitate their cooperation and thus bring about its benefits. These are interest-independent reasons, and consequently, Raz concludes, if the law's authority is legitimate, then the law is fulfilling well its purposes, which is to say, the reasons it generates for the subjects are interest-independent.

The question, then, of how well Raz's account fits the first feature comes down to whether these defenses are sound. Both, moreover, must be sound for the account to be cogent. Yet neither, in fact, is. Consider the first. Its pivotal thesis is that a claim to authority over someone is necessarily a claim to legitimate authority. If this thesis were true, then whenever a claim to authority over someone was made, it would make sense to ask whether the authority claimed was legitimate. Without doubt, it does make sense to ask this question when the authority claimed is delegated. Delegated authority is authority possessed by virtue of a right that has been conferred on the per-son or institution claiming to have that authority. Because one can always ask whether the conferral actually took place or whether the transaction it consisted in was valid or licit, it always makes sense to ask whether the authority claimed is legitimate. It also makes sense to ask this question when the authority, though not delegated, is conferred on the basis, say, of certain qualifications like being the eldest male child in a hereditary monarchy in which primogeniture is the rule of succession. In this case, it makes sense because one can always ask whether the person claiming the authority truly has the qualifications. The problem, though, is that not every case of author-ity over someone is a case of delegated or conferred authority, and in cases in which it is neither delegated nor conferred, it does not make sense to ask the question.

For instance, a believer who wondered whether God's authority over humankind was legitimate would be betraying some serious confusion about God, as if God ruled the universe by a right he had somehow acquired. God's claim to authority is not a claim to legitimate authority. Legitimacy is not something God needs to claim. Likewise, a parent who asserts her authority over her obstinate five-year-old with some such remark as "Because I'm your mother!" is not claiming legitimate authority over her child. What would be the point of that? It would, after all, have to be a very precocious five-year-old who could wonder whether its parents' authority was legitimate. In the small child's world, its parents have authority absolutely and not by virtue of custo-dial rights, say, that some state has granted them. The pivotal thesis, then, in Raz's defense of the first assumption is false.[28]

Raz's defense of the second assumption is no less defective. To hold, as he does, that the legitimacy of authority is a matter of how well the authority in question fulfills the purpose for which it exists is to treat the question of an authority's legitimacy as equivalent to the question of its rational justification. Specifically, given Raz's account of the purpose of governing authority, it is to treat the question of legitimacy as equivalent to the question of whether the subjects of this authority would be rationally justified in obeying it. Yet it is far from evident that a claim to legitimate authority over others is typically a claim to authority obedience to which would be rationally justified. It is not likely, for example, that when the House of York and the House of Lancaster were contesting which descendant of Edward III was the legitimate heir to the English throne, they were concerned with whose authority it would be more rational for the subjects to obey.[29] Sometimes questions of legitimacy turn on conformity to principles or rules that in themselves have no rational justification. Their normative force in a population consists in their having for generations been broadly accepted. Customs frequently have normative force in a society by virtue of broad acceptance by its members and a long his-tory of being kept and followed, and where they concern the determination of governing authorities, as the customs on which hereditary monarchies are

---

28. Of course, Raz could remake the defense by withdrawing this thesis and asserting instead that the law's authority was conferred or delegated authority, for if its authority were con-ferred or delegated, then its claim to authority over its subjects would be a claim to legitimate authority. But to make this assertion would be to deny the second feature of the law's authority. Moreover, it would require stretching the concepts of conferral and delegation far beyond the normal limits of their use. It is not, for these reasons, a plausible fallback.

29. Philip Soper, in "Legal Theory and the Claim of Authority," *Philosophy & Public Affairs* 18 (1989): 209–239, gives a similar example in criticism of Raz's account: "Second, it would seem to be one consequence of [Raz's] justification thesis that authority loses its legitimacy whenever a particular legislature is found to fall below the average in practical reasoning abil-ity—a situation that, at least in the United States, cannot be ruled out in advance even in high levels of government let alone local city councils" (p. 226).

founded do, the question of legitimacy is not answered by considerations of whether obedience to the authority would be rationally justified. Raz's mistake thus consists in confusing the question of legitimacy with that of rational justification.

One can trace this mistake to Raz's view that normative discourse about authority and obligation is always resolvable into discourse about reasons for action. Raz holds this view because he thinks any practical judgment of the form x ought to $\emptyset$ implies a judgment of the form x has a reason to $\emptyset$.[30] Hence, once he sets out the logical relation noted above between attributing to x authority over y in the normative sense and holding that y ought to obey x, the view immediately follows.[31] And because Raz thinks the relation holds only if the attribution of authority in the normative sense implies the attribution of legitimate authority, he is led to think that establishing the legitimacy of x's authority over y amounts to determining that y has reason to obey x. Or in other words, the question of an authority's legitimacy is the same as the question of its rational justification. The ultimate source of this mistaken identification, then, is Raz's thesis that any practical judgment of the form x ought to $\emptyset$ implies a judgment of the form x has a reason to $\emptyset$.

To see why this thesis is at the root of his mistake, one must first recognize an important ambiguity in practical judgments of the form x ought to $\emptyset$. On the one hand, they may be hypothetical, in which case their validity depends on x's having a desire or interest whose satisfaction would result from x's $\emptyset$ing. On the other, they may be categorical, in which case their validity is independent of x's desires and interests. "You ought to take an umbrella," for instance, is typically asserted hypothetically, for it is typically offered as advice to someone who it is assumed wants to stay dry. "You ought to give more to charity" is typically asserted categorically, for typically one thinks charitable action is called for by the external circumstances of the person to whom this directive is addressed and without regard to that person's desires or interests.[32] There is no question that one can always interpret a practical judgment of the form x ought to $\emptyset$ as x has a reason to $\emptyset$ when the judgment is understood to be a hypothetical one. Because the judgment in this case is made on the assumption that x has a desire or interest that would be satisfied by x's $\emptyset$ing, the interpretation is uncontroversial. But Raz cannot take the practical

---

30. Raz, *The Authority of Law*, p. 12; see also *Practical Reason and Norms*, pp. 15–33.
31. Ibid., p. 303.
32. On this distinction, see Philippa Foot, "Morality as a System of Hypothetical Imperatives," in her *Virtues and Vices* (Berkeley: University of California Press, 1978), pp. 157–173.

judgments the attribution of authority to the law implies as hypothetical, for then their validity will depend on the subjects' having certain desires or interests, and some outlaws may not have them. In other words, he cannot take these judgments as hypothetical without making the first feature of the law's authority inexplicable on his account. Hence, he must take them as categorical. And at this point, his mistake in identifying the question of an authority's legitimacy with that of its rational justification becomes obvious.

After all, it is not uncontroversial whether one can always interpret a practical judgment of the form x ought to $\emptyset$ as x has a reason to $\emptyset$ when the judgment is understood to be a categorical one. Quite the contrary. Such an interpretation is tantamount to saying that x cannot be fully aware of his circumstances and also utterly indifferent to $\emptyset$ing unless x is to some degree irrational, and opinion sharply and deeply divides on whether mere failure to take a positive attitude toward doing an action when one lacks the desire for or interest in any end the action would achieve can ever be irrational.[33] The question has been hotly debated since Hume's famous denial in his *Treatise*.[34] Nor does one need to take sides on this question to see Raz's mistake. Plainly, whether some person's or institution's authority over others is legitimate is not always a controversial question, and even when it is, the controversy does not typically concern philosophical uncertainties about the reason-giving force of categorical "ought's." On Raz's account, by contrast, the question is always controversial and always controversial in this way.

Hart explained normative discourse about authority, obligation, rights, and other features of law by distinguishing between internal and external statements.[35] When one makes the former, Hart declared, one makes them from an internal point of view. It is the view of someone who accepts the rules and standards the law comprises as guides to conduct. When one makes the latter, Hart continued, one makes them from an external point of view. This is the view of an outside observer, someone who notes facts about the legal system of the group he is observing but who does not accept its rules and standards as guides to conduct. It makes sense therefore to construe Raz's view that normative discourse about authority and obligation is always resolvable into discourse about reasons for action as intended as either a replacement for or a supplement to Hart's explanation. That is, it makes sense to take Raz to have

33. See Bernard Williams, "Internal and External Reasons," in his *Moral Luck* (Cambridge: Cambridge University Press, 1981), pp. 101–113.
34. Hume, *A Treatise of Human Nature*, bk. II, pt. 3, sec. 3.
35. See Hart, *The Concept of Law*, p. 99.

advanced this view either on the assumption that the subjects' responsiveness to interest-independent reasons, rather than some internal point of view, is the key to explaining normative discourse about authority and obligation in the law or on the assumption that such responsiveness explains what Hart meant by an internal point of view. On either interpretation, however, the view would fail. It falls short, as we've seen, of explaining the normative force that attributions of authority to law carry.

An emotion-based account of the law's authority does better. Because the internal point of view on Hart's explanation is the view of people committed to the law as a guide to their conduct, one can plausibly assume that some emotional bond to the law lies behind this commitment. Hart's internal point of view, in other words, can plausibly be understood as the product of an emotional bond to the law. On an emotion-based account, then, for those who have such a bond to the law, that the law has authority is a reason for obeying it, whereas for those—like outlaws, revolutionaries, and anarchists—who do not, it need not be a reason for obedience. This understanding of the normative force that attributions of authority to law carry is surely more plausible than one on which either outlaws, revolutionaries, and anarchists suffer from some cognitive defect, some ignorance of their circumstances or deficiency in their reasoning, or the authority of the law they oppose is illegitimate. Here too, then, in the matter of explaining normative discourse about the law's authority and the subjects' correlative obligations, the emotion-based account appears more cogent than a reason-based account such as Raz's.

VI

When the laws of Athens in Plato's *Crito* address Socrates and assert their authority over him, an emotional bond between Socrates and the law becomes evident.[36] The laws, in reproving Socrates for contemplating disobedience, remind him that they are his parents and that the disobedience he is contemplating would be a worse wrong than dishonoring his parents. Their metaphors and comparisons unmistakably show the strength and type of bond that exists between the laws and Socrates. This great work on the authority of law, with its passionate speech in favor of fealty to law, no less than Kafka's novel, testifies dramatically to the thesis I have defended in this paper.

36. Plato, *Crito*, 50a–54d.

7

All Kinds of Guilt

Why can a dog feel fear but not remorse? Would it be right to say, "Because he can't talk"?

— Ludwig Wittgenstein, *Zettel* §518

Wittgenstein's questions express two characteristically human conceits. One concerns our capacities for moral feeling, the other our possession of language. Wittgenstein, one might easily think, in joining these conceits as he does, is suggesting that the capacities for moral feeling presuppose the possession of language. It is tempting, that is, to read Wittgenstein here as first drawing our attention to affective capacities special to human beings and then making the point that possessing language is necessary to the realization of these capacities, much as the great thinkers of the rationalist tradition, in the interest of distinguishing human from animal psychology, traced these same capacities to the operations of reason. I suspect, though, that this is not Wittgenstein's point, that his point, rather, is that moral feelings require as their context certain practices, certain forms of life, participation in which is not possible if one doesn't possess language. If I'm right, then his point tells us less about the difference between human and animal psychology than one might have initially thought. For the same point could be made by asking why a dog can fear his master but not a plunging stock market and whether it would be right to say, "Because he can't invest." Financial fears too require as their context certain practices, certain forms of life, participation in which is not possible if one can't own property. But this

159

observation throws little light on human psychology and how it differs from that of other animals.

Wittgenstein uses remorse to make his point, but he might just as well have used guilt. At any rate, it is now common in moral philosophy to take guilt as the principal moral feeling expressing bad conscience. Thus, if we accept Wittgenstein's point, the one I am crediting him with having made at *Zettel* §518, then attributing feelings of guilt to someone implies, as their context, certain practices, certain forms of life, to which the use of language is essential. These are moral practices, of course. They consist, in particular, in the regulation of human conduct and human relations by requirements, rules, dictates, judgments, and other verbal expressions of a governing, moral authority. Guilt is the appropriate feeling one experiences in response to one's having ignored these requirements, broken these rules, disobeyed these dictates, etc., provided that one recognizes their authority and the authority of whoever stands behind or delivers them. This last proviso is crucial. Prisoners of war, after all, though subject to the rules of the prison camps in which they're held captive, are not prone to feel guilt over violating those rules. And their failure to feel guilt over these violations is not in the least incongruous or cause to wonder about their moral character, for it is perfectly in order for them not to recognize the rules' authority or that of the rules' enforcers. Guilt, then, is a feeling in which allegiance to the governing authority one has disobeyed is shown at the very same time as one acknowledges one's disobedience to that authority. The object of the feeling is one's disobedience; its required context is a practice, a form of life, whose requirements and rules one accepts as having moral authority.

Herbert Morris, in his provocative and poignant essay "Nonmoral Guilt," invites us to consider examples of guilt in which nothing answering to the idea of disobedience to authority appears to precipitate the emotion or serve as its object.[1] Guilt felt over a wish for another's misfortune, survivor's guilt and other feelings of guilt over good fortune that has come one's way and that has eluded or been denied others who are no less deserving, and guilt felt over historical wrongs committed by one's community or nation are the experiences Morris focuses on. The feelings in these experiences, he maintains, need not be regarded as products of irrational, groundless, or mistaken belief, or as symptoms of some pathological condi-

1. In *Responsibility, Character, and the Emotions: New Essays in Moral Psychology,* Ferdinand Schoeman, ed. (Cambridge: Cambridge University Press, 1988), pp. 220–241.

tion. Nor need they be regarded as manifestations of the self-deception that occurs when one displaces distressful feelings onto a convenient object in order to keep from having to acknowledge their true object. The experiences are thus offered as examples of appropriate feelings of guilt, despite their subjects' having done nothing wrong and being well aware of this. As such, they imply a kind of guilt that a person can incur even though he is not to blame for having done something wrong. Morris draws this inference for the purpose of refuting the prevailing view in moral philosophy that the only guilt a person ever truly incurs, leaving aside legal guilt, which is essentially a technical analog, is guilt that consists in being culpably responsible for wrongdoing. Characterizing this as moral guilt, Morris holds, on the basis of the examples he adduces, that there is nonmoral guilt as well.

The prevailing view in moral philosophy, the view that Morris criticizes, is not one I would wish to defend. At the same time, his examples appear to challenge the view I've drawn out of Wittgenstein's point, and the defensibility of this view does interest me. The Wittgensteinian view, if I may call it that, implies that feelings of guilt are necessarily moral feelings in the sense that they require, as their context, a practice that consists in the regulation of human conduct and human relations by requirements, rules, dictates, judgments, and other verbal expressions of a governing, moral authority. That is, they are necessarily moral feelings in the sense that one can understand them as feelings of guilt only against a background that comprises a moral practice of this sort. Morris's examples would then defeat this view if in fact the absence in them of anything answering to the idea of disobedience to authority showed that some feelings of guilt were understandable as such apart from this background. In this event, they would count as nonmoral feelings and thus, being also appropriate feelings, would be the basis for holding that there was nonmoral guilt in a different, thinner sense from the one Morris defined. The guilt would be nonmoral in this sense, for it would be incurred outside of any moral practice. The question, then, that interests me is whether Morris's examples count as nonmoral feelings of guilt in this different, thinner sense, whether, that is, they defeat the Wittgensteinian view.[2]

---

2. I call this a 'thinner' sense since what qualifies the feelings as nonmoral is the absence of a certain context, namely, that of moral practice, rather than the absence of their subject's being in a certain condition, namely, that of being culpably responsible for wrongdoing, which the subject could not be in unless that context also obtained. I don't mean to imply anything more than this difference in calling it a 'thinner' sense.

One can see the issue the question raises more sharply by comparing different accounts of how a child develops a capacity for feelings of guilt. Consider, for instance, Freud's.[3] On Freud's account, a child develops this capacity in acquiring a conscience, and it acquires a conscience through a process by which it internalizes parental figures as a way of resolving severe emotional conflict in its feelings toward its parents, a conflict that invariably arises out of the normal familial circumstances of early childhood. For Freud a conscience is an internal authority that makes stringent demands on its possessor, prods him to comply with those demands, and punishes him with severe criticism and reproach when he fails. Its model is the parental authority of early childhood, exaggerated and distorted by childish fantasy and fear, and accordingly, the internalization of parental figures that yields a conscience is to be understood as internalization of that authority. As Freud put it, conscience forms in the child when external authority becomes internal. On his theory, this development takes place with the formation in the child's psyche of a separate mental agency, the superego. The superego functions as a conscience, and feelings of guilt (a sense of guilt) are then defined, using Freud's theoretical constructs, as feelings that express tension between the ego and the superego. Thus, it can be seen that, on this account, feelings of guilt are conceived of against a background of subjection and resistance to governing authority.

Of course, Freud's is not the only account within psychoanalytic theory. There is also and notably Melanie Klein's.[4] On this account, a child develops a capacity for feelings of guilt before it comes to know and respond to its parents as governing authorities. Specifically, the child develops this capacity in infancy as a result of its coming to love its parents, particularly, its mother. The development of love alone, on Klein's account, predisposes the child to feelings of guilt, for the child's love implies both a powerful regard for its parents as objects of value and perfection and an abiding concern for preserving them and its bond to them. Accordingly, the child is set to feel guilt over its own aggressive and destructive actions toward its parents, actions to which

---

3. See, in particular, *The Ego and the Id*, ch. III, and *Civilization and Its Discontents*, ch. VII. For details of this explanation, see my "Remarks on Some Difficulties in Freud's Theory of Moral Development," *International Review of Psycho-Analysis* 11 (1984): 207–225; reprinted in my *The Sources of Moral Agency: Essays in Moral Psychology and Freudian Theory* (Cambridge: Cambridge University Press, 1996), pp. 65–93.

4. See, in particular, "A Contribution to the Psychogenesis of Manic-Depressive States," in Melanie Klein, *Love, Guilt and Reparation & Other Works 1921–1945* (New York: Dell Publishing Co., 1975), pp. 262–289.

it is inclined owing to a hostility toward them that is born of the distress and anger it feels when its needs and desires go unmet. In truth, though, these actions take place mostly if not exclusively in the child's fantasies, and their parental targets are likewise fantasized figures. Nonetheless, the actions give rise to feelings of guilt since the child at this early age is oblivious of the distinction between reality and fantasy. In its mind, it has truly attacked its parents and consequently feels responsible for damaging or destroying that which it holds most dear and is most concerned to preserve. Feelings of guilt and the desire to repair the damage and restore what was lost thus ensue. On Klein's account, the child reacts to its being responsible for this damage and loss with rage against itself and grief over the loss, a combination that makes for powerful feelings of guilt characterized by an urge to repair the damage and restore what was lost.

Klein's account, then, stands to Freud's as a variation on its main theme. Thus, like Freud's, Klein's is based on the child's ambivalent feelings toward its parents. But unlike Freud's, her account does not trace this ambivalence to the child's understanding of and response to its parents as all-important benefactors, on the one hand, and punitive authorities, on the other. Rather, she attributes it to the child's projection of the pleasures and distresses, joys and fears, of infancy onto the parental figures that inhabit its mind, projections that turn these figures into objects of glory and savagery, awe and anger, love and hate. Hence, following her account, one conceives of the child's feelings of guilt without supposing as background any practice in which the child is subject to some governing authority.

Typically, we regard feelings of guilt as a sign of socialization into such a practice. Typically, that is, we think feelings of guilt in children show that the children have at least a rudimentary knowledge of right and wrong. They know the difference between being naughty and being good and that what they've done is naughty. Freud's account squares with this typical thought. Klein's does not. Here, then, is the issue that the difference between them sharply defines. Do feelings of guilt imply that their subject has undergone the kind of socialization that yields rudimentary knowledge of right and wrong? Or can they be experienced apart from such socialization? The issue, moreover, arises for theories of moral development generally, and not just for those that fall within the psychoanalytic tradition. In cognitive psychology, for instance, it arises over the question of what cognitive capacities the power of moral judgment develops from, and one finds in this tradition as well theories on either side. Thus, Piaget's theory, given its program of Kantian constructivism, supports treating feelings of guilt as signs of a child's having begun to construct a moral world out of the authoritative rules that it has been made to obey,[5] whereas Martin Hoffman's theory, whose principal theme is that the power of moral judgment develops from the capacity for empathy, takes feelings of guilt as signs of a child's empathy with someone whose injury or suffering it attributes to its own actions.[6] Hence, on Hoffman's theory, these feelings are conceived of independently of the child's being subject to authoritative rules. The same issue, then, divides Piaget's and Hoffman's theories as divides Freud's and Klein's.

Morris's examples, it should be clear, bear directly on this issue. Their bearing on it can be seen in the question that interests me, the question of whether they count as nonmoral feelings in the thinner sense I specified earlier. For if they counted as nonmoral feelings in this sense, they would represent feelings of guilt that did not imply socialization of the sort that yielded rudimentary knowledge of right and wrong. Accordingly, they would support conceptions of guilt like Klein's and Hoffman's and oppose conceptions like Freud's. They would have this import, however, only if they could not be understood as moral feelings in the thinner sense. So the question we should examine is whether such an understanding of Morris's examples is possible, whether, that is, they can be understood consistently with the Wittgensteinian view.

In examining this question, we can leave aside Morris's examples of guilt felt over wrongs committed by one's nation or community. As examples of vicarious feelings, they spell trouble for the philosophical view of guilt Morris criticizes because their subjects are not responsible for the wrongs over which they feel guilt. But they don't represent a threat to the Wittgensteinian view because they in fact require, as their context, a practice consisting in the regulation of human conduct and human relations by requirements or rules of a governing, moral authority. The reason why is plain. As vicarious feelings, they mimic the feelings that the individuals responsible for the wrongs experience or should experience, and since the feelings they mimic require or would require, as their context, a moral practice of the right sort, they too require such a practice as their context. Let us then focus on Morris's other examples. In these, neither the cause nor the object of the feelings is an act

5. See Jean Piaget, *The Moral Judgment of the Child*, Marjorie Gabain, trans. (New York: The Free Press, 1965), pp. 121–138.
6. See Martin L. Hoffman, "Moral Development in Adolescence" in *Handbook of Adolescent Psychology*, Joseph Adelson, ed. (New York: John Wiley & Sons, Inc., 1980), pp. 295–343, esp. p. 312. See also "Development of Prosocial Motivation: Empathy and Guilt," in *The Development of Prosocial Behavior*, Nancy Eisenberg, ed. (New York: Academic Press, 1982), pp. 281–313.

of wrongdoing. Hence, there appears to be nothing in them that answers to the idea of disobedience to authority. For this reason, they represent a threat to the Wittgensteinian view.

Consider Morris's first example. Sometimes, because of anger, we may suddenly think, "How nice it would be if this person—the person with whom we are angry—were dead and we were rid of them"; and then, especially when the person is someone close to us, we realize the hatefulness of our thought and feel guilt. Such guilt can be felt over the thought alone. No expression of the thought in words or deeds is necessary. And because a thought, a mere wish for another's death, is not an act of wrongdoing, there is reason to think that the feeling may fall outside any practice in which human conduct and relations are regulated by the requirements or rules of some governing authority. The reason can be put as follows. Even sensible, mature people are liable to feel guilt over such wishes, and their feeling need not be taken as an indication of some irrationality or neurosis. At the same time, being sensible and mature, they realize that hostile wishes spawned by anger are better understood as spontaneous, involuntary thoughts than internal, controllable actions, and consequently they do not regard themselves as morally censurable for merely having wished another dead. What morality censures, they will think, are actions, states, and conditions over which the person it censures has control. It would thus censure any action they took that was prompted by and intended to fulfill their wish, for such an action would be subject to their powers of self-control. But, as they recognize, it does not censure the wish itself. Nonetheless, they feel guilt over it, and given that the feeling is normal and not irrational, it appears not to reflect any moral judgment. Hence, it is hard to see how anything answering to the idea of disobedience to governing authority could be either its cause or its object.

There is, however, a subtle flaw in this argument. The question we're examining is whether one can understand the feelings of guilt in Morris's examples consistently with the Wittgensteinian view, and to answer it we must see whether one can understand these feelings as having, as their context, certain moral practices. These, it is important to note, must be the existing practices of the society to which the subjects belong and not some ideal version of them. This is because, as we saw earlier, the requirements or rules of a governing authority that feelings of guilt, if moral, imply must be requirements or rules of a governing authority to which the subjects of those feelings have an allegiance, and having an allegiance to such an authority is not a matter of recognizing and aspiring to an ideal, no more than having a friendship with someone is a matter of recognizing an ideal companion and aspiring to his companionship. The distinction between existing moral practices and an ideal form of them corresponds to that between morality in the sense of the customary moral standards of some society and morality in the sense of a theoretical object, the ideal that philosophers construct and that moralists use to criticize such standards.[7] The theoretical object is commonly conceived of as a set of universally valid principles, whereas customary morality is commonly seen as parochial. The flaw in the argument, then, comes from confusing the two. Morality in the theoretical sense may not censure mere wishes, but it does not follow that our customary morality does not censure them. Hence, though sensible, mature people can firmly believe morality does not censure such wishes, they may still be liable to moral feelings of guilt over having them, for their belief may be about morality in the theoretical sense while their feelings reflect their adherence to a customary morality that deviates from the ideal at this point.

In fact, our existing moral practices do censure mere feelings and wishes. Take, for instance, the practices of marriage, family, and personal friendship in our society, perhaps in any society. In these practices, there are requirements of fidelity and loyalty, which are not satisfied by actions alone. George Fletcher, whose book on loyalty perceptively charts these and similar requirements across a broad range of relationships in which they apply, captures their core when he writes, "The minimal demand of loyalty is the maintenance of the relationship, which requires the rejection of alternatives that undermine the principal bond."[8] What Fletcher here calls the minimal demand is a demand for emotional commitment to the other party in the relationship, one's spouse, one's friend, one's kin. For without such a commitment, the relationship is not possible, the principal bond would not hold. Friends, spouses, the members of a close-knit family rely on each other for emotional support. Their relations, if sound, are built on trust in that each trusts the other to have the supportive feelings on which they rely and to be free of cruel and wounding feelings on whose absence they also rely. Indeed, one could not have such trust unless one supposed that the person one trusted was committed to having those supportive feelings and to being free of the cruel ones. It is this emotional commitment that is essential to being faithful and loyal. Consequently, the requirements of fidelity and loyalty include at their core a requirement of emotional commitment, a requirement to have certain feelings and to be free of certain others. The practices

7. The distinction is perspicuously drawn by Alan Donagan in *The Theory of Morality* (Chicago: University of Chicago Press, 1977), pp. 1–2.

8. *Loyalty: An Essay on the Morality of Relationships* (New York: Oxford University Press, 1993), p. 8.

of marriage, family, and personal friendship therefore involve requirements, requirements of emotional commitment, whose satisfaction is not assured by action alone.

To be sure, such commitments are primarily tested by actions. Falseness and betrayal are primarily shown in what one does and fails to do. But the presence or absence of the commitment can be detected in other ways. An involuntary smile at a friend's misfortune can be as telling as a deliberate sneer. This illustrates, then, how failure to maintain the emotional commitment, to satisfy the requirements of fidelity and loyalty, can be involuntary. To satisfy the requirements, one must have certain feelings and not have others, and whether one has the former or is free of the latter is typically not within one's power. Once this point is granted, it is then a short step to the conclusion that some feelings, some wishes, in being indicative or constitutive of inconstancy, disloyalty, or betrayal, are appropriate objects within the practices of marriage, friendship, and family of censure and resentment by those whose trust has been betrayed and feelings of guilt by the betrayer. Those practices thus supply the context necessary for understanding a person's feeling guilt over a wish for another's death consistently with the Wittgensteinian view.

How helpful is this way of explaining feelings of guilt over mere wishes for understanding the other examples from Morris's paper that challenge the Wittgensteinian view? These are examples of what Morris calls feelings of guilt over unjust enrichment, feelings whose object is some good fortune that has come one's way and that has eluded or been denied others who are no less deserving. Two friends compete for the same job; one is both more qualified and more in need of landing it, but as things turn out, it is given to the one who is less qualified and less in need of it. In the company of his friend, the successful applicant may feel some guilt over his good fortune, for his success, his friend's correlative failure, given that the reverse seems the juster result, has now come between them. At first blush, it may seem that, however one explains feelings of guilt over mere wishes consistently with the Wittgensteinian view, it will be of no help to understanding examples like this one. After all, the object of the feelings in these examples is something that has happened to the subject and not something originating in him. How, then, could one even begin to understand the feelings as signifying his having offended the requirements or rules of a governing, moral authority?

Yet on reflection one might have second thoughts. To make sense of these feelings, we must assume that some bond exists between the subject and the person or persons with respect to whose misfortune the subject feels guilt. Or at least we must assume that the subject must feel some connection to them.[9] Relationships such as those formed in a family or between friends or among comrades supply the context for the usual examples of such feelings. One powerful example, due to Martin Hoffman, is that of an American Navy pilot during the war in Vietnam who spent two years as a prisoner of war and who said on being released, "Getting released, you feel a tremendous amount of guilt. You developed a relationship with the other prisoners…and they're still there and you're going away."[10] What this example reminds us is that one of the requirements of these relationships, one of the requirements of friendship and comradeship, is sharing, both in good times and bad. We share our good fortune and successes with our friends, through shared joy and happiness, and they share in our misery through the sympathy they offer for our losses and failures. In Hoffman's example, however, the pilot is blocked from sharing his good fortune with his prison comrades, and his commiserating with them over their continued imprisonment after he's gone would also be awkward. The circumstances of his good fortune and their misfortune are such that he cannot meet the requirement of sharing that his relationship with them entails. Here, then, is one basis for his feeling guilt that allows us to understand the feeling consistently with the Wittgensteinian view.

A second basis can be seen if we suppose, as seems reasonable, that the pilot felt an immediate surge of joy at being released. Such joy would be in a sense a selfish emotion, since he could not share it with his comrades. Indulging it would certainly offend the requirements of the relationship he had formed with them, and it may be that merely having it does so as well. His feeling joy, then, would be a second basis for feeling guilt that allows us to understand the feeling consistently with the Wittgensteinian view.

Of course, this way of understanding the feeling would fail to comprehend Morris's examples if it implied that the object of the feeling was some wrongful action. Specifically, it would fail to capture what Morris sees as rendering the guilt in his examples nonmoral if the reason why an inability to share one's good fortune explained one's feelings of guilt were that one saw the inability as a failure to do what one ought to do. Morris, it should be noted, is careful to distinguish between feeling guilt over being unjustly blessed with good fortune and feeling guilt over failing to rectify the injustice

9. Thus, Morris writes about survivor's guilt and similar cases, "One's guilt would derive from being in an unjust position with regard to those with whom one identified" (p. 236) and "One's feelings would track the scope of one's identificatory ties with the less fortunate, those before whom one feels guilt" (p. 237).

10. Hoffman, "Moral Development in Adolescence," p. 313. Original source was *Newsweek*, 1972.

of that blessing.[11] It is the former feeling, he argues, that corresponds, when appropriate, to nonmoral guilt as he understands it, for unlike the latter feeling, it is necessarily experienced over something that happens to one independently of one's will. The latter feeling, by contrast, does not, even when appropriate, correspond to nonmoral guilt in Morris's sense, for a failure to rectify an injustice, given that one is morally obligated to rectify it, would be a moral wrong, a wrongful omission for which one was responsible, and so the guilt one incurred as a result moral guilt. Consequently, the inability to share one's good fortune cannot explain the former feeling if the object of the feeling it does explain is analogous to the object of the latter. It cannot explain the former feeling if the object of the feeling it does explain is some wrongful omission for which the subject is responsible. The question, then, is whether in explaining feeling guilt over good fortune by appealing to the subject's inability to share his good fortune, one provides a way of understanding the feeling that, while consistent with the Wittgensteinian view, misses Morris's point about the kind of object the feeling must have if, when appropriate, it corresponds to nonmoral guilt.

It should be clear, though, that feeling guilt over good fortune that one is blocked from sharing with others is not the same thing as feeling guilt over withholding from others a good that one is required to share. The object of the latter feeling is certainly a wrongful omission for which one may be responsible. But the object of the former is not well understood as a wrongful omission. The circumstance of being required to share something that is unshareable is a circumstance in which its possession alone means that any requirement to share it is perforce not met, and its not being met is independent of one's will. Hence, to say that one had failed to meet the requirement would be misleading. One feels guilt in this circumstance over one's condition and not over an omission for which one could be responsible. Explaining the feeling by appeal to its subject's inability to share his good fortune with others thus provides a way of understanding the feeling that is true to Morris's point about the kind of object the feeling has in the examples he gives of feeling guilt over unjust enrichment.

My aim here, it is worth stressing, has been to suggest ways to understand Morris's examples as moral feelings in the thinner sense I specified. I have in this way sought to defend the conception of feelings of guilt found in Freud's theory. A successful defense, it should be clear, does not mean that the conception tops the conception found in competing theories like Klein's. Both

---

11. Morris, pp. 236–237.

conceptions may be equally defensible for all I've said. What it means, rather, is that Morris's examples by themselves do not represent an argument for one conception and against the other. The examples do, by themselves, tell against the view that guilt is appropriately felt by someone only over his being morally guilty, where being morally guilty means being culpably responsible for wrongdoing. They do, as Morris has convincingly argued, give us sound reason to reject this prevailing philosophical view. Rejecting the tight fit between appropriate feelings of guilt and moral guilt that the prevailing view maintains, we must find some slack in our conceptual scheme. We might then along with Morris allow that there is a kind of guilt that is not moral guilt to which some appropriate feelings of guilt respond. But alternatively we may hold, following my suggestion, that there are authoritative moral requirements on feeling and condition as well as on action and that some appropriate feelings of guilt respond to offenses, albeit involuntary offenses, to these requirements.

8

Promises under Fire

Thomas Scanlon's account of the obligation to keep a promise, which he presents in chapter 7 of his book *What We Owe to Each Other*, has reinvigorated philosophical debate about the nature and grounds of this obligation.[1] In the chapter's introduction, Scanlon acknowledges the attractiveness of accounts like Hume's and Rawls's, on which the existence of social conventions that constitute the practice of promising is essential to generating the obligation to keep a promise. Although he once accepted these accounts, Scanlon no longer thinks they provide the best explanation of the wrong that one does when one wrongfully breaks a promise. A better explanation, he believes, is provided by an account of the obligation on which it is generated by a principle of duty that does not presuppose the existence of any social convention. My own belief is contrary to Scanlon's. Hume's account, I think, provides the better explanation. In this essay, I argue for seeing Hume's account as superior. My argument begins obliquely—and

---

1. Thomas Scanlon, *What We Owe to Each Other* (Cambridge, MA: Harvard University Press, 1998), pp. 295–327. Scanlon previously presented this account in "Promises and Practices," *Philosophy and Public Affairs* 19 (1990): 199–226.

some might think perversely—with sympathetic consideration of Hobbes's account of promises.

I

Hobbes's account of promises has never enjoyed a large following among philosophers. Their rejection of it is no doubt partly due to its affinity to his egoism. But even aside from this affinity, its peculiarities have made it seem implausible. They have pretty much reduced it to an account of merely historical interest. These peculiarities include such strange doctrines as that small children become subject to the authority of their parents as a result of their implicitly promising to obey them and that a coerced promise need not always be a nullity. I would not even begin to consider defending the first of these doctrines. Defending attributions of implied promises of obedience is already hard enough when the alleged promisers are sui juris. But I do think the second doctrine has more to be said for it than is usually thought and that its defensibility is worth considering. The impulse to reject it out of hand comes from an idealized view of morality that informs much of modern moral philosophy but that obscures its understanding of the actual moral practices and beliefs by which we conduct our lives.[2] Hobbes's doctrine about the validity of some coerced promises challenges this idealized view of morality at one of its principal nodes: the importance of voluntariness to the determination of the ownership of and responsibility for words and deeds. Thus, seeing what can be said for the doctrine, considering its defensibility, will help to estimate the disparity between the modern philosophers' ideal of morality and the actual moral practice by or through which people become bound to keep their word. And seeing to what degree some disparity between the two exists will help to resolve current disputes on the question of what explains the obligation to keep a promise.

Currently, philosophers divide on this question according as they follow Hume in thinking that what explains this obligation is the place in human life of certain social conventions, specifically, those that constitute the practice of making promises, or follow natural lawyers in thinking that what explains it are universal principles of duty that apply to making promises among other actions but whose validity does not depend on any social convention and so, a fortiori, on those that constitute the practice of making promises. Hobbes,

---

2. I have explored this theme in "All Kinds of Guilt," *Law and Philosophy* 18 (1999): 313–325 (ch. 7, this volume).

obviously, was no follower of Hume, having preceded him by a century, and though he might qualify as a natural lawyer, his qualifications are more nominal than real. Laws of nature, on Hobbes's theory, are not universal principles of duty. His account of promises, therefore, falls into neither of these camps. He neither thought that promises were the creatures of social conventions nor thought that universal principles of duty explained their obligatoriness. Hence, we cannot expect to find in this account direct support for either the Humean or the natural lawyers' position. If considering the defensibility of his doctrine that a coerced promise need not always be a nullity helps us resolve their dispute, the help must come from considerations in the doctrine's favor that are somewhat oblique to Hobbes's account. Nonetheless, the reasons Hobbes had for maintaining the doctrine shed light on this dispute.

The chief text in which Hobbes asserts the doctrine is found in chapter 14 of *Leviathan*. "Covenants entered into by fear," Hobbes wrote, "in the condition of mere nature, are obligatory. For example, if I covenant to pay a ransom, or service, for my life, to an enemy, I am bound by it. For it is a contract wherein one receiveth the benefit of life; the other is to receive money, or service, for it; and consequently, where no other law (as in the condition of mere nature) forbiddeth the performance, the covenant is valid."[3] Earlier Hobbes had observed that the way one became bound to do some action was to give voluntarily a sign indicating one's abandonment of the right to do other things and that such a sign was given through words or deeds or some combination of the two. What bound one to do the action, Hobbes further observed, was not the giving of the sign ("for nothing is more easily broken than a man's word") but fear of the evil consequences one would suffer if one reneged.[4] The sign expressed one's will, and on Hobbes's account of the will, fear and aversion no less than hope and desire could constitute it. The will, according to Hobbes, was the last appetite or aversion, hope or fear, in any deliberation that issued in action, and voluntary action was action that "proceedeth from the will."[5] Hence, promises that one made from fear, including fear induced by coercive threats, were voluntary in Hobbes's sense. They qualified as acts in which the promiser voluntarily gave a sign indicating his abandonment of the right to do things other than what he had promised to do, and they were therefore, at least in circumstances in which one had reason to fear the consequences of reneging, binding.

---

3. Hobbes, *Leviathan*, Edwin Curley, ed. (Indianapolis: Hackett, 1994), ch. 14, par. 27.
4. Ibid., ch. 14, par. 7.
5. Ibid., ch. 6.

This account, needless to say, has not persuaded very many people. Coerced promises are not voluntary in the ordinary sense of the term. In that sense, a voluntary action is necessarily uncoerced; a coerced action is necessarily involuntary. Hobbes, for this reason, is open to criticism for having defined voluntary action in a way that extends the term's range beyond what the ordinary notion comprehends. In particular, he is open to criticism for having erased, as a result of this definition, a relevant distinction between acts that, though they spring from fear, proceed from an uncoerced will and acts that, because they spring from fear induced by coercive threats, proceed from a coerced will. This distinction, on the ordinary notion of voluntary action, makes all the difference between a voluntary promise and an involuntary one and thus explains, so it is commonly thought, why the former but not the latter are regarded as binding. Kavka makes this criticism as well as any commentator when he writes:

> To see [what is wrong with Hobbes's account], it suffices to distinguish between promises made under two sorts of duress. A promise is coerced when the promisee threatens the promisor with some evil should the promise not be made, with the purpose of obtaining the promise. A promise is forced, by contrast, when the promisor enters into it to avoid some evil or danger not created by the promisee, or at least not created by the promisee with the intention of producing the promise. Coerced promises are not morally binding. Many, though not all forced promises are morally binding.... Thus, Hobbes is right that fear being the motive for making a promise does not in itself void it—everything depends on the nature and source of the fear.[6]

Of course, one might still want to know why "the nature and source of the fear" determines whether or not a promise made from fear is morally binding. One might still ask, why can't a coerced promise be morally binding when a promise made under pressure from some other kind of danger may be? Kavka gives what at first glance seems to be a very sensible answer. It "makes good practical sense," he says, to treat all coerced promises, but not all forced promises, as null. "[B]y treating coerced promises as null, we can deter potential coercers from threatening potential promisors" and in this way protect people from bullies. But we cannot protect people from all the dangerous and difficult situations that they face in life, and to treat promises made in all such situations as null would be to "deprive them of one tool for making the best of a bad situation."[7] Yet Kavka's answer, though it seems

6. Gregory S. Kavka, *Hobbesian Moral and Political Theory* (Princeton: Princeton University Press, 1986), p. 396.
7. Ibid.

sensible, runs into problems, for it ignores an important qualification that Hobbes placed on his doctrine. Specifically, Hobbes restricted the circumstances in which coerced promises could be binding to "the condition of mere nature," which for him was a condition of war. So while Kavka's point about the practical value of nullifying coerced promises makes good sense when applied to social relations in a civilized society, it does not make the same good sense when applied to relations between enemies in a war. To the contrary, enemies in a war, whose very relations consist in attempts to change each other's behavior through force and violence, may find it useful, as a way of reducing the destructiveness of their hostilities, to be able to make one another promises that they can regard as binding even and especially if the promises are coerced. Hence, to treat such promises as null would be to deprive people caught in a war of a tool for limiting the destructiveness of their situation.

Hobbes's example of a promise a victim of kidnapping makes to his kidnappers, who are his enemy in "the condition of mere nature," illustrates this point well. In this condition, where there is no government to prosecute and punish murder, the kidnappers have no incentive, apart from whatever exchange value the victim has for them, to keep him alive. Thus, his being able to promise to pay a ransom and have that promise seen as binding would be an invaluable expedient in these circumstances. By being able to be seen as making a valid promise and thereby binding himself to pay the ransom, he would be able to provide his enemy with a strong incentive to spare his life. He would be able, that is, to avoid a great loss at the cost of a smaller one. Hence, the same reason Kavka gives to explain why some forced promises are treated as binding applies to coerced promises in such circumstances as well.[8] Consequently, his answer falls short of explaining why a promise must be uncoerced to be morally binding.

A different answer draws on the special offensiveness of coercion in modern, liberal theory. A central theme of liberalism is that men and women are self-governing or autonomous agents. They attain this status with the full development of their rational powers, and in attaining it they not only become morally responsible for their conduct but also leave the custodial authority of their guardians and become sovereign, as it were, over their own lives. Accordingly, each assumes authority over his life in virtue of which his will, and not another's, determines the validity of such transactions as acquiring

---

8. For variations on this problem, see Thomas Schelling, *The Strategy of Conflict* (Cambridge, MA: Harvard University Press, 1960), pp. 43 ff.

and disposing of property, undertaking voluntary obligations, releasing others from obligations they have to one, and giving others the power to represent one and to act in one's name. Thus, respect for someone as a self-governing agent is the same as respect for the authority he has over his life and is shown by not interfering with the choices he makes in his exercise of that authority. Conversely, then, to coerce such a person is to show contempt for that authority. It is to force the person, either physically or by threats, to act as one demands, which is to say, to adopt one's will as his own, and such subordination of his will directly denigrates his authority. A coerced promise therefore cannot be binding if the promise is made by a self-governing agent, for its being binding is incompatible with such an agent's authority. It implies subservience to the will of another, which that authority necessarily excludes. The reason, then, why coerced promises cannot be binding while forced promises may be is that none of the latter, unlike all of the former, denigrates the promiser's authority as a self-governing agent. Taking any of the latter as binding does not contradict that authority, since the promiser, in making such a promise, does not subordinate his will.

This answer appears to avoid the problem that Kavka's answer ran into. Specifically, it appears to avoid the charge, to which Kavka's was liable, that the answer ignores the qualification Hobbes placed on his doctrine about coerced promises, that is, his restriction of the circumstances in which coerced promises can be binding to the condition of mere nature. Indeed, this restriction, one might argue, has no bearing on the answer's cogency. For the answer depends on the special offensiveness of coercion when it is used to dominate the will of a self-governing agent, and being in the condition of mere nature does not preclude someone from being a self-governing agent. Quite the contrary, what qualifies a person as a self-governing agent is his or her having fully developed and unimpaired rational powers, and since people can have such powers in the condition of mere nature, they can qualify as self-governing agents in that condition. Consequently, the answer's explanation of why coerced promises, unlike forced promises, are never binding applies to promises made in the condition of mere nature just as it applies to promises made in civilized society. In either case, taking coerced promises as binding contradicts the authority the promisers have as self-governing agents. So it makes no difference to the answer's cogency, the argument concludes, that Hobbes restricted the circumstances in which coerced promises could be binding to the condition of mere nature.

Yet despite this argument, one can still criticize the answer for missing the import of Hobbes's restriction. Here too the problem is one of failure to appreciate that for Hobbes the condition of mere nature was a condition of war. Coercing an enemy in war, even an enemy whose rational powers are fully developed and unimpaired, need not be specially offensive. To be sure, many wars are waged by aggressors whose aggression is specially offensive. But not all wars are wars of aggression, and not every side in a war is an aggressor. The point is that war itself, in whatever way it is waged and whoever wages it, necessarily involves coercion. When people go to war to settle their differences, their hostile actions are meant to coerce their enemy into accepting their demands. Coercion, in other words, is integral to war and part of its normal conduct. Hence, unless one is excessively high minded and regards war itself as beneath the dignity of any fully rational human being,[9] one must limit one's objection to using coercion to dominate the will of a fully rational human being as specially offensive to coercion in civilized circumstances. Coercion is specially offensive when it is used in such circumstances by someone who has no authority over the person he is coercing. But coercion when used in war to bring an enemy to heel is another matter. It need not be specially offensive, for it may be unexceptionable as an act of war. It may, that is, be what any participant in war would accept as fitting the situation. What this means, though, is either that enemies in war do not, in their relations to each other, act as self-governing agents or that in war an enemy's will can still be authoritative even if coerced. What it means, that is, is that coerced promises in war, for all that this second answer has shown, could nonetheless be binding.

Neither Kavka's answer nor the answer that derives from liberalism succeeds, then, in explaining why coerced promises cannot be binding when forced promises may be. Neither, therefore, succeeds in justifying the dismissal of Hobbes's doctrine for being blind to the relevance of coercion, as a source of fear, to whether a promise made out of fear is binding. There may, of course, be other ways to justify its dismissal. One may even be tempted to justify it on the grounds that the doctrine contradicts a basic, self-evident truth that no coerced promises by fully rational human beings could ever be binding. But the prospects of success in finding a satisfactory justification

---

9. War, of course, often involves the wanton use of violence, which does, in its connotation of madness, imply a loss of reason and a failure to conduct oneself as a fully rational human being. But one should not confuse this use of violence with its deliberate use to force another to accede to one's demands. Nothing in the latter connotes madness or implies a loss of reason and a failure to conduct oneself as a fully rational human being. Sadly, the deliberate use of violence against another for the purpose of settling differences that, if left unsettled, threaten to make one's circumstances intolerable is a part of human life and cannot be wished away as only representing the remnants of a prior bestial existence.

are dim, and we ought then to consider the possibility that Hobbes was not flatly wrong on this issue. To be sure, it would be hard to vindicate his capacious definition of voluntary action. It would be hard, that is, to abandon our ordinary notion of voluntariness as excluding coerced actions from being voluntary. But his doctrine about coerced promises might still be defensible even if the definition of voluntary action on which he based it is not. Perhaps, in war, some coerced promises are binding.

An example comes ready to hand. Surrendering in war entails a promise to cease fighting and to submit to capture. The promise is binding, though the act of surrender may be coerced. When one side in a battle inflicts such losses on the other that the latter, exhausted, unable to retreat, and fearful of destruction, gives up and raises a white flag, the flag is a sign of surrender. It expresses a promise to stop firing, to lay down arms, and to submit to capture. Having promised to stop firing and submit to capture, the surrendering side cannot then renew its attack when its enemy, believing that the battle has been won, becomes exposed as it moves forward. To do so would be to violate the obligation the surrendering side is under in virtue of its promise. It cannot, in particular, decide that because its surrender was coerced, it is under no such obligation and may therefore seize the opportunity of inflicting heavy losses on a now exposed enemy. Surrendering under fire is still surrendering. The promise it entails is still binding.

Enemies at war, as we noted earlier, benefit from being able to make promises that they can both regard as binding even and especially when the promises are coerced. Their mutually recognizing signs of surrender, like a white flag, as expressing a promise to stop fighting is a clear example. The aim in war is to force one's enemy to accept one's demands. Except for wars that are fueled by extraordinary hatred and tend toward genocide, destroying the enemy is not part of this aim.[10] Victory does not require it. And when each side in a war aims at defeating but not destroying the other, they share an interest in limiting the destructiveness of their hostilities. Having a way to signal to one's enemy acceptance of defeat in battle serves this interest since it makes it possible to end the hostilities with fewer casualties on either side than would result if the hostilities were to last until only one side remained standing. Or, to be more exact, it serves this interest when this way

10. For this reason, it was especially reprehensible and corrupting for the United States government during the Vietnam War to use "body counts"—numbers of enemy dead—rather than, e.g., extent of territory under its control as a way of persuading the American public that the war was being won.

of signaling acceptance of defeat is mutually understood as surrender and so as expressing a promise to stop fighting and submit to capture. For this reason, a conventional sign of surrender, like raising a white flag, is necessary, since no natural expression of the acceptance of defeat, such as throwing down one's weapons and falling to one's knees, could meet this condition. That is, none could secure the mutual understanding necessary for enemies jointly to end their hostilities before their battle turned into a slaughter. An action such as throwing down one's weapons would convey an intention to stop fighting, to be sure. But an intention to do something is not a promise to do it. One must convey something more than an intention to do some action to be understood as expressing a promise to do it, and this added meaning can only be conveyed by a conventional sign.

The example fits Hume's view of promises and what explains the obligation to keep them. On this view, one person makes a promise to another, to bring wine to a party, say, by giving the latter a sign that they mutually understand as meaning that he, the sign-giver, assumes an obligation to bring the wine. The act is part of a practice among a group of people that consists in their giving each other such signs for the purpose of binding themselves to do the actions that the signs mean they have promised to do. The group, in other words, follows certain conventions that constitute this practice and, accordingly, any of the signs by which they make promises has a conventional meaning. In the case of promising to bring wine to a party, the promiser gives a sign that conveys to its recipient not only his intention to bring the wine but also his intention to bind himself to bring it, and both understand that in conveying these intentions by giving this sign, he does bind himself to bring the wine. What they understand as binding him, though, is his giving the sign. His forming the intentions to bring the wine and to bind himself to bring it are not alone sufficient. Indeed, he would not be understood as having bound himself even if he directly told the person to whom he meant to be bound that he had these intentions. (Saying to someone, "I intend to bring wine to your party and to assume an obligation to do so," would simply invite puzzlement and the response, "Does that mean you promise?") Giving a sign that is mutually understood as creating the obligation is thus necessary.

More needs to be said, of course. That a group of people understand certain signs as meaning that whoever gives one of these signs to another assumes an obligation to do the action he has, in giving the sign, conveyed an intention to do is not sufficient to explain his actually being under an obligation to do the action. It is not sufficient, that is, if to say that he is under an obligation to do the action is to imply that it would be wrong for him not to do it.[11] For it is one thing for people to share an understanding of such sign-giving actions as binding and of breaking the promises they constitute as wrong, and quite another for those promises actually to be binding and for breaking them actually to be wrong. After all, the Hindus who practiced suttee understood marriage as creating an obligation on the wife's part to be cremated on the funeral pyre of her late husband and thought it wrong for widows to resist such self-immolation, yet a widow who resisted would certainly not be doing anything wrong. Clearly, then, the existence of conventions in virtue of which those who follow them share an understanding of their actions as creating obligations does not alone explain how the practice the conventions constitute in fact creates those obligations. Something else must be true of the practice for those who take part in it actually to assume obligations as a result. And in Hume's view, what else must be true is that the practice must contribute positively and importantly to the collective good of human beings. It must, when viewed from a universal and impartial standpoint, be seen as a boon to the general welfare of all whom the practice affects. This, in effect, is Hume's condition of justification on practices, and promising, because of how it facilitates cooperation among people, especially people who have no strong ties to one another, meets this condition.

Specifically, as Hume observes, it solves a problem that human beings who wish to cooperate with one other in mutually beneficial ways face on account of their lacking confidence in each other's reliability. The reason for this lack of confidence, Hume argues, is that people's goodwill toward each other is limited and weaker as the social distance between them is greater. The problem, in other words, would not arise if people's goodwill toward each other were unlimited in all cases, for a person could then be confident, when cooperating with others, that they would not abandon his interests whenever they could gain the benefits of his cooperation before he gained the benefits of theirs. But because people's goodwill is limited and weaker toward strangers than friends, a person would seriously risk being taken advantage of when cooperating with others who were not his friends and who could gain the

---

11. This qualification is necessary because 'obligation' is a word that has a descriptive as well as a normative use, and it is the normative use, the use that implies a person acts wrongly if he fails to perform his obligation, that is intended here. More generally, 'obligation' is part of the vocabulary of institutions, a vocabulary that also includes such terms as 'right', 'duty', 'responsibility', 'rule', etc., and one can use this vocabulary either to describe the institution from the outside or to make judgments from the inside. On this distinction, see H. L. A. Hart, *The Concept of Law* (Oxford: Clarendon Press, 1961). pp. 99–102, and J. L. Mackie, *Ethics: Inventing Right and Wrong* (London: Penguin, 1977), pp. 66–73.

benefits of his cooperation before he gained the benefits of theirs, at least if the only motive that could keep them from abandoning his interests in such circumstances were their goodwill toward him. So unless the fear and distrust that such risks create could be removed by giving people stronger motives to act in the interests of those with whom they were cooperating, cooperation, particularly among strangers, would be hard to get going and hard to maintain once it did get going. In short, the problem lies in the lack of trust necessary for people to engage in cooperative schemes, and it is Hume's view that the practice of promising fosters the stronger motives needed to solve this problem.

These new motives are of two kinds, self-interested and moral. In either case, the principal factor in the explanation of how the practice fosters the motive is that all who share the practice understand the sign-giving that constitutes promising as an act by which one assumes an obligation to do what one has promised to do. Accordingly, in the first case, making a promise gives one a self-interested motive to keep it since everyone has an interest in maintaining the trust of others, and violating an obligation to another is among the surest ways of losing people's trust. As Hume remarks, "When a man says *he promises any thing*, he in effect expresses a *resolution* of performing it; and along with that, by making use of this *form of words*, subjects himself to the penalty of never being trusted again in case of failure."[12] In the second case, making a promise gives one a moral motive to keep it since conscience or a sense of duty requires the performance of one's obligations. These motives, Hume holds, are more reliable springs of cooperative action than goodwill, particularly when the cooperators are mere acquaintances or strangers. Hence, the practice solves the problem of there being too little trust among people for them to engage regularly and productively in schemes of cooperation, since basing such schemes on promises creates the circumstances in which these new motives can operate and thereby enables one to have greater confidence in the reliability of others to act in ways that will benefit one than one would have if their goodwill toward one were their only motive to act in those ways once they had received the benefits of one's cooperation with them.

This account, then, applies directly to the practice of surrender in war. To begin with, surrender occurs in circumstances in which both the surrendering side and the side to which it surrenders have an interest in cooperating with each other to end their hostilities, yet obviously, being enemies, neither side could be confident of the other's reliability as long as it depended solely

---

12. Hume, *A Treatise of Human Nature*, 2d ed., L. A. Selby-Bigge, ed., with text rev. by P. H. Nidditch (Oxford: Oxford University Press, 1978), p. 522, italics in original.

on goodwill. In particular, the victorious side could not rely on the surrendering side's forbearance from renewing its attack, once the former had become exposed, if goodwill toward one's enemy were the only motive from which the surrendering side's forbearance could spring. For it goes without saying that enemies in war lack goodwill toward each other. Thus, the problem of there being too little trust for people to engage in fruitful schemes of cooperation arises acutely in these circumstances. Secondly, then, the practice of surrendering by giving a sign—raising a white flag—that means that the sign-giver assumes an obligation to stop fighting and submit to capture, being a specific case of inducing cooperation by making a promise, solves this problem. Raising a white flag creates circumstances in which both sides mutually understand that the surrendering side has assumed an obligation to stop fighting and submit to capture, and accordingly, it gives the surrendering side both self-interested and moral motives to do these actions. That it gives the surrendering side a moral motive is unmysterious. Conscience or a sense of duty operates in war as well as in peace. But that it gives this side a self-interested motive may not be immediately apparent. Because there is so little trust between enemies in war, one cannot simply attribute to the surrendering side an interest in maintaining its enemy's trust. A more involved explanation of its self-interested motive is therefore needed.

The motive arises from the interest that each side in a war has in its enemy's exercising restraint in its use of violence to achieve its ends. The hostility and enmity that war entails invariably tempts warmakers and their forces to use violence beyond what is necessary for victory or in ways that spread its destructiveness to civilian populations. So too the volatile mix of emotions that an intense battle between enemies produces makes either side prone to acts of wanton violence, prone, that is, to use destructive force to no good purpose or to maim and kill people who are not proper military targets. To be sure, the better disciplined an army is the more capable it is of restraining its hostile and aggressive impulses in the service of its ends. But it would be foolish for any side in a war to rely on the discipline of its enemy's army to provide a buffer against its provoking that army to retaliatory violence or merciless treatment in later dealings, and renewing an attack on an enemy, after having signaled surrender and thereby induced the enemy to become exposed, is bound to provoke such violence and merciless treatment, as it is bound to incite the enemy's wrath. The exercise of restraint in the use of violence is doubtless a prudent measure for conducting war, but it also reflects the recognition of one's enemy's humanity. And if one side in a war incites the wrath of its enemy, it risks losing its humanity in its enemy's eyes and therefore being seen as an acceptable target of unrestrained violence, even when prudence counsels against such violence. For this reason, each side in a war, though no longer in a position to have an interest in maintaining the other side's trust, does have an interest in maintaining the other side's recognition of its humanity.[13] Its signaling surrender thus gives it a self-interested motive to stop fighting and submit to capture.

Finally, it should be clear that the practice of surrendering in war meets Hume's condition of justification. Viewed from a universal and impartial standpoint, the practice will be seen to be of great benefit to human beings generally. Though many people never experience war directly, few, if any, live lives untouched by it, and consequently a practice that significantly limits its destructiveness is certain to benefit humankind immeasurably. On Hume's view, then, the practice is justified in view of its important contribution to the collective good of human beings, and its justification sustains, in particular, the shared understanding of signs of surrender as meaning that the sign-giver assumes an obligation to stop fighting and submit to capture regardless of whether his giving the sign is coerced. It sustains this understanding, for giving a sign of surrender is not likely to induce an enemy to stop fighting and expose itself to attack if the enemy cannot take the sign as a binding promise, and there would be little chance of its doing so if the shared understanding were that giving the sign constituted such a promise only if it was freely given. Indeed, because coercion is integral to war, signs of surrender would be largely useless for making binding promises if this were the understanding of them that enemies in war shared. The signs would therefore, if so understood, be largely useless as means to limiting the destructiveness of war. What makes them useful as means to limiting war's destructiveness is their being mutually understood by enemies in war as meaning, to the contrary, that the sign-giver assumes an obligation to stop fighting and submit to capture regardless of whether the sign was given freely. What justifies the practice thus justifies, in particular, this shared understanding of the signs it deploys.

In civilized society, where coercion outside of the law is incompatible with the habits of respect and deference essential to civilized life, the practice of promising would not be of as great a benefit to human beings if it allowed coerced promises to be binding. For allowing such promises to be binding would plainly strain those habits. This point, in effect, is Kavka's explanation of why all coerced promises but not all forced promises are null, and it is a

---

13. The importance of this interest is a major theme of Jonathan Glover's powerful book, *Humanity: A Moral History of the Twentieth Century* (New Haven: Yale University Press, 1999).

cogent one when restricted to the context of civilized life. Accordingly, the greater contribution to the collective good of human beings that in this context the practice of promising makes by excluding coerced promises from being binding justifies the shared understanding behind that exclusion. This shared understanding corresponds to a convention that partly defines the practice as it is followed in civilized society, just as the shared understanding of signs of surrender in war corresponds to conventions that define the practice as it is followed in war. That one context justifies conventions according to which all coerced promises are null, and another justifies conventions according to which some coerced promises are binding, supports Hume's view of the obligation a person assumes in making a promise as inexplicable apart from the conventions that constitute the practice the person followed. Hume, it is worth noting, makes essentially the same observation when he writes:

> We may draw the same conclusion, concerning the origin of promises, from the force, which is suppos'd to invalidate all contracts, and to free us from their obligation. Such a principle is a proof, that promises have no natural obligation, and are mere artificial contrivances for the convenience and advantage of society. If we consider aright the matter, *force* is not essentially different from any other motive of hope or fear, which may induce us to engage our word and lay us under any obligation. A man, dangerously wounded, who promises a competent sum to a surgeon to cure him, would certainly be bound to performance; tho' the case be not so much different from that of one, who promises a sum to a robber, as to produce so great a difference in our sentiments of morality, if these sentiments were not built entirely on public interest and convenience.[14]

II

While these considerations about the practice of surrender in war support Hume's view, they do not amount to a demonstration of it. Views opposed to Hume's might account equally well for the practice, and if they did, then these considerations would not serve to establish Hume's view as superior to any of them. The main view opposed to Hume's is that the obligation to keep a promise is a species of a more general obligation that one can understand independently of social conventions.[15] At one time, adherents to this opposing

---

14. Hume, *Treatise*, p. 525, italics in original.

15. Another view opposed to Hume's is that the obligation arises directly from a commitment implied by the intention the promiser expresses and the promisee tacitly, if not explicitly, accepts. See, for instance, Michael Robins, *Promising, Intending and Moral Autonomy* (Cambridge: Cambridge University Press, 1984), and Margaret Gilbert, "Agreements, Coercion and Obligation," *Ethics* 103 (1993): 679–706.

view explained the obligation to keep a promise as a species of the general obligation to be truthful, but forceful criticism of the analogy between keeping one's word and telling the truth on which this explanation rests has weakened considerably philosophical interest in it.[16] More recently, those drawn to the main view opposed to Hume's have sought to explain the obligation to keep a promise as a species of a different obligation, the obligation to meet expectations about one's future conduct that one has induced others to form and rely on.[17] Such an obligation, those who advance this explanation point out, is not anchored in any social practice, and therefore if the obligation to keep a promise is a species of it, no social practice, contrary to Hume's view, grounds the obligation to keep a promise. An especially powerful and subtle defense of this explanation is given by Thomas Scanlon, in chapter 7 of his book, and an examination of how well Scanlon's position can accommodate promises like those made by acts of surrender in war, while it won't resolve the dispute between Hume's view and the main view opposed to it, will bring out difficulties in the latter serious enough to put Hume's view in the stronger light.[18]

Scanlon presents the obligation to keep a promise as belonging to a family of obligations that includes the obligations to forbear from deception and manipulation of others. He begins by placing the obligation to forbear from making a lying promise within this family. If one makes a promise to another that one has no intention of keeping, then one is engaged in an act of deception since one will have led the person to form false beliefs about one's intentions. And if the aim of the promise is to induce the person to do something from which one will benefit, then one's action is a form of deceitful manipulation. Making a promise, however, is not essential to such deception or manipulation, for plainly one can, without making a promise, deliberately lead another to form false beliefs about one's intentions and to do so with the aim of inducing the person to do something from which one will benefit. Accordingly, the obligation to forbear from making a lying promise can be taken as a special case of a general obligation to forbear from deceitful manipulation of others, which Scanlon introduces the following principle, Principle D, to define:

16. For such criticism, see, e.g., Henry Sidgwick, *The Methods of Ethics*, 7th ed. (London: Macmillan and Co., 1907), pp. 303–304.

17. See, e.g., Neil MacCormick, "Voluntary Obligations and Normative Powers I," *Proceedings of the Aristotelian Society*, supp. vol. 46 (1972): 59–78; Judith Jarvis Thomson, *The Realm of Rights* (Cambridge, MA: Harvard University Press, 1990), pp. 294–391; Thomas Scanlon, *What We Owe to Each Other* (Cambridge, MA: Harvard University Press, 1998), pp. 295–327.

18. Scanlon, *What We Owe to Each Other*, pp. 295–327.

> One must exercise due care not to lead others to form reasonable but false expectations about what one will do when one has good reason to believe that they would suffer significant loss as a result of relying on these expectations.[19]

The obligation to forbear from making a lying promise is different, of course, from the obligation to keep a promise. So the question is how one can understand the latter as related to obligations not to deceive or manipulate others. Scanlon reasons as follows.

Suppose that one has led another to form a belief about one's intentions and has done so with the aim of inducing this person to do something from which one would benefit, but that later one decides not to follow through on these intentions. Suppose, for instance, that knowing that a colleague, with whom I share an office, wants to hear a lecture at a university across town but does not want to go by himself, I tell him that I am planning to go. I do this, let us further suppose, with complete sincerity but also with the aim of inducing him to buy the lecturer's books, which I know he will buy if he decides to go to the lecture—my colleague is the enthusiastic sort—and which I'd like to have in our office but don't wish to buy myself. In this case, telling him that I'm planning to go to the lecture would not obligate me to go even if it succeeded in getting him to stock our office with the lecturer's books. This is not to say, however, that I would have no obligation to him. Since I know, when I tell him of my plans, that he is likely to act on his belief that I am going to the lecture and likely, as a result, to incur substantial expenses beforehand, I have an obligation, if I later decide not to go, to tell him that my plans have changed. More generally, I have an obligation to keep him from suffering substantial losses that would result from the combination of his acting on the expectation I have led him to form and my then failing to meet it, and I can fulfill this obligation either by meeting the expectation, alerting him to the change in my plans before he has incurred these losses, or compensating him for them if the change occurs too late for such an alert to keep him from incurring them. Only if I do none of these things (or do not tarry in performing the second or third), will I have acted wrongly.

By contrast, if I promise my colleague that I will go to the lecture, then I have an obligation to go *tout court*. I could, of course, if there were a change in my situation that made going inconvenient, alert him to this and ask him to release me from the promise. But if he did not, then my failing to go to the lecture would be wrong. Nor could I avoid acting wrongly in failing to keep the promise by compensating him for any losses he incurred as a result

---

19. Ibid., p. 300.

of my failure. On Hume's view, the explanation of the difference is immediate. When I promise to go to the lecture, I invoke conventions according to which I assume an obligation to go by virtue of saying "I promise" or words to that effect, whereas when I merely tell my colleague of my plans to go, then I do not invoke any conventions according to which my actions bind me to do what I have told him I plan to do. Scanlon counters this explanation with one on which the obligation the promise creates is grounded on a principle whose validity does not depend on any conventions. What explains the difference between my promising my colleague and my merely telling him of my intentions, according to Scanlon, is that in promising I assure my colleague that I will go to the lecture, whereas in merely telling him of my intentions, I give him no such assurance. Giving him this assurance, Scanlon holds, is what binds me to my going, and since I could give it without making a promise or invoking some other convention, the act of invoking a convention is incidental to the obligation I assume in making the promise. On Scanlon's explanation, the practice of promising offers a convenient way of giving assurances to someone who wants them before he will act on the expectation that the assurer means to raise in him, but it is the assurances and not the promise that create the obligation. Hence, the practice is incidental to it.

The principle, then, on which Scanlon believes the obligation to keep a promise is grounded is, roughly, that one binds oneself to do a certain action X if, knowing that another wants assurance that one will do X before he is willing to act on expectations that one has intentionally raised in him, one gives him such assurance at the same time as one conveys to him one's intention to do X. Scanlon gives a more exact statement of the principle, which I display below. He calls this principle, F:

> If (1) A voluntarily and intentionally leads B to expect that A will do X (unless B consents to A's not doing so); (2) A knows that B wants to be assured of this; (3) A acts with the aim of providing this assurance, and has good reason to believe that he or she has done so; (4) B knows that A has the beliefs and intentions just described; (5) A intends for B to know this, and knows that B does know it; and (6) B knows that A has this knowledge and intent; then, in the absence of special justification, A must do X unless B consents to X's not being done.[20]

The principle differs from the principle on which the obligation to keep someone in whom one has intentionally raised expectations about one's future action from suffering a substantial loss as a result of one's failing to do that action is grounded. Scanlon calls this latter principle Principle L and states it as follows:

---

20. Scanlon, *What We Owe to Each Other*, p. 304.

188 Emotions, Values, and the Law

> If one has intentionally or negligently led someone to expect that one is going
> to follow a certain course of action, X, and one has good reason to believe that
> person will suffer significant loss as a result of this expectation if one does not
> follow X, then one must take reasonable steps to prevent that loss.[21]

By adhering to Principle L, one who has raised expectations in another with
the aim of inducing him to do something from which one will benefit avoids
acting manipulatively. And Scanlon's thought is that F, as a principle that
falls out of L for the case in which one gives another assurance when raising
in him expectations that would lead him to suffer significant loss if one did
not meet them, is also a guide to nonmanipulative conduct.

Principle F and the reasoning that leads to it make up the core of
Scanlon's position. While there is more to the position than this core, one
can usefully start with it in taking up the question of how well the position
accommodates promises made by acts of surrender in war. Consider, then,
Scanlon's statement of F. From inspection, it is clear that his position would
require modification to accommodate such promises. Because clause 1 of
the principle restricts its scope to voluntary actions, F does not apply to such
promises and therefore cannot ground the obligations they create. This
conclusion is then confirmed in the paragraph immediately following the
statement. Here Scanlon notes that one reason why all would regard F as a
reasonable principle for governing their conduct toward each other is that
the principle, owing to the "requirement of voluntariness," does not force
burdens on anyone. Anyone, that is, "could...avoid bearing any burden at all
simply by refraining from voluntarily and intentionally creating any expectations about their future conduct."[22] Scanlon, though, is also aware that this
"requirement of voluntariness" (i.e., the restriction clause 1 places on F's
scope) is too strong, and near the end of the chapter he revisits it and modifies his position to allow exceptions. Thus, with reference to the obligations
grounded on F, he writes:

> [C]oercion generally invalidates such obligations, but it does not always do so.
> Whether it does in a given case depends on whether the coercion removed
> alternatives to which the agent was otherwise entitled. Treaties entered into by
> defeated nations may all be coerced, for example, but this does not render them
> invalid when the terms are not unjust.[23]

---

21. Ibid., p. 300.
22. Ibid., p. 304.
23. Ibid., p. 326. N.B., Scanlon, in chapter 6 (pp. 279–280), departs from the ordinary conception of voluntary action by affirming a broader one on which an action is voluntary if the
agent is responsible for it in the sense that the action can be attributed to that agent. Actions that
result from forced choices are thus voluntary according to this conception, which means that

So too, since soldiers in war are not entitled to safety from their enemy's lethal attacks, Scanlon, by this modification, can bring coerced promises made by acts of surrender in war within the scope of F.

Whether he can do so unproblematically, however, is another matter. Bringing such coerced promises within the scope of F means that the principle governs the conduct of enemies in war toward each other. It means, in other words, that soldiers would be acting wrongly whenever, in accordance with clauses 2–6 of F, they led their enemy to expect them to do a certain action, succeeded in assuring that enemy that they would do this action, and then omitted doing it. Yet surely this result is too strong. Soldiers in war, while they have some obligations to their enemy, have no general obligation of fidelity or truthfulness to an enemy, and the obligation that F defines is a general obligation of this sort. Of course, you might think that in war one's enemy is never so credulous as to be receptive to one's assurances, except when one invokes an established convention like raising a white flag, and consequently one could never incur an obligation to one's enemy that was grounded on F except by invoking some convention. You might think, that is, that one could never have good reason to believe that one had successfully assured an enemy of one's intention to take a certain action except when one provided assurance by invoking an established convention, and, hence, one could only satisfy clause 3 of F and so create an obligation grounded on F by invoking a convention. For this reason, the criticism of F as too strong may seem hasty. But it is not. What gives the criticism its bite is that F belongs to a family of principles that define general obligations of fidelity and truthfulness and owes its intelligibility to its being related to the other principles in this family. To bring coerced promises made by acts of surrender in war within the scope of F implies, then, that these other principles too govern the conduct between enemies in war. And it is plain that they do not.

Manipulation and deception of an enemy are as much a part of the conduct of war as the direct use of lethal force. Misleading one's enemy about one's position and giving false signs of one's plans while camouflaging one's true position and activities are basic military tactics. Washington, for instance, as every American schoolchild learns, achieved his first important victory over the British by crossing the Delaware River late on Christmas night 1776 and then making a surprise attack at dawn the next

---

coerced actions are voluntary according to it. But plainly he returns to the ordinary conception in chapter 7 since the "requirement of voluntariness" that clause 1 of F represents implies that coerced actions are not voluntary.

morning. Presumably, Washington and his men, to conceal their plans, gave false signs of an intention to remain in camp, which is to say that for the purpose of being able to attack their enemy without warning they deliberately led that enemy to expect them to stay put. Such action would violate Principle D, and the subsequent attack violated L. But Washington surely had no general obligation to the British forces to forbear from giving them false signs of his intentions or to warn them of the losses they would incur as a result of his acting contrary to the expectations he encouraged them to have. D and L surely have no standing as principles governing conduct between enemies in war.

To be sure, to say this is not to say that any act of deception or manipulation of an enemy in war is permissible. Though enemies in war have no general obligations to each other of the sort defined by D and L, they are subject to some constraints on their deceptive and manipulative actions. While deceiving one's enemy about the movement of one's troops and munitions is generally permissible, it would be wrong to conceal that movement by using trucks bearing medical insignia like a red cross.[24] Enemies in war benefit from mutual forbearance from attacks on their medics and their medics' vehicles, and accordingly, they benefit from a conventional sign like a red cross that they can use to identify its bearers as medics and medical transports so as to give them immunity from attack. And what justifies this convention, just as what justifies the conventions for surrender, is that it serves the interest that all whom war affects have in limiting war's butchery. To understand victory in war as not requiring that one's enemy be destroyed is implicitly to understand it as not requiring that the enemy be stripped of his humanity as a prelude to such destruction, and a convention of war that grants immunity from attack to medics and their vehicles vitally contributes to maintaining each side's recognition of the other's humanity. Hence, when either side invokes the convention by using a red cross to identify its medics and their vehicles, it assumes an obligation to be truthful in its use of this sign.

In war, then, though enemies have no general obligation to forbear from deceiving and manipulating each other despite circumstances in which deception or manipulation would seriously endanger its target, they are not completely free to engage in such deception and manipulation. Conventions of war create some obligations to one's enemy to be truthful and to honor one's promises. These obligations lie outside of Scanlon's position, for they

---

24. I owe this example and its analysis to Ann Davis.

are not grounded on principles, like D and F, that define such obligations independently of conventions. Perhaps, then, what Scanlon needs to do is to screen off wartime obligations from obligations made in civilized society.[25] That is, rather than bring coerced promises made by acts of surrender in war within the scope of F, what he needs to do is to screen off the obligations such promises create from those that voluntary promises between people who are not at war create. War, after all, is different. Its morality, so to speak, is different from the morality of civilized life, and it is natural, therefore, to think that this difference would justify Scanlon's treating separately the obligations that coerced promises made in war create from those that voluntary promises made in civilized society create. At the same time, war may not be so different that one cannot learn from the former something about the nature of the latter. It may not be so different, in other words, that one cannot learn from the former something about the general nature of the obligation to keep a promise that goes against Scanlon's position.

Thus, consider again the obligation to stop firing and submit to capture that raising a white flag creates. Raising the flag signals an intention to perform these actions, and it also gives to the enemy assurance of the firmness of this intention. On the account Scanlon favors, raising the flag is a convenient way of providing this assurance but nothing more. Yet in this case it seems to be more. As we observed earlier, the lack of trust between enemies in war is so great that it would be futile to try to assure one's enemy of the firmness of one's intentions by means other than invoking a convention established for this purpose, and consequently, the role that raising a white flag has in providing assurance to the enemy must be more than the incidental one that Scanlon's account assigns to it. Its role, rather, must be to signify something the enemy can take to be a reason to be assured, and what gives the enemy such a reason is the fact of surrender and, in particular, the

---

25. Such a division between principles of obligation may seem particularly well suited to a contractualist theory of morality. The general thrust of contractualism certainly suggests a theory that conceives the principles on which obligations are grounded as principles to which a group of people wanting to form an association for mutual benefit on fair terms of cooperation would agree. Accordingly, the theory could hold that such principles were limited to governing conduct by members of a civilized society toward each other but not conduct between enemies at war. Scanlon, however, rejects this conception of the principles of obligation and the corresponding understanding of their scope. It is too narrow. Such principles, he holds, govern the conduct of a broader class, specifically, all beings "who are capable of judging things as better or worse and, more generally, capable of holding judgment sensitive attitudes," and who have a good, are conscious and are capable of feeling pain. See *What We Owe to Each Other*, pp. 177–187.

obligation to stop firing and submit to capture that surrender entails. On this account, then, raising the flag provides assurance to the enemy because the enemy both understands it as signifying that one has assumed this obligation and knows that this understanding is mutual. Accordingly, the assurance it provides is not the source of the obligation the act creates but rather the other way round. The obligation is the source of the assurance. And to make this point is just to affirm, in the case of surrender, Hume's general thesis about promising, that it fosters in promisers motives in view of which the promisees can be confident of the promisers' acting as they have promised and that mutual recognition of a promiser's having, as a result of making a promise, assumed an obligation to do this act explains how the promise fosters these motives.

The case, not surprisingly, directly challenges Scanlon's position. What is more important, though, is that it illustrates the quite general challenge that Hume's thesis poses to Scanlon's position. For it exemplifies how, on Hume's account, obligations that promises create explain the assurances that promises provide rather than, as Scanlon proposes, the other way round. Hume's account construes the signs by which one makes a promise as, in the first instance, signs for undertaking obligations, in view of which they provide assurances, and given the cogency of this account, it is then incumbent on Scanlon to justify his construing these signs as, in the first instance, signs for giving assurances, which then create obligations. In short, it is incumbent on Scanlon to answer the charge, which Hume's view inspires, that his position gets things backward. And though Scanlon is aware of this charge and of its Humean inspiration, his answer to it nonetheless fails to vindicate his account.[26]

Scanlon gives this answer in replying to an objection G. E. M. Anscombe raised to accounts like his. The objection, which is that such accounts are "subject to a fatal circularity," is substantially the same as this charge, so one can easily adapt his reply to fit the latter.[27] In replying, Scanlon points out that when one person P makes a promise to another Q, P already has obligations to Q that give Q reasons to believe that P will keep his promise. In particular, P has an obligation of truthfulness to Q that is defined by Principle D. Hence, if Q believes that P takes this obligation seriously,

26. Ibid., p. 307.
27. Ibid. Anscombe's objection is found in her "Rules, Rights and Promises," *Ethics Religion and Politics: Collected Philosophical Papers* (Minneapolis: University of Minnesota Press, 1981), pp. 97–103.

then Q will have a reason to believe that P would not try to induce him to form expectations about his, that is, P's, future conduct if P himself were at all uncertain about meeting them and therefore that P would not make this promise unless he had a firm intention to keep it. Consequently, the promise provides assurance to Q as a result of Q's believing that P has, and recognizes himself as having, general obligations to be truthful in his dealings with Q, and since these obligations precede the promise and do not depend on the conventions that constitute the practice of promising, they explain how a promise can provide assurance to its recipient independently of any special obligation the practice generates. In other words, this explanation of the assurance a promise provides does not presuppose the very obligation the assurance is supposed to explain. It thus avoids the circularity that Anscombe saw in accounts like Scanlon's. It thus meets the charge of getting things backward, since the promise explains the provision of assurance in virtue of which the promiser assumes an obligation and not the other way round.

This explanation, as we already know, fails in the case of a promise made by an act of surrender in war. Though such a promise provides its recipient with assurance, it would be a mistake to trace that assurance to the recipient's having a reason to believe that the promiser recognizes and takes seriously the obligation of truthfulness that D defines. For the promiser is the recipient's enemy, and enemies in war understand all too well that neither has a general obligation of truthfulness to the other of the sort that D defines. Might there, then, be in civilized society similar circumstances, ones in which a promise creates an obligation but the promiser does not have the general obligation of truthfulness to its recipient that D defines? Are there not some relations in civilized society sufficiently adversarial to create such circumstances? Consider, for example, workers and bosses locked in an angry dispute over wages, or parties to a nasty civil suit seeking an out of court settlement, or a married couple going through a less than amicable divorce. Certainly, in tough negotiations between people pitted against each other in these ways, it is common practice to try to persuade one's adversary to expect to have to settle for less than what he would get if he bargained harder. That is, it is common practice to try to lead one's adversary to believe falsely that one is unwilling to compromise beyond a certain point—to lower one's offer, to accept a smaller settlement, to pay no more in child support. Of course, if both sides are savvy, then neither will be deceived by the other's bluff. But even when one side is easily taken in by the other's false pretense of being unyielding, the deception is acceptable practice. Its being a violation of D, however, implies that Scanlon's explanation runs into trouble in the case of the promises such adversaries exchange when they reach agreement and settle.[28]

This case, like the case of a promise made by an act of surrender in war, is one in which the principals are assured by the promises they exchange even though neither previously had a reason to believe that the other would regard it as wrong to deceive him about certain intentions he had that bore on the outcome of their contest. Should you ask why either of these adversaries now has a reason to be confident of the other's having sufficient motives to forbear from deceiving him about his intentions when before they exchanged promises neither had a reason to be confident of the other's having such motives, I would answer, following Hume, that the promise each makes creates an obligation that he can recognize as requiring him to act on the intentions he has led the other to believe he has when before he made the promise there was no such obligation. These observations go directly against Scanlon's explanation of the obligations these adversaries assume by their exchange of promises. His explanation, briefly, is that they can recognize a prior obligation of truthfulness that requires them to forbear from deceiving each other about intentions they have that bear on the outcome of their contest and that therefore gives each a reason to be confident of the other's having sufficient motives to keep a promise. Unlike the Humean answer, then, this explanation does not present the obligation to keep a promise as the source of motives in view of which each can have confidence in the other's reliability

28. Similarly, a common practice in highly competitive activities (even those that are not cutthroat) is to deceive your opponent about your strategy. In democratic elections, for instance, you may try to persuade your opponent that your plan for winning a majority includes capturing a particular block of voters when, in fact, you are convinced that this block will not give you enough votes to be worth targeting. Since the point of the deception is to induce your opponent to expend valuable time and resources needlessly, it too is a violation of D.

Scanlon does note, in a passage about the possibility of permissible deception, that some forms of competition may give rise to it. He writes, "The more interesting class of cases...goes beyond actual consent [to being deceived], however. These would be cases in which there is good reason to structure certain forms of interaction (some forms of economic competition perhaps) in a way that permits some forms of deception but not others (a qualified form of *caveat emptor*, so to speak). I am not certain whether there are such cases or not. Leaving these special institutional cases aside, however, I do not believe that from a general moral point of view there is an important difference between lying and other forms of deception" (*What We Owe to Each Other*, p. 320). Scanlon may, then, be acknowledging cases of acceptable deception like the example of concealing one's electoral strategy through various feints. But what Scanlon does not note is the implication of this concession for his reply to Anscombe's objection. A qualification of D's application to some interpersonal activity should, given Scanlon's reply, similarly qualify the assurance a promise between people engaged in those activities provides, yet obviously it doesn't.

not to act contrary to intentions he has led the other to expect him to act on. Rather, it presents the obligation as superfluous in this respect, because it takes the prior obligation of truthfulness that each has to the other as yielding such motives. But once the folly of placing confidence in an adversary's or enemy's recognizing an obligation to forbear deceiving one about his intentions becomes apparent, the explanation loses its grip.

In this opposition between the two explanations, one can see the classical dispute between the positivism of thinkers like Hume and the rationalism of thinkers in the modern tradition of natural law. Hume denied the fundamental assumption behind the latter's program. He denied, that is, that one could by careful reflection on the idea of interpersonal relations and the most general conditions of human life grasp universal principles of right and wrong that would define the strict obligations of justice we owe to each other. Hume thought, instead, that such obligations presupposed the invention by human beings of certain institutions and practices, like property, trade, promising, and civil government, and that the strictness of these obligations was evidence of the role of human artifice in their origins.[29] In Hume's view, the moral motives to perform these obligations depend on appreciation of the place in human life of the institutions and practices they presuppose. In the program of the natural lawyers, by contrast, the moral motives to perform these obligations spring directly from grasping the validity of the principles of right and wrong that define them. The theory of obligation that Scanlon has developed and that includes his explanation of the obligation to keep a promise continues this program and advances it considerably. Its accounts of the obligations of justice are illuminating and deep, especially when applied to relations of fellowship among people. Difficulties in these accounts, however, or at least in the account of the obligation to keep a promise, emerge when they are applied to relations of hostility. These difficulties, I believe, tend to undermine the general view of the nature of moral motives Scanlon's shares with other theories in the modern tradition of natural law. Whether Hume was closer to the truth on this question is hard to say. But that his account of promises and the obligation to keep them does not run into these difficulties gives some reason to think that he was.

---

29. Hume, *Treatise*, pp. 529–531.

9

Moral Agency
and Criminal Insanity

Horrifying crimes often seem incomprehensible. Their monstrous character and gruesome consequences freeze our thoughts, leaving us at a loss to
explain how a human being could act with such wanton or heartless violence. Stunned at the horror of such action, we may begin to form the idea
of a malign will bent on causing death and destruction and then invest this
idea with the intense fear and revulsion that the horror excites. Thus, from a
powerful mix of feelings, an idea of an evil will can take hold of our imagination and suggest an explanation of what otherwise seems inexplicable. And if
we are unsophisticated about such primitive mental processes, we will now
think that we have the explanation we wanted for these grisly crimes. There
is evil in the world, and they are its manifestations.

Filmmakers are especially good at creating the frightening and repellent
images that give us the idea of evil.[1] One need look no further for examples
than the recent popular fantasy, *Lord of the Rings*, from Tolkien's trilogy.
Its many monsters embody evil or, in the case of several shrieking, spectral

---

1. See Noël Carroll, "Horror and Humor," in *Beyond Aesthetics: Philosophical Essays*
(Cambridge: Cambridge University Press, 2001), pp. 235–254, esp. fn. 15.

riders, exude it. Once the lights in the theater go down and we become immersed in the film's depiction of Tolkien's story, we see these monsters as instruments of evil: a collective scourge against which the opposing forces of good must do battle. This view is the product of imagination well wrought by the filmmaker's art as well as Tolkien's. Escaping into their imaginary world, we regress, as it were, slipping into a kind of thinking appropriate to young and credulous minds. To be sure, such thinking may have once, long ago, been the standard of mature minds. Perhaps, in the ancient world, when Zoroastrian and Manichean beliefs dominated various cultures, it was a testament to human intelligence. Perhaps, then, it befits a particular stage of civilization. But it does not befit ours. In today's world, rather, its home is the Saturday morning cartoon show and Hollywood productions like *Lord of the Rings*. It would be out of place in the conduct of civic affairs. In particular, it would be out of place in the determinations of public policy concerning the prevention and punishment of crime and the treatment of violent and disruptive individuals. To regard crimes, even horrifying crimes, as manifestations of evil and to think of their perpetrators as agents of evil is to invite back into the institutions of the criminal law barbarous and inhumane practices of an earlier time whose removal counts among the most important advances in these institutions' development.[2]

These advances correspond to more sophisticated beliefs about human behavior and a more analytical understanding of evil and what accounts for its occurrence in the world. Specifically, they correspond to the view of human beings as possessing free will and the belief that evil comes into the world when a person, in the exercise of his free will, purposefully or knowingly harms another. On this view, to say that someone possesses free will is to say that he has a power to originate actions independently of the impact of external events on his thoughts and feelings. A person, in other words, by virtue of this power, is the originating cause of his voluntary actions. External events are merely part of the circumstances of his actions and do not constitute

---

2. The possibility of such retrogression was brought home to me a few years ago in the aftermath of the killings at Columbine High School. The comments of public figures whose opinions matter were often reported in the news, and I remember one nationally prominent politician, whose ambitions for high office were obvious and whose prospects of gaining it strong, being asked by the press for his thoughts on this horrible event. Did he think it showed that something is seriously wrong in America? Are there too many guns around? Is there too much violence in popular culture? Is the culture's materialism and consumerism instilling in too many young people an uncertain moral compass? The politician demurred. We should not, he said, look to social conditions for the answer to why this event occurred. People just need to realize that the world contains evil.

their causes. Further, in being the originating cause of his voluntary actions, a person is also the originating cause of their natural consequences. Accordingly, when, through the exercise of a free will, the person acts violently and destructively and thereby inflicts injury and suffering on others, he becomes the originating cause of the evil that his actions' harmful consequences define. He is thus seen as responsible for evil, and seeing him in this way is importantly different from seeing him as being actuated by evil. It helps to preserve the view of him as human. The latter, as we noted before, tends to turn him into a monster. Hence, we count seeing a person as being responsible for his actions in virtue of their having resulted from his exercise of a free will as an advance in human thought. Among other things, it supports more just and humane policies concerning the prevention and punishment of crime. It supports, in particular, the practice in the criminal law of holding people responsible for their actions only if they did them voluntarily.

Nonetheless, this view is also more appropriate to an earlier time. It belongs to a tradition of conceiving of human beings as neither wholly animal nor wholly divine, but rather something in-between. For to regard human actions, no matter how intelligent and deliberate they may be, as uncaused by external events is to take them as exceptions to the rule that the conditions and forces of nature explain events occurring in the natural world. Correspondingly, it is to attribute to ourselves a power that puts us outside of that world, even while our actions are occurring within it. It is, in other words, to think of ourselves as having supernatural powers. Such metaphysical exceptionalism about human beings is no longer viable. It too represents a kind of primitive thinking.

To advance beyond such thinking, then, it is necessary to come to an understanding of intelligent and deliberate human action as a natural phenomenon, as something that not only takes place in the natural world but is also explainable by its conditions and forces. Achieving such an understanding without at the same time having to conclude that the criminal law must abandon its practice of holding people responsible for their actions is no simple matter. The problem has vexed thinkers from various fields for a good long time. I will call it, with apologies to W. V. O. Quine, the problem of naturalized responsibility. It is one of the main problems at the intersection of law and psychology.

The problem arises most acutely in debates over the law's allowing insanity as an exculpatory defense to a charge of criminal wrongdoing. The issue in these debates is not whether mental illness can ever so affect a person's behavior that she is not responsible for it. It is generally agreed that it can and that it would be grossly unjust for the law to punish people for such behavior. The issues, rather, are whether the law needs to have a separate insanity defense to protect the mentally ill from such punishment and, if it does, what criteria of insanity it should adopt for the purpose of so protecting them. Someone who breaks into a neighbor's unoccupied house during a psychotic episode in which, in the grip of a hallucination, a stranger appears to be coming at him with an ax and the house appears to be a place of safety would not have to turn to a separate insanity defense to be excused from responsibility for home invasion. Having acted in the genuine belief that his life was in sudden danger from an ax-wielding assailant, he could avail himself of the same legal defenses that are available to people of sound mind who invade others' property in the mistaken belief that it is necessary to save themselves from some imminent threat to their lives. But not every act of wrongdoing that results from mental illness and whose punishment we would find troubling so clearly qualifies as involuntary action, and some, perhaps, clearly qualify as voluntary action. It is in view of these that the issues of whether the law needs a separate insanity defense and, if so, what its criteria of insanity should be arise.

The issues, then, usher in the problem of naturalized responsibility as a result of how they are understood. The general reluctance to punish acts of wrongdoing that result from mental illness—and the corresponding sentiment in favor of excusing their doers from responsibility for them—springs from a common view of the actions as beyond the actors' control. Consequently, the debates on these issues tend to focus on the ways mental illness can disable people from controlling their actions. They tend, that is, to take the ability to control one's actions as the principal *sine qua non* of responsibility and thus to define the issues as whether and how mental illness impairs that ability in ways the criminal law would not recognize if it did not have a separate insanity defense. Whence the problem of naturalized responsibility surfaces. For it is not easy to understand people's ability to control their actions without falling back on the idea of their having the power to determine them independently of external causes.

In this essay, I want to take a fresh look at these debates. It is my belief that they offer hope of a solution to the problem. To see this, however, one must look at the debates without redefining the issues in them as issues about whether and how mental illness impairs a person's ability to control her behavior. For once one allows this redefinition, the debates cease to be a potential source of new ideas on the topic. Instead, they become at best a source of new and exotic examples of familiar ideas about the machinery of human action and the requirements of criminal responsibility. Of course, you might already think that any effort to find new ideas on the topic in the way I propose is vain, that the connection between responsibility for one's actions and the ability to control them is too tight to be ignored. It is my hope, though, to persuade you otherwise.[3]

I

To make the case for the law's allowing a separate defense of insanity to a charge of criminal wrongdoing, one needs to give some reason why the law cannot rely on its traditional defenses—mistake, ignorance, duress, necessity, and so forth—for providing those who suffer from mental illness with adequate protection from being punished for actions that are more appropriately seen as symptoms of disease than exercises of criminal will. One needs, in other words, to point to something about action resulting from mental illness that, in many cases, removes the actor's responsibility for it but that none of the traditional defenses covers. These defenses assume a certain standard of action and that the defendant's behavior conformed to it. Thus, one needs to point to some way in which mental illness renders the behavior of its sufferers deviant relative to this standard. One thing the defenses assume, for instance, is that the defendant's actions sprang from comprehensible if not completely rational motives. This is evident from reflection on what a cogent presentation of one of these defenses entails. Specifically, it entails explaining why one acted as one did so that a jury can understand how in so acting one came to violate the law unwittingly or unwillingly. Consequently, an argument for a separate insanity defense might be based on the deviance of the motives

---

3. An apparent alternative to my proposal would be to define different senses in which a person was said to have the ability to control his actions, one of which permitted a solution to the problem of naturalized responsibility. One such program is developed with great subtlety in John M. Fischer's book *The Metaphysics of Free Will: An Essay on Control* (Oxford: Blackwell, 1994), pp. 131–189. See also John M. Fischer and Mark Ravizza, *Responsibility and Control: A Theory of Moral Responsibility* (Cambridge: Cambridge University Press, 1998), pp. 28–41. Fischer distinguishes two types of control, guidance and regulative, and works out a solution to the problem of naturalized responsibility on which the type of control we attribute to people in attributing to them the ability to control their actions is guidance control. Fischer's program, however, is not a real alternative. It is either based on misdirection or entirely consistent with my proposal. That is, either 'guidance control' is a term expressing the everyday notion of mechanistic control, the notion expressed in such sentences as 'A thermostat controls the heat in the building', in which case it expresses a notion that is not relevant to the problem of naturalized responsibility, or it is a technical term that is meant to replace the everyday notion of volitional control, the notion expressed in such sentences as 'I control whether the heat in the building goes up or down', in which case its adoption presupposes rather than provides a solution to the problem.

that often operate in actions traceable to mental illness. One might argue, that is, that such actions are unsuitable for regulation by the criminal law because the motives from which they spring are irrational and sometimes even incomprehensible. Hence, it would be both pointless and cruel to punish any such actions.

This argument looks to the deterrent purpose of the criminal law to make the case for the insanity defense. Spelled out more fully, the argument is this. The criminal law is designed to keep people who see some advantage in trespassing on the interests or rights of others from pursuing that advantage. Guided by this purpose, the law prohibits a great variety of harmful and unjust actions and sets penalties for engaging in these actions as a means of deterring anyone who is inclined toward doing them from acting on that inclination. The general assumption is that people are rational actors in the economist's sense: they act on decisions reached from calculating the costs and benefits of the various courses of action open to them. Thus, the would-be offender, it is assumed, will see the penalties the law imposes on harmful and unjust actions as disadvantages and will, in the usual case, regard them as severe enough to outweigh whatever advantages attract him to acting in ways that would harm others or violate their rights. Mentally ill offenders, however, are far from the usual case. Their offenses, if products of their illness, do not as a rule conform to the economist's model of rational action. Indeed, their offenses often make no sense in terms of some advantage they might have hoped to gain from committing them. They often, in other words, appear to lack the kind of motive whose operation the law is designed to suppress.

Consider, for example, a sad case that was in the local news of Chicago and its suburbs some years ago.[4] It is a case of what one might call melancholic homicide. In March 1999, a forty-one-year-old woman, in the middle of a rocky divorce, drugged and then smothered to death her three young children. Afterward she tried unsuccessfully to take her own life by cutting her wrists. Having survived, she was subsequently tried and convicted of murder. Her defense was a plea of insanity based on her having

4. Janan Hanna and Eric Feskenhoff, "Mom Charged in Slayings," *Chicago Tribune*, 7 March 1999, sec. 1, p. 1. (The sad case of Andrea Yates, which received much more coverage in the national news, has many of the same elements as the one I am about to describe, but it also has one important difference. Yates's illness included psychotic episodes, for which she was being treated at the time she killed her children. The psychosis, while it makes her mental illness more severe and thus makes her plea of insanity even more compelling, complicates her case in a way that makes it less useful for my discussion than more straightforward cases of severe depression. The mother in the case I'm about to describe did not have a history of having suffered from any psychosis.)

suffered from severe depression at the time she killed her children. From the evidence presented at trial, it is plain that she did suffer from severe depression at the time and that killing her children was a product of this illness. It is also hard to see from this evidence any advantage she could have hoped to gain from killing her children or, indeed, any motive behind the killings of the sort that concerns the criminal law. The prosecution argued that she killed to spite her husband, and such revenge is, of course, possible, as is a misplaced concern for her children's welfare. Certainly, no one would deny that severe depression brings plenty of anger and despair. Still, to treat the anger and felt desperation it brings as revealing desires (or as the economists would say, preferences) of a rational actor disposed to weigh the benefits of their satisfaction against the costs that acting on them would incur is to misconstrue them. They are not, as the upshots of severe depression, rooted in the beliefs and values on which rational decisions are made, and one cannot, therefore, expect penalties designed to influence such decisions to have a similar influence on the motivational currents of these emotions.

Or consider an example of Joel Feinberg's, the case of *State v. McCullough*, an early twentieth-century case of theft in which kleptomania was accepted as grounds for acquittal.[5] The defendant was a high school student who had stolen a great many things, all of which had little value and which he hoarded for no apparent purpose. His stash included combs, jack knives, old clocks, watch chains, razors, harmonicas, bicycle wrenches, rulers, bolts, padlocks, oil cans, old keys, and so forth. Given both the relative worthlessness of this stash and his failure to put any of it to good use, it would appear that he repeatedly committed acts of theft without seeing any advantage in acquiring the things he stole. It would appear, that is, that behind his thievery there was no motive of the sort that concerns the criminal law. The acts were the product of some strange urge to steal and not part of a plan, say, to make himself rich.

In short, then, the deterrent purpose of the penalties the criminal law sets for breaking the law rests on assumptions about the kinds of motive on which lawbreakers act, and mentally ill offenders, in many cases, do not act from such motives. Subjecting them to punishment is therefore pointless and cruel. It is pointless because their behavior does not issue from the sort

---

5. Joel Feinberg, "What Is So Special about Mental Illness?" in his *Doing and Deserv-ing: Essays in the Theory of Responsibility* (Princeton: Princeton University Press, 1970), pp. 272–292. Feinberg gives as the citation for this case 114 Iowa 532 (1901).

of calculation of costs and benefits whose terms the law seeks to alter by announcing penalties for lawbreaking and imposing them when it occurs, and it is cruel because by punishing mentally ill offenders for acts that result from their illness, the law appears to be punishing sickness rather than ministering to it. The argument, once it is evident how mental illness can produce undeterrable acts of lawbreaking for which none of the criminal law's traditional defenses provide an excuse, seems unassailable. And by focusing on the question of deterrability, it finesses that of responsibility. By basing the case for a separate insanity defense on the irrationality of the motives from which the actions of mentally ill offenders spring, it sidesteps the issues about the voluntariness of the offender's actions and the extent to which they come within the person's control on which the question of responsibility traditionally turns. Thus, the argument not only seems unassailable but also progressive.

Nonetheless, I think it falls short of justifying a separate insanity defense. The problem lies in the very finessing of the question of responsibility that seems to recommend it. This move essentially involves replacing the question of responsibility with that of deterrability, and these are not equivalent questions. Nor does the latter encompass the former. However it is settled, the former may still remain open. Consequently, a gap exists between the argument's premises and its conclusion. A criminal offender may be responsible for his conduct despite being immune to the deterrent force of the penalties the law imposes on such conduct, and if he is, punishment may be neither pointless nor cruel.

This observation, moreover, is not just an abstract possibility. Mentally ill offenders, after all, are not the only class of lawbreakers whose members, in many cases, fail to fit the assumptions on which the deterrent purpose behind the law's penalties rests. Religious fanatics, zealous revolutionaries, and fiery anarchists also fail to fit these assumptions. Their zealotry blinds them to concerns of ordinary people and leads them to put little or no value on their own well-being. As a result, the deterrent force of punishment cannot reach them. To be sure, unlike the mentally ill offenders we considered earlier, these subversives still qualify as rational actors in the economist's sense. One can still regard them as acting on decisions made by calculating the costs and benefits of the various courses of action open to them. The reason they do not fit the assumptions on which the deterrent purpose behind the law's penalties rests is that they do not see these penalties as costs or at least as costs of sufficient severity to outweigh the benefits of subversive action. Being single-minded in their pursuit of the overthrow of government, they take anything that furthers this pursuit as negating or trumping such costs. Hence, they too are undeterrable offenders.[6] They too do not act from motives of the kind the criminal law is designed to suppress. Yet who could deny that they are responsible for their actions? Nor does it seem altogether pointless or cruel to punish them. It is not as though one could seriously say that by punishing them the law appears to be punishing political differences rather than settling them. By punishing them, rather, the law appears to be imposing penalties necessary to assuring people that resorting to violence in the pursuit of political ends will not be tolerated.[7]

Of course, you might think there is a world of difference between punishing rational actors who are undeterrable and punishing irrational ones. And this may be so. But the distinction, as we have drawn it in characterizing certain subversive offenders as rational and certain mentally ill ones as irrational, depends on the economist's model of rational action, and it is hard to see in this model, taken by itself, anything implying that those who fit it are appropriate subjects of punishment and those who don't are not. The model helps to explain why mentally ill offenders like the melancholic mother

6. In making this point, I am assuming that being deterrable means something more than being able to control one's actions. If it meant nothing more than this, then my criticism here would lose its force. But then the target of the criticism too would be of no interest since it would not be an argument from which one could learn how to conceive of responsibility for action without recourse to questions of whether the actor had the ability to control his actions. Hence, if the argument has interest, being deterrable must not be reducible to being able to control one's actions.

Admittedly, reducing deterrability to the ability to control one's actions is common in legal writing. The reduction, at any rate, is implicit in the familiar test of whether the offender would have committed the crime if a policeman had been at his elbow. One can, however, understand deterrability as a distinct notion from that of being in control of one's actions. Thus, as a matter of ordinary use, we say that someone cannot be deterred from doing X when the person is bent on doing it regardless of the obstacles she faces. This doesn't mean that the person will try to do X in every situation in which she perceives that she might do X (as if trying to do X were an automatic response to any such situation). Putting off the attempt until the circumstances are more favorable is consistent with being bent on doing X, though it must also be true that sooner or later one will make the attempt and will continue to make attempts despite failures. Hence, on this notion of deterrability, being undeterrable is consistent with being in control of one's actions in any particular set of circumstances, including those in which a policeman is at one's elbow. Accordingly, it is persistence rather than automaticity that indicates undeterrability, and in criticizing the argument I am assuming that it presupposes this notion of deterrability in its point about the undeterrability of certain mentally ill offenders.

7. Note that providing assurance to the law-abiding that breaking the law will not be tolerated is a different basis for justifying punishment from deterrence. On the role of punishment in providing assurance to the law-abiding, see Herbert Morris, "Persons and Punishment," in his *On Guilt and Innocence: Essays in Legal Philosophy and Moral Psychology* (Berkeley: University of California Press, 1976), pp. 31–58, esp. 33–34, and John Rawls, *A Theory of Justice* (Cambridge, MA: Harvard University Press, 1971), pp. 268–270, 314–315.

and the kleptomaniac high school student in our two examples fail to fit the assumptions on which the deterrent purpose of the penalties the criminal law imposes rests, but it does not, as far as I can see, offer a reason independent of undeterrability for exempting such offenders from being liable to punishment. Hence, if such an exemption is warranted on account of their being irrational, it must be warranted in virtue of a different sense of irrationality. Yet what this different sense could be is far from clear.

One person who has tried to capture it is Feinberg.[8] Taking the actor's motives as the relevant determinant of rationality and the economist's model as his starting point, Feinberg suggests three qualifications of the model. First, the motive, to be rational, must represent one of the actor's interests. Merely being one of his desires is insufficient. Second, it must cohere with the actor's other motives, particularly those central to his character and to the life he is living. And third, it must not be hidden from the actor or so deeply hidden that he has no insight into it. This last qualification, Feinberg thinks, is perhaps the most telling. The clearest indication of the mentally ill offender's irrationality, he tentatively suggests, is the offender's inability to comprehend his own motives. But I doubt the criterion of rationality implied by this suggestion will do. Surely many zealous revolutionaries are driven by deep-seated difficulties in dealing with authorities, difficulties the origins of which long precede their political awakening and into which they have absolutely no insight, yet it would be a stretch to exempt such people from being liable to punishment on the grounds of their having acted from irrational motives. Nor do the criteria implied by either of Feinberg's other two suggestions offer much hope. Well-heeled people who shoplift on the spur of the moment may be acting on mere desires or sudden urges to get away with something and completely out of character, but the law is not about to exempt them from being liable to punishment on the grounds that the desires prompting their shoplifting are irrational.[9]

8. Feinberg, "What Is So Special about Mental Illness?" pp. 280–289.
9. In fairness to Feinberg, it should be pointed out that he is not proposing these qualifications of the economist's model as each a distinct criterion of rationality. Rather, he is attempting to abstract from his several examples of mentally ill offenders, all of whom suffer from some obsessive-compulsive disorder, a profile of the mentally ill offender whose offense is voluntary but, because of its irrationality, undeserving of punishment. The qualifications then correspond to elements in the profile. The general idea that guides Feinberg in his construction of this profile is the thought that these offenders are pathetic rather than vicious, more to be pitied and helped than scorned and punished. Feinberg's aim is to defend his "prephilosophical attitude" that there is a morally significant difference between "mental illness and plain wickedness." The profile he constructs is intended to capture this difference, and the difference alone, apart

II

Having found that one cannot finesse the question of responsibility in arguing for a separate insanity defense, let us then turn to argument that deals directly with the question. The criminal law's interest in the question reflects its general concern with protecting the innocent from being punished, and this concern in turn reflects its commitment to justice, specifically to upholding both in its design and in its operations certain principles of retributive justice. To attribute this commitment to the criminal law is not, however, to deny that its main purposes are to deter crime, to incapacitate criminals, and to reduce social unrest. Rather, it is to say that the law recognizes an imperative to limit or regulate the pursuit of these purposes by principles of retributive justice. Following H. L. A. Hart, let us suppose that the main purposes of punishment in the criminal law are the ones just mentioned and that the principles of retributive justice regulate how the law distributes the burdens of punishment in its pursuit of these purposes.[10] Accordingly, the principles are, first, that punishment should be imposed on people who are guilty of some offense and on no others and, second, that the severity of the punishment imposed on someone should be proportionate to the degree of that person's guilt. Only the first principle bears on our study. The second becomes relevant when arguments for a separate insanity defense are extended to address the related issues of diminished responsibility.

That the criminal law makes responsibility for an act of wrongdoing a condition of being liable to punishment for that act follows from its commitment to upholding the first of these two principles. This principle restricts those who are liable to punishment to persons guilty of some offense, and in upholding it the law aims at imposing its penalties only on those who deserve punishment. To say this much is only to make explicit what the

---

from any consideration of deterrability, is the ground on which Feinberg makes his argument for a separate insanity defense. See ibid.

While this gives a fairer account of Feinberg's argument, the argument itself is still unsound. In particular, the idea that Feinberg takes as his guide is clearly unreliable. Consider one of his examples, a fetishist whose fetish leads him to shoplift women's bras. Though we can certainly grant Feinberg that this man is most unhappy and deserves our pity, nonetheless we have no reason to suppose that the man's shoplifting is morally any different from other incidents of shoplifting in which the thief steals items associated with sex in order to avoid embarrassment. How many young men, for instance, in the more puritanical regions of America have shoplifted condoms in order to avoid embarrassment at the cash register?

10. See H. L. A. Hart, "Prolegomenon to the Principles of Punishment," in his *Punishment and Responsibility: Essays in the Philosophy of Law* (Oxford: Oxford University Press, 1968), pp. 1–27.

notion of being guilty of wrongdoing implies. At the same time, it is a matter of justice (and not merely an implication of the notion of being guilty) that guilt be attributed to someone for some act of wrongdoing only if the person is responsible for the act. Justice, that is, requires that responsibility for wrongful action be the basis for one's deserving punishment for it. The idea here is that one deserves blame and punishment for wrongful action, just as one deserves praise and credit for worthy action, only if one is genuinely the author of the action. And this is not a vacuous idea, as is evident from brief reflection on how easily we come to feel pride in or guilt over the good and bad actions of people with whom we are affiliated but for whose actions we are not in the least responsible. The criminal law thus seeks to realize this idea by restricting liability to punishment not to lawbreakers generally but to lawbreakers who are responsible for their offenses.

A contrast with institutions in which penalties are imposed on rule breakers without regard to their responsibility nicely illuminates this point. Consider, for instance, how rules regulate the play in such organized sports as hockey and basketball. In either, penalties are imposed for infractions of the rules, and part of the purpose of imposing them is to deter players from breaking the rules. At the same time, the officials who determine when a player has broken the rules have no interest in whether the player deserves the penalty. They have no interest in the question of the player's guilt or innocence. Players thus incur penalties for both accidental and deliberate infractions. Charging, for example, which is an infraction of a rule in basketball against knocking into a player from the opposing team who has firmly positioned herself in one's path, is penalized regardless of whether the offending player charged into the opponent intentionally or by accident. It is therefore of no consequence within the game whether that player was or was not responsible for her play. By contrast, the criminal law generally excuses from punishment offenders who because of some faultless mistake or accident are not responsible for their actions. Thus, its restricting liability to punishment to lawbreakers who are responsible for their actions distinguishes it from other institutions that also regulate conduct by rules to which penalties for their violation are attached.

To make an argument, then, for a separate insanity defense that deals directly with the question of responsibility, one must look to the law's commitment to upholding principles of retributive justice. In particular, one must point to some way in which mental illness can render its sufferers undeserving of punishment for an offense they committed yet at the same time unexcused by any of the law's traditional defenses from responsibility for that offense. For in that case, one will have pointed out how, in the absence of a separate insanity defense, a mentally ill offender could be liable to punishment for some offense though he did not deserve it, and therefore one will have established that the criminal law's adherence to the first of our two principles of retributive justice requires the availability of a separate insanity defense. That the offense in question is a symptom of some disease suggests how such an argument would go. Considered as a symptom of a disease, the action is appropriately seen as an effect of some dysfunctional mechanism within the mind. Accordingly, it appears as the upshot of a chain of causes that extend back to the onset of the disease and not as behavior the actor initiates in the execution of his intentions. It does not, in other words, appear to issue from the actor's exercise of his agency, but rather to originate in causes that are ultimately alien to his agency. Hence, the action should not be attributed to the offender as its author, and accordingly he does not deserve punishment for it.

This argument, what I'll call the argument from etiology, is much too sweeping as it stands. Its pivotal assumption is that an action's being the product of mental disease is incompatible with its issuing from the actor's exercise of his agency, and this assumption is plainly false. Mental illness can, to be sure, so impair a person's agency that his actions do not issue from its exercise, but it can also merely influence how the person exercises his agency without at the same time vitiating his authorship of the actions that result from that exercise. Thus, the works of a novelist may show signs of mental illness. Indeed, the illness may so influence the novelist and so inform his works that they could justly be called its products. Nonetheless, he would still be their author. No doubt someone in the psychobiography trade, for example, has attributed the hypermasculinity of Hemingway's novels to Hemingway's having suffered severe, lifelong pathological anxieties about his sexual functioning or his sexual identity. I have no idea whether such a diagnosis is credible, let alone true, but even if it were true and the novels were the product of such a severe, life-long neurosis, this would not diminish in any way Hemingway's authorship of them. It would not make him any less deserving of his Nobel Prize.

So the argument from etiology has to be modified. One cannot base the conclusion that the law must allow a separate insanity defense to protect mentally ill offenders from being liable to punishment they do not deserve just on the observation that their offenses are the symptoms of mental illness. One must also show something further about the illness, that it so impaired the offender's agency, say, as to render it idle. The illness could do so, for instance, by rendering the offender passive with respect to the internal forces that bring about his commission of the offense. The offense, in this case, would be like action done under the influence of hypnosis or some powerful psychoactive drug, for typically when an action is done under either of these influences, its actor is passive with respect to external forces that induce him to act. Hence, the action does not issue from the actor's exercise of his agency. He is not its author.[11] Similarly, then, if an offender's mental illness renders him passive with respect to the forces that induce him to act, he is not the author of his action and does not, for this reason, deserve punishment for it. One way to modify the argument, then, is to qualify the kind of mental illness of which an excusable offense is a symptom to that which can have such a deleterious effect on a person's agency.

Of course, this modification would fail to yield an argument in support of the law's allowing a separate insanity defense if rendering a person passive with respect to the forces that induced him to act were the same thing as rendering him incapable of resisting those forces. For in that case, the forces would not only have induced action but compelled it, and a mentally ill offender whose illness rendered him subject to forces that compelled him to act would not need to avail himself of a separate insanity defense to gain legal protection from punishment. He could avail himself instead of the same defenses that are available to people who violate the law under duress.[12] But the two are not the same. A person who is passive with respect to the forces that induce him to act may nonetheless be capable of resisting those forces. Kleptomaniacs are a case in point. They are, after all, able to moderate their urge to steal to avoid detection. The urge, in other words, does not compel theft. Hence, to characterize their illness as rendering them passive with respect to that urge is not to imply that they are incapable of resisting it. It is to imply, rather, that they failed to resist it, and, in consequence, their behavior issued from forces external to their agency.

Admittedly, there is a problem with taking this feature of offenses that are symptomatic of mental illness as what qualifies those offenses as excusable.

---

11. I am drawing here from Harry Frankfurt's "Identification and Externality," in his *The Importance of What We Care About: Philosophical Essays* (Cambridge: Cambridge University Press, 1988), pp. 58–68.

12. What is more, if the two were the same, then my study would be at a dead end. The idea of being unable to resist a force that is inducing one to act is a specification of the more general idea of being unable to control one's behavior. Hence, to use it to determine when an offense that is a symptom of mental illness is excusable on account of that illness would be to make the issue of whether to allow in the criminal law a separate insanity defense turn on the idea of the offender's being so impaired by his illness as to be unable to control his conduct. And that would block my attempt to study this issue without redefining it as an issue about whether and how mental illness so impairs its sufferer's ability to control his behavior.

The problem is that the same feature seems to characterize offenses that are due to weakness of will, and weakness of will is not grounds for excusing offenses that result from it. To the contrary, it is a deficiency that normally warrants blame. This problem is not insuperable, however. Typically, when a person's actions are due to weakness of will, they are not just actions the person thinks he ought not to do. They are also actions whose ends, though he regards them as less valuable or important to achieve than ends he could have achieved had he done something else, are nonetheless seen by him as ends whose achievement is not without value or importance. This second characteristic distinguishes typical cases of weak-willed action from actions that do not issue from the actor's agency but are due instead to forces external to it and with respect to which the actor is passive. For it is one thing to regard the ends one pursues as ends whose achievement is less valuable or important than the achievement of other ends one could pursue, and another to regard them as foreign. Only when one regards them as foreign does one see them as ends whose achievement would be valueless or meaningless in the context of one's life. Only then does one experience the desire to achieve these ends as a force external to one's agency.

Many people, for instance, standing on a precipice or a bridge high above the ground or water below experience an urge to jump.[13] They don't jump, not because they regard some end that jumping would achieve as less valuable or important than that of remaining alive and in tact, but because they know the urge is crazy. Acting on it makes no sense in the context of their lives. If one of them, on experiencing such an urge, did jump, a description of him as weak willed would be inapt. He may be acting voluntarily, to be sure. The urge need not compel him to jump. But he would not be pursuing an end whose achievement interests him but that he regards as less valuable or important than the achievement of some other end he could pursue. The end does not interest him in the least. The urge has no place in the network of desires and interests that his agency compasses. We can thus distinguish weak-willed actions from voluntary actions that do not issue from the actor's exercising his agency, even if in both cases the action is contrary to the actor's judgment about what ought to be done. Or if you think the category of weak-willed action is broader and includes both, we can make the point differently. For we can draw the same distinction within that category. We can distinguish, that is, between those weak-willed actions that issue from the

13. The example is essentially Sartre's. See his discussion of anguish in *Being and Nothingness*, Hazel Barnes, trans. (London: Routledge, 1989), pp. 30–31.

actor's exercising his agency and those that do not. However we introduce the distinction between the former and the latter, once we see how it is drawn, the problem why the latter should be excusable when they are symptomatic of mental illness while the former are not dissolves.[14]

This first modification of the argument from etiology is alone sufficient for the purpose of finding an argument for a separate insanity defense that deals directly with the question of responsibility. But for the larger purpose of drawing from debates about this defense a solution to the problem of naturalized responsibility, it will be useful to consider another modification, one that corresponds to a second way in which mental illness can so impair an offender's agency as to make him undeserving of punishment. Specifically, illness that deadens or destroys an offender's grasp of the moral aspects of his circumstances and the courses of conduct he is contemplating may so impair his moral judgment as to bring into question whether the exercise of agency from which his offense issued was an exercise of moral agency. And in bringing into question whether the act issued from an exercise of moral agency, the illness brings into question whether the offense has the moral character necessary to warrant punishment. For the issue is whether the offender, having broken the law, deserves punishment for his offense, and this issue concerns the moral character of the action.

Comparison with our hypothetical Hemingway may be helpful here. The issue in his case, if there were an issue, would be whether he deserved his Nobel Prize in view of the influence of severe pathological anxieties on his literary work, and this issue would concern the artistic character of that work. Accordingly, the question would be whether these anxieties so impaired his artistic agency as to raise doubts about attributing the work to the exercise of that agency. And this, of course, could not be a real question since there could be no doubt about the artistic character of Hemingway's work and so its origins in the exercise of artistic agency. The parallel question in the case of some mentally ill lawbreakers, by contrast, is a real question since mental illness can so impair a person's moral agency as to raise doubts, when he breaks the law or in some other way acts contrary to basic principles of right and wrong, about the moral character of his action and its origins in the exercise of moral agency. Another way to modify the argument, then, is to qualify the kind of mental illness of which an excusable offense is a symptom as illness

---

14. See the appendix to "Reason and Motivation," in my *The Sources of Moral Agency: Essays in Moral Psychology and Freudian Theory* (Cambridge: Cambridge University Press, 1996), pp. 155–159, where a similar distinction is drawn between weak-willed actions and omissions due to depression.

that erodes or kills the sensibility and intelligence an agent must have to be a moral agent.

The argument, once modified in either of these two ways, supports the criminal law's allowing a separate insanity defense, provided, of course, that its major premisses are true, that mental illness can so impair a person's agency as either to render him passive with respect to the forces that induce him to act or to deprive him of the sensibility and intelligence necessary for his agency to qualify as moral agency and that some lawbreakers whose offenses result from such impairments would be liable to punishment if no separate insanity defense were available. These are not controversial propositions, however. Opposition to a separate insanity defense does not arise from any serious disagreement with them. Thus, it is plausible to suppose that the development in the criminal law of such a defense represents general acceptance of this argument. It is plausible, that is, to suppose that the support for a separate insanity defense that led to its adoption and has subsequently sustained it despite recurrent calls for its abolition represents a common perception of some mentally ill offenders whose offenses would not be excused by any of the law's traditional defenses as not deserving punishment because of their illness and its role in their conduct. And on this supposition it stands to reason that the debates within the criminal law over the proper test for determining criminal insanity are debates over what sort of impairment to moral agency a mentally ill offender must suffer from, as a result of his illness and at the time of his offense, to be excused from responsibility for that offense.

The most famous of these tests is the McNaghten Rule, which the English House of Lords adopted in 1843. The Rule, stated in full, is that the offender, to be excused from responsibility by reason of insanity, must, at the time of the action, have acted under a defect of reason that arose from some disease of the mind, and as a result he must have either not known the nature and quality of his action or not known that the action was wrong.[15] On standard interpretations of the Rule, its test of insanity is whether, due to mental illness, the offender has suffered certain cognitive impairments, impairments of his knowledge of right and wrong, in particular. To many people, then, the test has appeared to ignore the possibility of there being noncognitive volitional impairments and emotional disorders that result from mental illness and that render their sufferers no less innocent of wrongdoing than the cognitive impairments the test recognizes. As a result, the McNaghten Rule

15. See James Fitzjames Stephen, *A History of the Criminal Law of England* (New York: Burt Franklin, 1883), vol. 2, p. 158.

has come in for heavy criticism. Indeed, because of the Rule's early and firm entrenchment in the development of the Anglo-American law of insanity as a separate defense, the criticism has more or less defined the debates over the proper test for determining criminal insanity. Accordingly, they have largely consisted of arguments either about amendments to the Rule or about alternatives to it, whether the Rule should be amended to include an irresistible impulse test, say, and whether a wholly new alternative would give better coverage to the range of impairments that the law should recognize as determinants of insanity.

This dissatisfaction with the McNaghten Rule is well represented, for example, by the leading alternative to it, the two-pronged test put forth in the American Law Institute's Model Penal Code. This test, stated in full, is that the offender, to be excused from responsibility by reason of insanity, must, at the time of the action and as a result of mental disease or defect, have lacked substantial capacity either to appreciate the criminality or wrongfulness of his conduct or to conform his conduct to the requirements of law.[16] The Code's drafters make clear, in an explanatory note, that the reference in the test's second prong to a lack of a capacity to conform one's conduct to the requirements of law is meant to specify, as determinants of insanity, volitional impairments that can arise independently of failures to appreciate the criminality or wrongfulness of one's conduct.[17] In addition, the drafters point out that the use of the word 'appreciate' in the test's first prong is meant to cover emotional dispositions as well as "simple" cognitive capacities so that certain emotional disorders too will be sufficient determinants of criminally insanity.[18] Thus, the Model Penal Code's test purports to make good on the inadequacies for which the McNaghten Rule has been heavily criticized.

These criticisms of the Rule have, unfortunately, been made on the basis of unreflective assumptions about the separability of cognitive impairments from volitional and emotional ones. Because the McNaghten Rule focuses exclusively on the question of the offender's knowledge of the nature and quality of his action and whether it was wrong, its critics have tended to view the Rule as ignoring the volitional and emotional components of the action. And in taking this view, they have then implicitly assumed that knowledge is

---

16. *Model Penal Code and Commentaries (Official Draft and Revised Comments)*, pt. I, §4.01 (Philadelphia: ALI Institute, 1985), p. 163.

17. Ibid., pp. 163–164, "Explanatory Note." See also "Comment" that immediately follows.

18. Ibid., p. 169, "Comment" ("The use of 'appreciate' rather than 'know' conveys a broader sense of understanding than simple cognition.")

something inert in human psychology, that it has no internal connections to volition or emotion. For if it had such connections, then defects in a person's knowledge could have consequences for the volitional and emotional components of his action, and therefore it might not be necessary to formulate a test that recognized noncognitive volitional impairments and emotional disorders as determinants of insanity. They have implicitly assumed, in other words, that a whole tradition of thinking about human action stretching back to Plato is defunct. To the contrary, though, the issues that Plato first raised about the place of moral knowledge in human action and the extent to which volition and emotion incorporate rational thought are still alive. The point, of course, is not that the critics of McNaghten are wrong to conceive of human action in opposition to this tradition or that the assumptions on the basis of which they have made their criticisms are false. The point, rather, is that the assumptions, being unreflective, have made their criticisms shallow, and as a result, the debates to which they contribute have been largely stagnant. There is theoretical depth to the opposition between the McNaghten Rule and its alternatives that the criticisms miss and that needs to be plumbed if the debates are to move forward.

What gives theoretical depth to the opposition is the notion of moral agency essential to the argument behind the development in the criminal law of a separate insanity defense. For this is a theoretical notion. The question of what makes men and women moral agents is an old one that has long been treated theoretically in philosophy and psychology. It springs from an interest in distinguishing human beings from other animals and also in distinguishing those human beings whom it makes sense to hold responsible for their actions from those, like the very young and the utterly demented, whom it does not. The latter lack the capacities that people must have for it to make sense to hold them responsible for their actions, capacities that equip people for understanding the moral character of their actions and for being motivated to act accordingly. Full possession of these capacities is what qualifies a person as a moral agent, and accordingly, the question of what makes men and women moral agents is a question about what these capacities are. The different theories that have developed in philosophy and psychology from the study of this question reflect different conceptions of moral agency, and seeing how these conceptions inform the McNaghten Rule and its alternatives is sufficient for grasping the theoretical depth that exists to the opposition between them.

In modern moral philosophy, the study of this question has largely concentrated on the role and importance of reason in moral thought and moral motivation. The overarching issue is whether reason alone, if fully developed and unimpaired, is sufficient for moral agency, and the study divides chiefly into two schools of thought. One, aptly dubbed rationalism, holds that reason alone, when fully developed and unimpaired, suffices for moral agency. The foremost defenders of this view in the modern period are Kant and Reid, but it is the hallmark of rationalist philosophy generally, in a tradition that begins with Plato. On this view, reason works not only to instruct one about the moral character of one's actions but also to produce motivation to act morally. It is both the pilot and engine of moral agency, not only guiding one toward right action but also producing the desire to act rightly. Human beings, on this view, are thus moved by two fundamental kinds of desire, rational and nonrational. Rational desires have their source in the operations of reason, nonrational in animal appetite and passion. Accordingly, moral motivation, on this view, is a species of rational desire, and reason not only produces such desire but is also capable of investing it with enough strength to suppress the conflicting impulses of appetite and passion. Moral agency in human beings thus consists in the governance of appetite and passion by reason, and the possession of reason is therefore alone ordinarily sufficient to make one a moral agent.

The chief opposition to this view comes from empiricist philosophers like Hume and John Stuart Mill. They deny that reason is ever the source of moral motivation and restrict its role in moral agency to instructing one about the moral character of one's actions. On this view, all desires originate in animal appetite and passion, and reason works in the service of these desires to produce intelligent action, action that is well aimed for attaining the objects of the desires it serves. As Hume put it, in a famous declaration in his *Treatise on Human Nature*, "Reason is and ought only to be the slave of the passions."[19] The upshot of this doctrine is that the primary forms of moral motivation, the desire to act rightly, the aversion to acting wrongly, are not products of reason but are instead acquired through some mechanical process of socialization by which their objects become associated with the objects of natural desires and aversions. Moral agency in human beings thus consists in cooperation among several forces, including reason, but also including a desire to act rightly and an aversion to acting wrongly that originate in natural desires. Consequently, because the acquisition of these desires is not guaranteed by the maturation of reason, the possession of reason is never alone sufficient to make one a moral agent.

This anti-rationalist view is typically inspired by, when not grounded in, the methods and theories of natural science as applied to human psychology. In this regard, the most influential elaboration of the view in twentieth-century

19. Hume, *Treatise*, bk. II, pt. 3, sec. 3.

thought is Freud's.[20] Applying the general principles of personality development central to his mature theory, Freud gave an account of the child's development of a conscience and a sense of guilt that explained the independence and seeming authority of these phenomena consistently with their originating in instincts and drives that humans like other animals possess innately. On Freud's account, conscience and a sense of guilt were products of a superego, which develops in children through internalization of parental authority. This internalization occurs in response to severe emotional conflict that characterizes the child's ambivalent relations to its parents at an early stage in its life, and it results in the incorporation of the parents' authority within the child's personality as an independent policing and censuring force. Freud's account in this way spoke directly to the challenge that the rationalist view represents, for rationalists traditionally—and here Kant is an exemplary figure—make the independence and seeming authority of conscience the basis for attributing the phenomena of conscience, including their motivational force, to the operations of reason.[21]

The theoretical depth to the opposition between the McNaghten Rule and its alternatives should now be evident. Seeing it comes from seeing that the conception of moral agency that informs the McNaghten Rule is opposed to the one that informs its alternatives, and it should now be evident that, contrary to the presupposition of the criticisms of the Rule from which these alternative developed, the Rule does not share the anti-rationalist conception on which those criticisms are based and which thus informs the alternatives. Rather, its exclusive focus on questions about the offender's knowledge at the time of his action suggests that it is informed by a rationalist conception of moral agency. This suggestion, moreover, is implied by the Rule's original statement, in which the lack of knowledge required for insanity is linked to mental disease by a defect of reason. It is also implied by the remark immediately preceding this statement, in which responsibility is expressly made contingent on the possession of reason.

20. See Sigmund Freud, *The Ego and the Id*, chs. 3 and 5, and *Civilization and Its Discontents*, chs. 7 and 8, in *The Standard Edition of the Complete Psychological Works of Sigmund Freud*, James Strachey, gen. ed. (London: Hogarth Press, 1969, 1953–1971), vol. 19, pp. 28–39, 48–59, and vol. 21, pp. 123–145. For discussion of Freud's account, see John Deigh, "Remarks of Some Difficulties in Freud's Theory of Moral Development," *International Review of Psycho-Analysis* 11 (1984): 207–225; reprinted in my *The Sources of Moral Agency*, pp. 65–93.

21. See Kant, *Critique of Practical Reason*, L. W. Beck, trans. (Indianapolis: Bobbs-Merrill, 1956), pp. 17–51. For discussion of the opposition between Kant and Freud on the nature of conscience, see my "Freud, Naturalism and Modern Moral Philosophy," in *The Sources of Moral Agency*, pp. 113–132.

Of course, one could insist on reading 'reason' as it occurs both in this prefatory remark and in the Rule's original statement to mean the notion of reason contained in the anti-rationalist conception. Accordingly, the Rule would still be open to the very criticisms that inspired its alternatives since on this reading no defect of reason implies volitional or emotional impairments. But once the possibility of a rationalist reading surfaces, this anti-rationalist reading loses its appeal. The criticisms of the Rule to which it leads now stand instead as arguments against it. Stephen makes essentially the same argument when he distinguishes between narrower and wider interpretations of the Rule and argues that on the latter the Rule covers everything the law ought to cover in allowing a separate insanity defense, whereas on the former it falls so short of what the law ought to cover as to be an implausible construction of what the judges who authored it intended.[22] Stephen, though he favors for reasons of expository clarity a different formulation of the test, endorses the Rule on its wider interpretation, and his endorsement, forty years after the original statement, stands as further, powerful confirmation of a rationalist reading.[23] The rationalist conception of moral agency is plainly at work in his account of what the law ought to be.[24] Indeed, his account of how the power of judgment works to suppress desires, emotions, and other impulses that would prompt wrongful conduct if acted on is a précis of Reid's account of how reason regulates human conduct.[25] Thus, Stephen's wider interpretation of the Rule, given his endorsement, inherits that conception.

Appreciation of this theoretical dimension to the debates in the criminal law over the proper test for determining insanity should then move them past fruitless disputes about what sort of impairment to moral agency a mentally ill offender must suffer from to be excused from responsibility for his offense. That is, once this dimension is appreciated, the issue in dispute should no longer be whether a proper test must recognize volitional and emotional

---

22. Stephen, *A History of the Criminal Law of England*, vol. 2, pp. 159–168.

23. Ibid., p. 168.

24. Ibid., p. 171. ("All that I have said is reducible to this short form:—Knowledge and power are constituent elements of all voluntary action, and if either is seriously impaired the other is disabled. It is as true that a man who cannot control himself does not know the nature of his acts as that a man who does not know the nature of his acts is incapable of self-control.")

25. Thomas Reid, *Essays on the Active Powers of the Human Mind* (Cambridge, MA: MIT Press, 1969), pp. 200–347 (essay III, pt. 3, and essay IV). For evidence of the continued vitality of the rationalist conception in English philosophy at the time Stephen wrote and afterward, see Henry Sidgwick, *The Methods of Ethics*, bk. I, ch. 3, and my essay "Sidgwick on Ethical Judgment," in *Essays on Henry Sidgwick*, Bart Schultz, ed. (Cambridge: Cambridge University Press, 1992), pp. 241–258; reprinted in *The Sources of Moral Agency*, pp. 181–197.

impairments, as well as cognitive ones, as sufficient determinants of insanity, for both the McNaghten Rule and its leading alternatives should be seen as covering the same range of impairments. Rather, the issue in dispute should be what conception of moral agency ought to inform a proper test of insanity, what theory of moral agency ought to shape the law in this area. Admittedly, seeing what the choices are, you might think that replacing the one issue with the other is not likely to have any substantial effect on the debates, that all that is likely to result is the exchange of one kind of criticism of McNaghten for another. Instead of derogating the Rule for being blind to the possibility of volitional and emotional impairments that can render a mentally ill offender undeserving of punishment, critics of McNaghten are likely just to derogate it for implying an obsolete conception of moral agency. I won't comment here on whether the rationalist conception is obsolete, except to note that it currently enjoys a considerable following among moral philosophers. It does seem to me, though, that apart from this question, bringing the issue of how the law should conceive of our moral agency forward, putting prominently on the table the question of what the capacities are by virtue of whose full possession a person is appropriately held responsible for his or her actions, would have a clarifying effect on these debates.

III

It is time to return to the problem of naturalized responsibility that I raised at the beginning of the paper. I suggested that looking at the legal debates over the law's allowing a separate insanity defense to a charge of criminal wrongdoing offered hope of a solution. These debates concern mentally ill offenders who, owing to the way their actions result from their illness, do not deserve punishment for them but who, in the absence of such a defense, would be liable to such punishment, nonetheless, because of the inapplicability of the law's traditional defenses to those actions. In some cases, such as our examples of the melancholic mother and the kleptomaniac high school student, the traditional defenses are inapplicable because the actions are voluntary, and in these cases, at least, as cases in which a separate insanity defense protects the offenders from liability to punishment, it follows that the offenders are excusable from responsibility for their actions despite their having control over them and being aware of what they were doing. It is these cases, therefore, that offer guidance on how responsibility for action can be understood without reference to the ability to control one's actions. Thus, insofar as such reference in accounts of responsibility makes the problem of naturalized responsibility resistant to resolution, it is these cases that offer guidance on how to avoid this impasse.

Specifically, if the argument for a separate insanity defense that I have developed in view of them succeeds in justifying such a defense, then it succeeds as well in spelling out conditions of responsibility for one's actions that are free of the deadlock that comes with tying such responsibility to the ability to control one's actions. These conditions, according to the argument, are the capacities whose full possession qualifies a human being as a moral agent, and although the question of what these capacities are is the subject of theoretical dispute, not all sides to the dispute give answers that are inconsistent with understanding human action as taking place in the natural world and explainable by its conditions and forces. It is true that the rationalist side to this dispute has traditionally given such answers, for traditionally the rationalists' attribution of the phenomena of moral agency to the operations of reason has been preparatory to their putting these phenomena beyond the reach of the conditions and forces of nature. So I cannot with confidence point to rationalist theories of moral agency as suggesting a solution to the problem.[26] Anti-rationalist theories are different, however. As I mentioned earlier, they have typically been inspired by the methods and theories of natural science as applied to human psychology. In these theories of moral agency, one can, I believe, find hope of a solution to the problem of naturalized responsibility.

26. At the same time, I don't mean to rule them out. See, e.g., for a possible solution whose author may be intending a rationalist account of responsibility, Susan Wolf, "Sanity and the Metaphysics of Responsibility," in *Responsibility, Character and the Emotions: New Essays in Moral Psychology*, Ferdinand Schoeman, ed. (Cambridge: Cambridge University Press, 1988), pp. 46–62.

10

Liberalism and Freedom

I

It is a commonplace of intellectual history that what chiefly separates the political thought of the moderns from that of the ancients and the medievals is a concern with individual freedom. Rousseau, in the most famous line from the *Social Contract*, expressed this concern brilliantly when he wrote, "L'homme est né libre et partout il est dans les fers."[1] One can only marvel at how much of modern political philosophy Rousseau crystallized in these twelve words. It is the birthright of every human being to be free, and it is the task of political philosophy to find an arrangement of the institutions and practices of political society that will secure that right for each of its members. A society that falls short of this ideal is an unjust society. It denies some of its members this right. It keeps them in chains.

Liberalism is the tradition that we most closely identify with the search for this ideal. Its hallmark is the defense of individual liberty against various

---

1. "Man is born free and everywhere he is in chains." Rousseau, *Social Contract and Discourses*, G. D. H. Cole, trans. (New York: E. P. Dutton, 1950), p. 3.

forms of tyranny that are justified and prosecuted in the name of some other, allegedly higher ideal: higher, its proponents will argue, because it is of greater importance in the grand scheme of things than the life of an individual or because it is of greater importance than liberty to an individual's life. Liberalism opposes all such claims, and it has been the primary bulwark against the authoritarian, totalitarian, and supremacist programs to which they give rise. At the same time, though liberalism is first among movements and theories of modern political thought in its concern with individual liberty, the concern is not exclusive to it. Anarchism too, in some of its forms, springs from this concern. And it is also a principal theme in Marx's early writings, the essay "On the Jewish Question," the *Economic and Philosophical Manuscripts of 1844, The German Ideology.*

Of course, there are large disagreements across these movements and theories not only about what interferences with action count as violations of individual liberty but also about the very notion of individual liberty: whether it is an essentially negative notion, as Hobbes argued, or has some positive element in it, as Rousseau thought. What is more, large disagreements on these questions exist within liberalism itself. The dispute between libertarians and welfare state liberals that resurfaced a quarter century ago in the United States and Britain with the return to popularity of anti-government politics is perhaps the foremost example.[2] It defined one of the major splits within the British Liberal party in the late nineteenth and early twentieth centuries, divided as the party was between its traditional and radical wings. The former contained the classical or laissez-faire liberals for whom, following Locke, individual liberty was secured for all by instituting limits on the powers of government so as to protect private, voluntary transactions from government interference. The latter contained the reform liberals for whom, following T. H. Green, individual liberty was secured for the members of the weaker classes by protecting them from falling into servitude and wage slavery as a result of their poverty and ignorance. The reform liberals' program called for the government to interfere with contracts between workers and owners of private businesses in the interests of the former, and it thus put the reform liberals at loggerheads with the traditional wing. The earliest legislation that the reform liberals successfully got enacted included restrictions on the hours that a business owner could employ women and children and requirements that a business owner maintain a safe and sanitary workplace. It also included

---

2. For a deft treatment of this dispute, see Jim Sterba, *Justice for Here and Now* (Cambridge: Cambridge University Press, 1999), pp. 41–76.

compulsory education laws, which at the time were seen as interfering with the freedom of parents to contract with business owners for the labor of their children.

The reform liberals, it is important to keep in mind, endorsed such legislation on the grounds that it was necessary for securing individual liberty for the workers and their children in whose interests these laws were enacted. They could not have advocated it as part of a liberal program otherwise. That it was necessary for meeting these people's basic needs, for instance, would not have been a distinctly liberal basis for the laws, since that would be consistent with the illiberal regime of noblesse oblige. How they saw the laws as securing individual liberty for these workers and their children is therefore crucial to understanding the grounds of welfare state liberalism since later reforms that are even more distinctive of this political program, reforms such as those achieved through laws establishing a minimum wage, entitlement to compensation for on the job injuries, and unemployment and old age insurance, had a similar justification.

Green's important lecture on liberal legislation supplies the key argument.[3] In brief, Green's argument was that individual liberty is realized only through the development of those human faculties by whose exercise men and women could "make the best of themselves," and such development is not possible in the conditions of poverty and ignorance to which British factory workers, railway workers, miners, and their families seemed condemned as a result of being left on their own to sell their labor to the owners of private businesses. In these conditions, Green argued, workers were ruled by their primitive desires and inclinations. They lacked the maturity of judgment and strength of character essential to realizing a fully human existence, and consequently their actions were closer to mere animal behavior than to the conduct of a truly free agent. Merely removing legal constraints on their conduct so that they might act on their desires and inclinations as they pleased, Green pointed out, would not enable them to advance beyond such an impoverished life and limited selfhood. Rather, such advancement required positive action by the state. It required the state to create the conditions necessary for their developing those faculties without which a human being could not enjoy the blessings of individual liberty.[4]

3. T. H. Green, "Liberal Legislation and Freedom of Contract," in *Lectures on the Principles of Political Obligation*, Paul Harris and John Murrow, eds. (Cambridge: Cambridge University Press, 1986), pp. 194–212.
4. Ibid., pp. 199–201.

Mill's influence on Green's thought is apparent in this argument. The argument's appeal to the development of our distinctively human faculties echoes Mill's own appeal to self-development in chapter 3 of *On Liberty*. Mill, of course, was concerned with how custom and popular opinion worked to stunt such development and crush its expression in a man's or woman's individual personality, and the argument at the heart of *On Liberty* is an argument for absolute freedom of purely personal conduct, freedom to live one's life by one's own lights and plans, as a necessary condition for self-development and the individuality that results from it. He was not then concerned with how economic forces could work to prevent people from developing their intellectual and moral powers. In particular, he was not concerned with how such forces could keep people who lacked independent means—manual laborers, tenant farmers, their families, and the like—desperately poor and without hope of bettering themselves or improving the lives of their children. Nonetheless, there is no reason to suppose that one could not remake Mill's argument into one that applied to the circumstances of the desperately poor or that doing so would violate its spirit. There is nothing, that is, in Mill's argument that opposes an analogous argument in support of state regulation of economic forces for the purpose of creating conditions in which people otherwise at the mercy of those forces and thus reduced to a cruel and brutish existence could develop their intellectual and moral powers and realize a more distinctively human life. In this way, one can see Green's argument as just such an extension of Mill's.

Unlike the original, however, Green's argument was meant to support political action that collided directly with the politics of classical liberalism. Green, that is, unlike Mill, had this clash in mind in developing the argument of his lecture, and to emphasize it, he explicitly defined a notion of individual liberty in contradistinction to the notion favored by the classical liberals. True freedom, Green declared, was a positive power or capacity to act in pursuit of morally and socially worthy ends.[5] It was not merely freedom from constraint or compulsion, not merely freedom to do as one pleased. Accordingly, in presenting his argument, Green set the positive liberty whose conditions were forwarded by the reform liberals' political program in opposition to the merely negative liberty whose security was the uppermost concern of classical liberal thought, and having set up this opposition, he then maintained that only the former met the ideal of human freedom.

5. Ibid., pp. 199.

Does this show that Green in fact did more than merely extend Mill's argument? Does it show that he went beyond its terms? It would be easy to think that he did since the principle of liberty that Mill defended in his essay plainly concerns negative liberty. Yet this thought would be a mistake. While it is true that the principle Mill defended concerns negative liberty, the argument he gave in its defense is that its realization in society is a necessary condition of the development and exercise by individuals of powers and capacities of the kind Green identified with positive liberty. Hence, Mill too can be read as making the advancement of positive liberty the ultimate appeal in his argument.[6] To be sure, Mill himself did not speak of positive liberty or identify liberty with any set of powers or capacities. But his reliance on a similar ideal of human freedom to the one Green endorsed is unmistakable. It is evident, for instance, in such theses and remarks from chapter 3 of *On Liberty* as that human well-being requires the development and exercise of capacities for making choices that express one's individuality, that "the proper condition of a human being, arrived at the maturity of his faculties, [is] to use and interpret experience in his own way" and that "individual spontaneity" must be seen "as having intrinsic worth...and deserving...regard on its own account."[7] As several recent commentators have noted, the ideal to which Mill appeals is what we now commonly refer to as autonomy, and autonomy on our common understanding of it is a form of self-command or self-determination and therefore a form of positive liberty.[8]

Green's argument, by invoking a distinction between positive and negative liberty, thus explains how the reform liberals kept individual liberty at the forefront of their politics while rejecting the doctrines of classical liberalism that called for the immunity of private, voluntary transactions from state interference. The explanation, though, is open to being misunderstood. The language of positive and negative liberty is notoriously imprecise and cannot alone serve to capture the difference between the notion of individual liberty

---

6. Of course, Mill said that utility was the ultimate appeal of his argument. But he quickly added, "it must be utility in the largest sense, grounded on the permanent interests of man as a progressive being," and utility in this largest sense can encompass positive liberty. *On Liberty*, David Spitz, ed. (New York: W. W. Norton, 1975), p. 12. On this point, see Richard Wollheim, "The Ends of Life and the Preliminaries of Morality: John Stuart Mill and Isaiah Berlin," in his *The Mind and Its Depths* (Cambridge, MA: Harvard University Press, 1993), pp. 22–38.

7. Mill, *On Liberty*, pp. 54–55.

8. See, e.g., Gerald Dworkin, "Paternalism," in *Morality and the Law*, R. Wasserstrom, ed. (Belmont, CA: Wadsworth, 1971), pp. 107–126; and Fred R. Berger, *Happiness, Justice and Freedom: The Moral and Political Philosophy of John Stuart Mill* (Berkeley and Los Angeles: University of California Press, 1984), pp. 232–237.

that gave impetus to the reform liberals' political program and the notion that defined these core doctrines of classical liberalism. After all, even Locke, whose political philosophy is the most authoritative source of these doctrines, did not consider individual liberty to be merely negative. He neither took it to be the absence of compulsion and constraint nor identified it with freedom to do as one pleased. Liberty, Locke declared early in the *Second Treatise*, is not license.[9] One does not exercise it simply by doing what one wants or desires. To the contrary, its exercise requires that one act under the direction of reason, which Locke understood to be the direction of laws that one can know only through reason.[10] The point, of course, is not that Locke too should be read as a theorist of positive liberty. It is rather that the disagreement between reform and classical liberals over the ideal of human freedom is much richer than the simple opposition between positive and negative liberty suggests.

Classical liberals are concerned with the distribution of individual liberty under the rule of law. Locke's distinction between liberty and license reflects this concern. For Locke, the rule of law is in the first instance the rule of reason as informed by the Natural Law. Accordingly, Locke connected liberty with actions done in the light of reason, for he understood liberty as something only people who are capable of acting under the guidance of law can enjoy. Specifically, his view was that liberty is something one exercises in voluntary actions, actions that proceed from one's volitions, and volitions are formed through rational thought about one's circumstances. Actions done, unthinkingly, on impulse or from some overwhelming desire do not proceed from the actor's volitions and therefore, no matter how happily the actor does them, are not exercises of liberty. Locke likened such actions, instead, to the actions of beasts, who, because they lack reason, are incapable of acting under the guidance of law and are thus incapable of acting voluntarily. The general idea, which his theory presents and which other strands of classical liberalism endorse, is that the enjoyment of liberty is the special privilege of human beings who qualify as legally competent actors by virtue of their capacity for voluntary action. They, then, enjoy liberty to the extent that they exercise this capacity and are not coerced by others. The main agent of such coercion is, of course, the state, and hence the enjoyment of liberty chiefly depends on the reasonableness and justice of the state's laws. Here, then, is the nub of the classical liberal's defense of liberty: the voluntary actions of

9. John Locke, *Second Treatise of Government*, C. S. MacPherson, ed. (Indianapolis: Hackett, 1980), §6.
10. Ibid., §57.

individuals must be protected from the state's use of its coercive power in ways that are neither reasonable nor just.

The reform liberals, by contrast, did not regard all voluntary actions as exercises of individual liberty. They did not think the enjoyment of liberty consisted in acting from volitions formed in uncoercive circumstances. In their view, it depended on how those volitions, or as they would say, choices, were formed. To be sure, a person is not free if his actions are coerced. But in addition, they maintained, a person is not free if his actions proceed from choices he makes as a result of general ignorance, weak-mindedness, uncritical or naïve beliefs, addictions to crude or infantile pleasures, or the steady undercurrent of fear and anxiety that comes with living in severely deprived or hostile circumstances.[11] Thus, the reform liberals, by taking a person's enjoyment of individual liberty to depend on how the choices from which his actions proceed are formed, advanced a notion of individual liberty that presupposed complexity and depth to human psychology significantly greater than what the classical liberal's notion implied or what classical liberals, in their defense of liberty, entertained.

In this respect, the simple, seventeenth-century faculty psychology that informs Locke's theory is telling. On this basically Cartesian psychology, the human mind is constituted by two principal faculties, understanding and will, which operate on the sensory and affective experiences to which it is subject, transforming them into opinion and action.[12] One exercises one's understanding in interpreting the experiences and judging their practical import, and then, on the basis of these judgments, one exercises one's will in forming the volitions from which one's actions proceed. What is missing from this psychology is any mention of character or individual personality as a factor in the formation of volitions. And the reason why is clear. The psychology is too simple. It lacks the conceptual resources necessary for understanding a person's volitions as determined, at least in part, by his character or personality. A fortiori, it lacks the conceptual resources necessary for understanding a person's voluntary actions as reflections of strengths or weaknesses in his character or as reflections of his having a more or less well-ordered personality. Hence, any notion of individual liberty that includes the idea that a

11. Perhaps the boldest statement of this idea is found in L. T. Hobhouse's *Liberalism*, where he writes, "It is also possible...to foster the development of will, of personality, of self-control, or whatever we please to call the central harmonizing power which makes us capable of directing our own lives. Liberalism is the belief that society can be safely founded on this self-directing power of personality" (Oxford: Oxford University Press, 1964), p. 66.

12. See Locke, *An Essay Concerning Human Understanding*, bk. II, ch. 21.

person is freer to the degree that his character is sound, his personality well ordered, which is to say, to the degree that he is in command of his opinions and actions, entirely escapes its grasp. What it supports is a notion that makes acting at the direction of one's volitions and in the absence of coercion the test of liberty and thus suits a political philosophy that takes the reach of the state's coercive laws as the main measure of individual liberty. On such a philosophy, the degree to which a person exercises self-command in the formation of his volitions never enters the picture. The classical liberal's unconcern with how a person's volitions are formed is well expressed by Locke's famous assertion that 'person' is a forensic term.[13]

The difference, then, between the notion of individual liberty that gave impetus to the reform liberals' political program and the notion that supports the core doctrines of classical liberalism is traceable to a difference in the way an individual's will is conceived. The latter notion is supported by a conception of the will as a basic human faculty distinct from other basic human faculties such as understanding and feeling. The former, by contrast, follows from a conception of the will as a synthesis of various faculties and capacities that a person exercises in making choices and that help to constitute his personality. This difference in conception of the will corresponds, then, to a difference in how particular exercises of the will are understood. On the conception of it as a basic faculty distinct from other basic faculties, particular exercises are likewise understood as distinct, basic mental acts, and the term 'volition' is the appropriate quasi-technical one for such acts. On the conception of the will as a synthesis of various faculties and capacities, particular exercises are understood as mental processes that combine a number of different mental operations rather than as individual mental acts. Accordingly, the use of the word 'volition' as a quasi-technical term ceases to be appropriate, and the language of choice and decision making, which is better suited to the idea of a process involving the exercise of various faculties, is favored instead. The point rings clearly in Mill's emphatic description of the faculties that are called upon in making a personal choice of a life plan.

> He who lets the world, or his own portion of it, choose his plan of life for him has no need of any other faculty than the ape like one of imitation. He who chooses his plan for himself employs all his faculties. He must use observation to see, reasoning and judgment to foresee, activity to gather materials for decision, discrimination for decision, and when he has decided firmness and self-control to hold to his deliberate decision.[14]

13. Ibid., bk. II, ch. 27, sec. 26.
14. Mill, *On Liberty*, p. 56.

This shift from the language of volitions to that of choices and decisions marks a recovery of Aristotelian ideas about human psychology. For Aristotle's psychology, unlike the Cartesian psychology that Locke had adopted, does not include a basic faculty of the will whose exercise is the source of all voluntary actions. Rather, on Aristotle's psychology, voluntary actions—more exactly, those actions that would count as voluntary on a Cartesian psychology— follow from the actor's deliberative choices, and the actor comes to these choices through the exercise of various intellectual and moral capacities.[15] In this psychology, unlike Locke's Cartesian psychology, a person's deliberative choices issue from the complex of intellectual and moral capacities that forms his character. They do not issue from a separate, basic faculty for producing voluntary actions. There is no such faculty. The complexity of the human soul, on Aristotle's psychology, contrasts strikingly with its simplicity on Descartes'.

The recovery of Aristotelian ideas in the philosophy that inspired the reform liberals' program is evident in another way as well. For the necessity of the development of the intellectual and moral capacities to the realization of one's humanity is also a central theme in Aristotle's thought. On his theory, the development of these capacities, when full and balanced, yields the moral and intellectual excellences that constitute the ideal the theory seeks to establish, and this ideal is entirely consonant with the ideal of human freedom expressed in the arguments from which the reform liberals drew inspiration. The influence of Aristotle's ideas about human psychology on the argument of chapter 3 of On Liberty, though perhaps not direct, is nonetheless substantial. Their influence on Green's thought is no less profound. The understanding of individual liberty that these thinkers advanced and that gave impetus to the reform liberals' program, the program on which welfare state liberalism was founded, arises out of these Aristotelian ideas. And in contemporary political thought, the same understanding has now resurfaced in the capabilities approaches of Amartya Sen and Martha Nussbaum, each of whom has pressed it in the service of advocating liberal reforms to economic and political policies in international development.[16]

15. On Aristotle's views of voluntary action, see Martha Nussbaum, *The Fragility of Goodness* (Cambridge: Cambridge University Press, 1986), pp. 264–289.

16. See, e.g., Amartya Sen, *Inequality Reexamined* (Cambridge, MA: Harvard University Press, 1992), and Martha Nussbaum, *Women and Human Development: The Capabilities Approach* (Cambridge: Cambridge University Press, 2000).

II

Contrary, then, to popular belief, the philosophical dispute between classical and welfare state liberalism did not originate in the Harvard Philosophy Department in the 1970s. This belief or something like it has contributed to the misconception of the dispute as a quarrel between liberals who love liberty and liberals who love equality. It is a misconception because, as Sen has instructively pointed out, the opposition between liberty and equality it assumes is a false dichotomy.[17] Classical liberals no less than welfare state liberals value equality in the possession of liberty, just as welfare state liberals no less than classical liberals value individual liberty. Both are champions of equal freedom. Both maintain that everyone has an equal right to be free. They differ, as our review of the arguments the political program on which welfare state liberalism was founded makes clear, in how they conceive of individual liberty and in what they count as its violation. And they do not necessarily differ in their support for equality in the distribution of other social goods except insofar as such distribution is necessary for securing equal individual liberty. Or in other words, any difference in their support for equality in the distribution of other social goods, except insofar as such distribution is necessary for securing equal individual liberty, is inessential to understanding the difference between them.

The essential difference between them, therefore, is not reflected in disputes, such as that between Rawls and Nozick, over whether distributions of wealth in a society must, to be just, conform to some egalitarian standard like Rawls's difference principle. To be sure, welfare state liberalism, because its conception of individual liberty presupposes self-development, the acquisition of the central human capabilities, to use Nussbaum's helpful terms, supports government enforced transfers of wealth for the purpose of securing for everyone who needs them the goods necessary for developing and exercising these capabilities. But such transfers are consistent with huge disparities in the distribution of wealth. Hence, they are not undertaken to achieve and maintain some egalitarian pattern in this distribution, and transfers of wealth that are undertaken for that purpose should have no place in a liberal political program if they entail loss of individual liberty by those whose estates are reduced by these transfers.

Indeed, one can construct, following Sen's well-known criticism of Rawls's account of primary goods, examples supporting this point. Sen's criticism is

---

17. See Sen, *Inequality Reexamined*, pp. 21–23.

that Rawls's concern with achieving an egalitarian distribution of primary goods, and so in particular, wealth and income, is insensitive to human diversity.[18] The value of those goods varies with the needs and abilities of those who possess them, and thus a transfer of wealth, as required by the difference principle, from someone A, who was better off as measured by the bundle of primary goods he or she possessed, to someone B, who was worse off by the same measure, could turn out to impair A's ability to function physically or mentally while merely improving B's bottom line. Hence, the transfer would achieve its aim of greater equality in the distribution of wealth at the cost of A's liberty, and no liberal theory of justice should endorse this.

This last point, to be sure, does not immediately apply to Rawls's theory. Rawls, after all, did not follow Green and other reform liberals in rejecting the notion of individual liberty contained in the core doctrines of classical liberalism. To the contrary, he accepted it, and as a result could, by pointing to his doctrine of the priority of liberty, deny that his theory called for imposing losses of individual liberty on some in order to increase the wealth of others.[19] But what this response would do is to bring out Rawls's understanding of his theory as one that supports the institutions of the welfare state and at the same time retains, as the sole notion of individual liberty, the notion that is central to doctrines that such liberalism opposes.[20] What it shows, then, is that Rawls, having excluded the possibility of appealing to an ideal of individual liberty to justify the institutions of the welfare state, must turn instead for their justification to an ideal of equality in the distribution of social goods. Thus, his theory comes to represent a conception of welfare state liberalism that, in opposition

18. Ibid., pp. 79–84.

19. John Rawls, A *Theory of Justice* (Cambridge, MA: Harvard University Press, 1971), pp. 201–205, 243–251. Note that Rawls implicitly repudiates the reform liberals' notion of liberty when he writes (p. 204) that poverty and ignorance reduce the value of their sufferers' liberty but not their liberty itself.

20. Rawls nonetheless avoids a direct clash between the ideal of individual liberty and that of equality in the distribution of social goods by limiting the former to what he calls basic liberties. These include freedom of speech and assembly, freedom of conscience and thought, the right to vote and hold public office, and so forth. He does not explicitly include freedom of contract among these basic liberties. He mentions "the right to hold (personal) property" but leaves what this right entails unspecified. Nonetheless, his theory as a whole makes it plain that he does not think this right precludes the state's interfering with a person's control over his estate or his labor for the purpose of achieving greater equality in the distribution of wealth and income. His doctrine of the priority of liberty, in other words, does not protect freedom of contract from being interfered with by the state for the purpose of promoting greater equality in the distribution of wealth, and it therefore follows that freedom of contract is not one of the basic liberties. See ibid., p. 61.

"Freedom ... [is] the liberation of powers of all men equally for contributions to a common good."[22]

The common good, as the reform liberals conceived of it, comprises the good of every member of society. Each member's good, that is, contributes to it. On this conception, then, the common good is not the same thing as the good of the society, at least not if the latter is understood to be something distinct from and possibly superior to the good of each member. Society, in the reform liberals' view, is nothing over and above its individual members, and its common good, therefore, is not found by looking past the good of each member to the good of the larger whole to which each belongs. It is not something one puts ahead of one's own good in the way each member of a well-disciplined sports team puts the good of her team ahead of her own good. Rather, it is found by identifying one's own good with the good of one's fellow members in view of the interests and goals one has in common with them. In this respect, then, not only does each member's good contribute to the common good, but each contributes equally. Each is equal in weight and worth to that of every other member. It counts the same as the good of every other member, though, of course, in any given situation the best means to advancing the common good may incidentally entail benefiting some more than others.[23]

In this conception of the common good, one can again see traces of Mill's influence, specifically, his ideas about the growth of social feelings as a vehicle of moral progress. Writing in chapter 3 of *Utilitarianism* about "the natural basis of sentiment for utilitarian morality," Mill declared, "This firm foundation is that of the social feelings of mankind—the desire to be in unity with our fellow creatures," and he then went on to explain the growth of social feelings as a development in strength and scope of the disposition in human beings to identify their interests with the interests of others with whom they were joined in social relations.[24] This disposition thus matches what Green described as the power to contribute to a common good, the power whose development and exercise Green saw as the chief vehicle of social progress

---

22. Ibid., p. 200. See also Hobhouse, *Liberalism*, pp. 67–69.

23. See Green, *Prolegomena to Ethics*, §245, in *Lectures on the Principles of Political Obligation*, p. 279, and Hobhouse, *Liberalism*, pp. 67–69. Against the communitarian view that the common good must be identified with the good of a collective or community and that therefore liberalism can have no conception of the common good, see Will Kymlicka, *Liberalism, Community and Culture* (Oxford: Clarendon Press, 1991), pp. 76–79, and David McCabe, "Private Lives and Public Virtues: The Idea of a Liberal Community," *Canadian Journal of Philosophy* 28 (1998): 557–585.

24. Mill, *Utilitarianism*, George Sher, ed. (Indianapolis: Hackett, 1979), pp. 30–32.

and the advance of human freedom. At the same time, his conception of the common good differs significantly from the utilitarian notion of the highest good, and not just in its being relativized to a particular society. It differs as well in its not being a purely aggregative notion. Specifically, on the reform liberals' conception, the common good represents a unification of the interests of all members of society and not merely a summation. To take the common good as an end is to aim at an equitable satisfaction of the interests that all members of the society share rather than at the maximal satisfaction of interests that all members have aggregatively. Promotion of the common good, in other words, does not entail promotion of the greatest good.

The two standards thus represent two conceptions of social good. The difference between them is that the reform liberals' standard reflects greater or at least more direct concern than the utilitarians' with taking equality in treatment, and not just equality in consideration, as a guide to the promotion of social good. Because the reform liberals' standard represents a conception of social good on which interests that are regarded as equal in weight and worth are united and not merely added together, its promotion avoids the disparities in treatment and consequent divisiveness that can too easily result from aiming at promoting aggregative social good without regard to that good's distribution. Hence, to take the common good as an end is to aim at satisfying the interests that the members of society share without treating the interests of some as having less inherent worth than those of others or allowing the interests of some to be sacrificed on the altar of maximization, a sacrifice that in this context would be yet another way of treating some members' interests as less important than others. Accordingly, in promoting the common good, no difference in the extent to which some members' interests would be satisfied as compared with those of others can be due to the interests of some members being counted as less worthy of satisfaction than those of others or less important in social life. All such differences, instead, must be due to factors that result incidentally from the choice of means to this end. In this way, participation in institutions and practices that aim at promoting the common good, on the reform liberals' conception of it, need not cause those participants who benefit less than others to think of themselves as having subordinated their own interests to the interests of those who benefit more.

It follows that to live in a society in which some members' interests count more than others, in which the laws and customs treat the honor and well-being of some as more worthy of protection and promotion than the honor and well-being of others, and in which the institutions and practices mostly operate by design for the benefit of some and not others, would be to live in a society in which social engagements did not offer opportunity to act in concert with others in the promotion of the common good. It would be to live under social conditions that were unconducive to one's developing the moral and intellectual powers one needs to engage wholeheartedly in such activities. Hence, given the reform liberals' view of such powers as essential to self-development, it would be to live under social conditions unsuited to the enjoyment of individual liberty as they conceived of it.

Worse still, these conditions would foster types of personality in which the moral and intellectual faculties were arrested in their development or distorted in ways that crippled their possessors for engagement in social life. The types are well known from history and literature. On the one hand, when a sense of superiority is bred into people as a result of their enjoying from birth institutional privileges from which others are excluded, the upshot often is to create in them an inner need to see those they regard as beneath them supplicate and suffer. Having a sense of superiority, they need to have it confirmed in the behavior of their "inferiors," and under the pressures of this need they develop dependencies that leave them excessively self-involved and unfree. On the other, when people come to see themselves as inferior to others as a result of being excluded from institutional privileges that those others enjoy, they can easily fall into states of humility and subservience that leave them without initiative and prey to the control and manipulativeness of others. Alternatively, though, if they retain a sense of their own worth, they may then be consumed by an anger that, because it would be imprudent to vent it on the distant keepers and beneficiaries of the institutions that oppress them, is displaced onto local objects in destructive and self-destructive ways. In either case, the conditions of caste and exclusion give the members of the lower caste little chance of developing the energetic and balanced personalities on which the enjoyment of individual liberty depends.

The reform liberals' program thus included legislation intended to root out entrenched privilege from society's institutions and practices. Male privilege and class privilege, in particular, were both objects of reforms eliminating barriers to the participation in public life by women and the lowborn and to their occupation of positions of advantage and influence in social and economic affairs. And efforts at establishing state provision of free, universal education were likewise aimed at eliminating the entrenched privileges of sex and class. All of these efforts were backed by the analyses of such privilege as creating conditions hostile to freedom, as denying those condemned to social and political inferiority the opportunities necessary for self-development, and as also productive of disordered personalities that left their possessors unhappy and unfree. Thus, Hobhouse, writing about liberalism's dismantling of "those restraints on the individual which flow from the hierarchic organization of society, and reserve certain offices, certain forms of occupation, and perhaps the right or at least the opportunity of education generally, to people of a certain rank or class," could declare, "Once more the struggle for liberty is also, when pushed through, a struggle for equality."[25]

By extension, then, the same analysis can apply to large disparities in the distribution of wealth within a society. Because such disparities can take on the character of class divisions, they too can be a threat to individual liberty. Where wealth so influences the operations of society's institutions as to cause them to deliver disproportionately more benefits to those with large estates than to those with modest ones, and where it so influences legislation and social convention as to have the laws and customs of society tailored to treat wealthier people as worthy of greater protection of their honor and promotion of their well-being than the less wealthy, the same conditions deleterious to individual liberty arise as are created by entrenched privileges of sex and class. And where, as a result of these distortions in the workings of the society's institutions and practices, laws and customs, the wealthier members are encouraged to see their good fortune as a badge of superiority and the poorer ones to see their comparative lack of wealth as a social stigma, the same types of disordered personality, the same social pathologies, arise within these populations. Consequently, efforts at curbing disparities in the distribution of wealth so as to keep them from becoming so large or pronounced as to create social conditions unsuitable to the enjoyment of individual liberty became part of the reform liberals' program. A prime example, precisely because of the privileged character of inherited wealth, was legislation imposing stiff inheritance taxes on large estates.

It is the corruptive power of wealth when amassed by private individuals, therefore, the tendency of concentrations of great wealth in private hands to take on the trappings of aristocracy, that justify, on the reform liberals' theory of the welfare state, efforts at curbing large disparities in the distribution of wealth. This threat of corruption is most serious when it centers on public institutions, a point of particular importance on the reform liberals' theory. On their theory, public institutions, above all, must work and be seen to work in ways that count everyone's interests as equal, for these institutions, more than any others, afford citizens the most direct and fundamental opportunities for acting in concert with other citizens in the promotion of their common good. These institutions, that is, more than any others, afford citizens with the most direct and fundamental opportunities for engaging in the kind

25. Hobhouse, *Liberalism*, p. 21.

of activities through which individual liberty is realized. Thus, disparities of wealth must not be allowed to become so large as to enable wealthier citizens to use their greater wealth to influence the workings of these institutions in ways that tilt the results to their advantage and to disadvantage of poorer citizens. They cannot be allowed to become so large as to enable them to use their wealth to increase significantly the prospects of electing officials who will act in their special interests, to induce lawmakers directly to shape legislation in ways more favorable to those special interests, or to harness the power of the courts in the service of those interests. Such uses of wealth, the tendency to which is perhaps inevitable in its amassing, destroys the common good as an end toward the promotion of which citizens can see themselves acting through their participation in these institutions.

Rousseau, in the *Social Contract*, offered that wealth should not become so unequal in its distribution as to enable a wealthy citizen to buy a poor one.[26] He did not object to such inequality as unjust in itself. He saw it instead as destructive of the General Will and so of the liberty that depends on it. Equality, he said, is an object of legislative interest not because it is good in itself but because liberty cannot exist without it.[27] The reform liberals did not endorse Rousseau's peculiar test for when inequality in the distribution of wealth has become too great to be allowed. They did not make it part of their program. But their ideas and sentiments on the question of how much inequality in the distribution of wealth to allow were otherwise the same.

26. Rousseau, *Social Contract and Discourses*, p. 50.
27. Ibid., pp. 49–50.

Index

to classical liberalism, endorses an ideal of equality in the distribution of such goods, income and wealth, in particular. And it is reasonable to suppose that the now common understanding of welfare state liberalism as differing from classical liberalism in being committed to an ideal of equality that comes into conflict with that of individual liberty arises for the same reason. That is, it arises because of an assumption that the notion of individual liberty informing the latter ideal is the notion contained in the core doctrines of classical liberalism, for given this assumption, one then naturally supposes that to justify the institutions of the welfare state appeal to the former ideal is necessary.

This understanding of welfare state liberalism, as the discussion of section 1 makes clear, departs from the ideas on which the reform liberals grounded their political program. It departs from them, moreover, in two ways. Not only does it incorporate the classical liberals' notion of individual liberty and not the notion the reform liberals favored, it also elevates the ideal of equality in the distribution of social goods to an ideal worth realizing for its own sake. It treats this ideal as a separate standard from that of individual liberty. This separation of the two represents a revision of liberal thought. To be sure liberalism, whether classical or reform, is an egalitarian philosophy. It bows to no other tradition in its commitment to promoting equal individual liberty for all. At its core is the doctrine that every man or woman has an equal right to freedom. What is more, it promotes equality in the distribution of other social goods wherever inequalities in their distribution threaten some with loss or curtailment of this right. But until recently, liberal thinkers did not regard inequalities in the distribution of such social goods as income and wealth as injustices independently of their being a threat to human freedom. They did not support measures to make the distribution of wealth in a society more equal simply for the sake of achieving greater equality in its distribution. Liberalism is self-identified as a progressive philosophy. The aim of expanding people's individual liberty is a progressive aim. It is an article of liberal faith that humanity advances through the promotion of freedom for all. The aim of making the distribution of wealth more equal is not, as a final aim, obviously a progressive one. It is not obvious that realizing this aim in itself makes human life better.

The distinction between promoting greater equality in the distribution of wealth as an ideal worth realizing for its own sake and promoting it as necessary for protecting people, the poorer members of society in particular, from loss or curtailment of their right of freedom is crucial to seeing why the now common understanding of welfare state liberalism represents a fundamental change in liberal thought from the ideas on which the reform liberals grounded their political program. For the distinction explains how the reform liberals could be strong supporters of greater equality in the distribution of wealth without ever regarding contingent inequalities in its distribution as in themselves unjust. It explains, in other words, how the strength of one's commitment to reducing such inequalities need not depend on one's regarding them as inherently bad. One might see them, instead, as conditions that threaten people's liberty, particularly those whose share of this good is the least bountiful. Hence, the crux of the difference between the now common egalitarian understanding of welfare state liberalism and the understanding of the reform liberals lies in the place in a liberal theory of the ideal of equality in the distribution of wealth and not in the strength of the commitment to that ideal. The former understanding, because it incorporates the classical liberals' notion of individual liberty, places the ideal in competition with that of securing equal individual liberty for all. The latter, by contrast, places it in a position of support. On the reform liberals' understanding, promoting greater equality in the distribution of wealth advances the cause of freedom.

The key concept in the argument on which reform liberals based this view is the concept of the common good. Human beings, they held, are essentially social. Political societies are not, as some theorists suppose, organizations humans form to escape the dangers and deprivations of a solitary life, and theorists who start with this supposition misconceive political phenomena from the get-go. Conceiving human beings as social, then, the reform liberals understood the intellectual and moral capacities whose development was necessary to enjoying liberty as primarily, though not exclusively, capacities for engaging in social life. Such engagement consists in acting in concert with other members of one's society for the promotion of a common good, a good in which everyone shares, and consequently one's enjoyment of liberty is conditioned on one's living a life in which such activities are prominent or in which one can see the activities that are prominent as contributing to social good. Green, for instance, identified the objects of such activities with the morally and socially worthy ends in the pursuit of which, he maintained, people developed the powers to make the best of themselves and so achieve freedom. "When we measure the progress of a society by its growth in freedom," he wrote, "we measure it by the increasing development and exercise *on the whole* of those powers of contributing to social good with which we believe the members of the society to be endowed; in short, by the greater power on the part of the citizens as a body to make the most and best of themselves."[21] And again, at the beginning of the next paragraph, he asserted,

---

21. Green, "Liberal Legislation," p. 199 (original italics).